THE DOLLS OF
Jules Nicolas Steiner

by Dorothy A. McGonagle

Historical Perspective
by Barbara Spadaccini Day

Photography by the Author

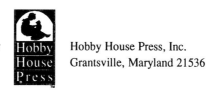

Published by   Hobby House Press, Inc.
Grantsville, Maryland 21536

Dedication

for Jerome

Additional copies of this book may be purchased at $39.95

from

Hobby House Press, Inc.
1 Corporate Drive
Grantsville, Maryland 21536
1-800-554-1447
or from your favorite bookstore or dealer.
Please add $6.50 per copy for postage.

© 1988 by Dorothy A. McGonagle
Second Printing March 1996

Printed in the United States of America

ISBN: 0-87588-312-5

Table of Contents

Acknowledgements

A book of this sort requires the encouragement, support and good humor of a great number of people, a gift I have been fortunate to have received. Notable amongst the people I wish to single out is my dear and constant friend, June P. Kibbe, who was the first to say the word "book" and who has throughout remained a pillar and a consultant in matters diverse and esoteric. I am also indebted to Dorothy and Jane Coleman who shared their home and their knowledge and who unlocked the mysteries of the Library of Congress as well as to Barbara Spadaccini Day, whose willingness to talk Steiner at any international hour has been astounding, and whose historical chapter here brings insights into the 19th century French doll industry.

A multitude of generous friends shared their dolls for research and photography, opening their homes and their collections to my husband, Jerome, and me. Many of their dolls are pictured here, but those that are not are just as important to me for they all form the basis of the research required for this book. Special thanks go to the following: Lorna Lieberman, Curator of Dolls at the Wenham Museum who shared both Museum treasures and her own for my research; Beulah Franklin, Dorothy Dixon and Winnie Langley who willingly undressed their very special dolls for research for this book; Nancy A. Smith and Maurine S. Popp whose continued interest, support and suggestions have been invaluable. Sincere thanks also go to the Musée des Arts Décoratifs in Paris and The Strong Museum in Rochester, New York, Margaret Whitton, Elizabeth Pierce, Hannah Shrand, H. & P. Bitterman, Constance W. Fielden, Pearl D. Morley, Lynn Eckhardt, Louise Lund, Sylvia MacNeil, Mary Thomas Justice, Mary Christie, Ferné Young, Yvonne L. Baird, Fidelia Lence, Chantal Dagommer, Claude Detave, Agnès and René Goulignac, Gail Cook, Patricia Gallagher, Arthur & Shelley Fields, Karen Copher, Tom Bugenhagen, Zelda H. Cushner, Anita Hirsh, Ann Park, Helen Read, Velma J. Ross, Marie Kranich, Maree Tarnowska, Clifford & Heather Bond, Albert Bazin, Gérard Etienbled, John Diamond, Richard Wright and Rick Saxman, Maxine Look, Ann Lloyd, Ralph W. Griffith, Dolores Gilbert, Howard & Jan Foulke, François Theimer, Marvin Cohen Auctions, Richard W. Withington, Mary Lou Rubright, Sidda Sandel, Shirley Buchholz, Anarene Barr, and Olivia Bristol.

Thanks are also due the following for their various research and translation assistance: Steve Lowe, Susan McGonagle Beran, Richard White and Katherine Singley. David Claxton, Mary Isaac, Mary Kahler, Penelope Phelps, Gill Stribling-Wright, and Dr. James A. Robison are among those whose contributions have been special.

I am sincerely grateful to my Publisher, Gary R. Ruddell, and his fine staff at Hobby House Press, Inc., for all their efforts to make this such a beautiful book. The art and typesetting staffs at Hobby House deserve much credit, as does my Editor, Donna H. Felger — H is for helpful, which she has been beyond words! For the second printing it has been a pleasure to work with Mary Beth Ruddell.

Lastly, and in many ways most importantly, my family is to be lauded for their patience and efforts to bring this to a conclusion. There were periods when the words "wife" and "mother" like "book" were but ephemeral concepts. I thank you Jerome, David, John and Rebecca for being the fine and reliable realities of my life!

Frontispiece

Drawing of the Steiner premises at 60 rue d'Avron, based in part on a turn-of-the-century insurance plan. It suggests the flavor of the property in Jules Nicolas Steiner's golden years and completes the progression of addresses begun on the end papers. Both are the work of Jerome G. McGonagle.

AUTHOR'S NOTE

Nothing will ever be attempted if all possible objections must be first overcome.
SAMUEL JOHNSON

The dolls of Jules Nicolas Steiner have long fascinated and intrigued me. When I first began to assemble information and photographs to present to the National Convention of UFDC (United Federation of Dolls Clubs, Inc.) in San Antonio in 1984, I considered titling the lecture "Jules Steiner, Insomniac," for I could envision Jules Steiner lying awake nights devising methods to make his dolls walk, talk or cry, to make the eyes move and the like. With more careful examination of his dolls, though, came the realization that Steiner was a pragmatic entrepreneur with a gifted eye for detail, for quality, and also for what would sell. Additionally, and classically, I became aware that the more I learned, the more there was to learn, a task hindered by my limitations with the French language. Happily, Barbara Spadaccini Day, assistant to the curator of the Toy Department at the Musée des Arts Décoratifs in Paris generously shared with me patents, department store catalogs, advertising and various other nuggets of research. She aided in the translation of these and agreed to contribute an historical account of the Maison Steiner enriched by her knowledge and understanding of the French doll and toy industry and of the subtleties in French business advertising and interrelationships. In the process of research we uncovered important new information.

My husband and friend, Jerome, has shared every step and should by rights share authorship, but he is humble. Yet without him this would be much less of a book, for his ideas, observations and speculations are often excellent. His love of history and his feel for the time and place is reflected in "An Historical Prelude" which follows these notes, in the map, in the drawing on the endpapers and in his artistic rendering of the factory address on the Frontispiece.

A study of the varied dolls of Jules Nicolas Steiner is complicated by the fact that his years of production were long and records short. Further, I like all things logical and orderly, with chronological, numerical and alphabetical consistency in mold marks, numbers and dates of production — a fantasy here. The reality is that some molds and body types were used for long periods and others briefly; there are overlaps and there are gaps. However, to wait until all the gaps are filled would mean this book might never come to exist. Fortunately, the dolls, by a careful study in conjunction with the patents tell much of their history and of their age. In this way we can also learn much of the man, Jules Nicolas Steiner, himself a 19th century Renaissance man. The spelling of "Nicolas" appears to American eyes to be incorrect. It is, however, the proper French spelling and the way it appears on his birth certificate, patents and other legal documents. While sometimes seen hyphenated, it more frequently is not.

Throughout the text, and particularly in the translation of the patents, the word "bébé" has not been translated because "bébé" is in our vernacular to describe a French doll in the form of a child. However, sometimes in the French "bébé" is used to describe more a baby doll than a child doll. Contradictory though it may seem, "poupées" has ordinarily been translated to "dolls" when it is used as a general term, but at times "poupées and bébés" is left untranslated in order to show the differentiation made by Jules Steiner. This is the sort of thing that makes me wish I were writing in French!

The book is divided into five sections. Each color section consists of 16 COLOR PLATES, which are extensively described in the black and white pages which follow it.

Section One looks at a variety of dolls produced by Jules Steiner, especially those with the ingenious patented mechanisms utilizing key-wound clockworks as they evolved through the 19th century. Also examined in this section are some early bébés, including the wonderful "bisque hip" or Motschmann-type and those with the first of the innovative articulated composition bodies but bearing no marks on their bisque heads.

The second and third sections study in detail the Series and Figure faces and the differences and similarities among these molds.

The fourth section considers some of the novelty items which the pragmatic Jules Nicolas Steiner designed or adapted for his use as well as some rarities, special variations and ethnic-costumed dolls with international appeal.

The fifth and concluding section contains a comparative study of the mold marks, bodies and other details of features, followed by trademarks, some advertising and patents.

Steiner's prodigious output, often not chronologically consistent, has led to the aim herein: to give a more orderly view of the phantasmagoria of Jules Nicolas Steiner's creativity.

AN HISTORICAL PRELUDE

by Jerome G. McGonagle

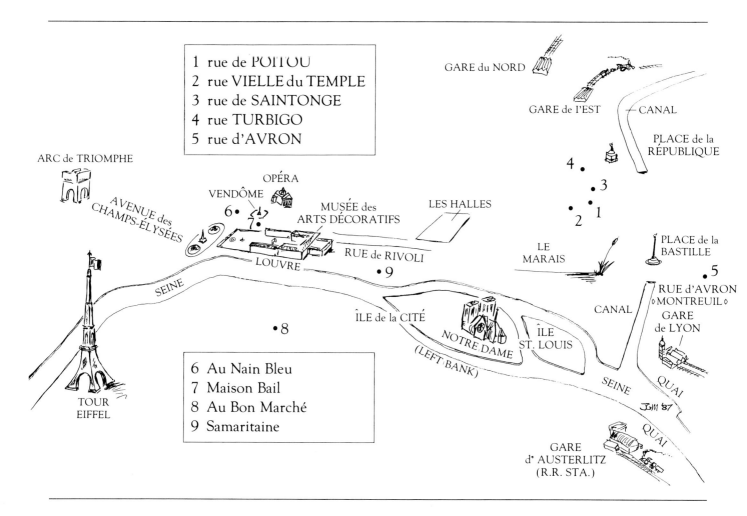

1 rue de POITOU
2 rue VIELLE du TEMPLE
3 rue de SAINTONGE
4 rue TURBIGO
5 rue d'AVRON

6 Au Nain Bleu
7 Maison Bail
8 Au Bon Marché
9 Samaritaine

Before studying the work of Jules Nicolas Steiner, it is interesting to look at the world into which he was born, in March of 1832, and at the interest in mechanical and musical devices prior to that time. From the time of the Renaissance, Western man had been intrigued by the possibilities of clockwork mechanisms. Five centuries of developments and improvements had culminated in relatively inexpensive novelties and toys available to the masses in the late 18th, 19th and early 20th centuries. (Batteries not included!)

Grand wizards of clockwork marvels toured the palaces and towns of western Europe entertaining and sometimes frightening the more simple citizens with their automated marvels. The image of Frank Morgan as the "Wizard of Oz" peeking out from behind his curtain comes to mind as one reads accounts of Von Kempelen,

Vaucanson, Droz and Laschot, Maillardet, Maelzel and others. This roster includes the name of a Steiner family, makers of automatons in Zurich at the end of the 18th century. Curiously for our research, the Steiner name is common in the nearest French city to the Swiss border, Dijon, Jules Nicolas Steiner's birthplace.

The early 19th century brought political and economic revolution to Europe. Toys originally available to princes were now available to the grandchildren of the very peasants who had driven the wizards and their "devilish creations" from their villages. Ambitious free thinkers and inventors such as Jules Steiner were on the leading edge of development and manufacture to supply a growing international market demand for marvelous trifles. Clockwork was king and JNS was a Master.

In 1863 Steiner is listed in the Didot-Bottin commercial directory as "fabricant de jouets et fantaisie, Rue Saintonge, 25." I like that "fantaisie;" it says so much about JNS. The dictionary definition reads: imagination, whim, caprice; (musical) fantasia. But beyond the whimsical, a study of the patents in the appendix reveals the man, the man who was concerned with the world around him. Think of it — if these are things he patented, what wonders did he create that were unique but never patented?

Paris mid-century was certainly an exciting place for young Jules. He was established in the ancient "Le Marais" (the marshes) section, now the Third Arrondissement. It is on the right bank of the Seine, just north of the Île de la Cité. Even today on major boulevards there are signs that point in the direction of the quarter of clock makers. Coincidentally, the northeast corner is the section of toy makers and sellers. "Le Marais" houses the oldest Jewish population of the city and is a wonderful helter-skelter world of small businesses and apartments. The diagonal streets shoot off in all directions while being tightly laced with byways and intriguing alleys. Just imagine the population now riding the Metro, out of sight, filling the streets on foot and horseback, going about their business! Jules Steiner's success can be traced by his address changes over the years, always within the district (as seen on the map), but always toward a more prosperous location. Bracketed by the important rail stations, the River Seine and the canals, Steiner's neighborhood was a hub of commerce. Worked from photographs of the actual buildings, my drawing on the endpapers reflects his first six addresses in a "fantaisie" grouping.

Steiner's final move was to 60 rue d'Avron, a scant two miles from his beginnings just beyond the Place de la Bastille. This walled-in three-quarter acre plot contained several buildings including his living quarters; these I have recreated in the rendering here from an insurance plan of 1901 and from an engraving done after Steiner's heirs sold the property. It was to this address that JNS brought both the Silver Medal won at the Paris Exposition of 1878 and the coveted Gold Medal he won in 1889. That Exposition in Paris introduced the Eiffel Tower to the world; curiously there are several parallels in the lives of its creator, Alexandre Gustave Eiffel, and Jules Nicolas Steiner.

Both Eiffel and Steiner were born in 1832 in Dijon, France. Each had an interest in aeronautical design and engineering. Steiner, the clock maker and doll maker, and Eiffel, the engineer, each designed compressed air systems for use in their respective fields, in the manufacture of doll bodies and in bridge construction. Eiffel reached the pinnacle of success at the Exposition of 1889 with his tower, as did Steiner there with the Gold Medal for his dolls. Although their fields were different and even though Eiffel's life was perhaps more glamorous — he is also remembered for his design of the framework for the Statue of Liberty — it would be interesting to know if they knew each other, being contemporaries with so much in common. In any event, the last half of the 19th century was a wonderful time to be alive and to contribute to their respective worlds as did these visionary men.

It has been my privilege to touch the past in an attempt to help recreate that time and place, to set the stage as it were, for the study of the man, Jules Nicolas Steiner. His works and his creativity have reached across a century to inspire both my life and Dorothy's.

An Historical Perspective:

In Search of Steiner

by Barbara Spadaccini Day

Very little is known about the man Jules Nicolas Steiner, one of France's foremost doll makers in the 19th century. Of the main group of toy and doll makers in the second half of this century well known to collectors, he was one of the first to appear. He was part of the second generation of doll makers who were to be in business for some 40 years and whose names posterity has retained. The names of the makers belonging to the first generation are for the most part forgotten, unknown. Their dolls were made in a more artisan way, in lesser quantities, not signed, thus unidentifiable.

Industrialization, commercialization, exportation together with the propagation of wealth amongst the middle class and a tangible expansion of the bourgeosie and upper middle classes under the Second Empire (1852 to 1870) developed a larger market and brought about an awareness of trademarks and names.

Awards were given in industrial exhibitions, national and international, and with the growing attraction for toys, special sections were created for them. France had been holding her own internal trade exhibitions since the late 18th century but toys were only noticeably present in them from the late 1830s onwards. The first world exhibition took place in London in 1851 in the specially erected Crystal Palace, a structure of glass and metal girders; French exhibitors were present. Children accompanied their parents when visiting these fascinating windows of progress.

The use of publicity and the development of department stores and specialized toy shops were other factors of competition. In the early stages, the doll as a manufactured object profited by this situation. Later, towards the end of the century, with the further evolution of techniques for mass production, standards dropped.

Seen in retrospect, this half a century from approximately 1850 to 1900 was the golden era of doll making and Jules Nicolas Steiner was very much an integral part of it, innovating in domains and techniques that were new. No other French doll maker in this period offered such a diversity of heads, the most visible and prized part of the doll.

Before he came on the scene, toy making in Paris was very much orientated towards producing small mechanical toys. Steiner himself started his career in the toy field as a maker of mechanical toys.

From the mid 1820s dolls must have been produced locally in Paris for there are at least three mold makers advertising their trade and wares as well as a maker of *bustes de poupées*. One only need go through the patents from the mid forties onwards to realize to what extent dolls, the method of making them, the materials used and their articulations were a major preoccupation. Advertising is explicit in the trade directories of that period about the origins of the dolls for sale: they could be French or German.

The Revolution of July 1847 obviously slowed down or arrested much of the production. The years that followed the Revolution with Louis Napoléon as president of the Republic, then later as Emperor, seem to herald in a turning point in the doll making world. It appears to be the end of an era and the dividing line between the first and second generation of doll makers already mentioned.

Was Jules Nicolas Steiner in Paris during these troubled times? We know he spent the first four years of his life in or around Dijon where he was born in March 1832. His mother Louise Steiner was 25 when she legally acknowledged the birth of her son, endowing him with a surname. Jules Nicolas was then four years old. When did he come to Paris? Did he come many years before his first patent was registered in the Patents Office in Paris? He was 23 years old when this took place. On these patent papers taken out in 1855 for a mechanical doll he is noted as being an *horloger* — clock maker. He is not listed under his name or trade at the address given on the patent, neither before nor after that date. There is, however, at that address of 16 rue de Poitou an indication that he might have worked there if we take into account his profession of clock maker. There are several people listed there for whom he might possibly have been employed. Or is this only a coincidence and he just lived there? Or was he already established as his publicity claims some 30 years later *maison fondée en 1855* firm founded in 1855?

Where did Jules Nicolas Steiner learn his profession of clock maker? In Paris? Was he predestined to this by his mother's Swiss origins from the canton of Vaud? Dijon is not far from the French clock making region of Besançon and from the long established famous clock making districts in Switzerland, la Croix, Neuchâtel, la Chaux-de-Fonds. Did he accomplish his apprenticeship in one of these towns, French or Swiss?

For the moment conjectures about it are open. J.E. Gerken says in *Wonderful Dolls of Papier Mâché* on page 49 "since Steiner is presumed to have been apprenticed to Munnier (sic)" without giving the source of this interesting information. If founded, it would establish that Steiner was in Paris some years before being granted the 1855 patent. A Monnier as a shop selling toys as well as a Munier making dolls are listed at two distinct addresses a decade earlier. But would Steiner have received an apprenticeship as a clock maker from either Munier or Monnier? (There appears to be some confusion around these two names with a tendency to amalgamate them into an entity.) Clock maker is how he is listed in the directory in 1858. The address given in it is identical to that of his second patent and that supplied by R. Capia in *Poupées*, 1984, as the address at the time of his marriage: 108 rue Vieille du Temple, proving with three entries that it is the same Jules Nicolas Steiner. Steiner is a fairly common name in France; even today there are many more Steiners listed in the Paris telephone directory than Jumeau or Bru.

Jules Nicolas Steiner akin to A.N. Theroude was prolific in inventiveness. When he later states in his publicity that he had taken out 22 patents, it avers to be exact if are counted in this number the addenda to his initial patents and those granted in nearby countries. Not all of them are pertaining to dolls and their improvements; some concern mechanical toys, one was for a machine worked by compressed air for producing molded dolls and bodies, others are for mechanisms that have nothing to do with toys.

Genesis of the Business

1858 appears to be an important year in the life of Jules Nicolas Steiner: a second patent granted for the breaking mechanism of toy boats in March in which he establishes himself as a *fabricant de jouets mécaniques* — maker of mechanical toys; in May he takes a wife, a dressmaker (Capia, *Poupées*, 1984) and his first entry appears in the Commercial Directory under clock making as a *horloger-mécanicien*. For doll collectors Jules Nicolas Steiner has stepped out of the shadows proving his existence, perhaps not yet as a doll maker for which he is renowned but in a vast all-englobing domain as a toy maker. From now on it is possible to follow his trace and career.

Numerous patents are granted in the two decades following 1850; many of them concern the mechanical functioning of toys, some of which are dolls. Steiner, like Theroude, Cruchet and François Guillard, is preoccupied about endowing the doll with a resemblance of speech and distinct pronunciation of the two syllables: mama papa. According to Henri Nicolle in 1868 the true paternity of this invention should be granted to Cruchet. This endowment is often combined with other mechanical devices of movement.

The question of how, when and why the baby form of the doll came into being is more precise today. It is not all important in knowing what European country and which maker introduced it first on the market. It is almost a certitude that its original source is Japan. Steiner was probably following a trend in form with his doll composed of a juxtaposition of rigid and flexible parts, but he did not invent it.

In the rapport of the 1855 International Exhibition, the first of its kind to be held in Paris, François Greffier was awarded an honorable mention for his "Dolls Japanese type known under the name of babies...this industry which is just beginning in France appears to have a promising future." Greffier was also present in the 1867 International Exhibition: "The dolls exhibited by Mr. Greffier are made entirely by him. The material used for the composition of his heads is his own invention and appears to be as fine and as strong as that employed by the Germans." Perhaps the dolls sold by Monnier were made by Greffier. Did Steiner use these dolls associating the parts with the mechanisms of his first inventions? His first patent like many of his subsequent patents concerned the mechanical system and not the formal aspect of the doll.

Although one can never qualify Jules Nicolas Steiner as a simple assembler of parts because he was in the true sense a maker of dolls, it is possible that at this time of his career he did not himself produce his own heads. Evidently the question arises: who supplied Steiner with the bisque parts and heads? Where did he obtain the early wax-over composition heads? Germany? A possibility especially in the beginning years. France? Personal supposition tips the scales of the balance a little more in favor of this probability.

Of course, there were importations from Germany, especially up to the time of the French-Prussian War in 1870. This is evident in the directories from the late 1850s when bisque and porcelain heads were being employed, gradually taking precedence over other mediums. Barrois, Blampoix aîné supplied heads. From research on François Gaultier, Florence Poisson reveals that Dalloz — successor to Blampoix aîné — was on the 1881 list of doll makers owing money to François Gaultier. It appears that Blampoix and Barrois were middle men. It is hardly plausible that Barrois selling German as well as French heads as stated in the directory would have made his own. Or did he, in spite of representing German makers? This almost rules out the above two names as being actual manufacturers but does not exclude the possibility that Steiner could have used one or the other as a source for the early bisque heads, or else Gaultier who says his firm was founded in 1860. Greffier could have been the maker of the early non bisque Steiner heads. Reasonably, not excluding the partial use of German heads, if there were mold makers in Paris producing molds for dolls, there were people on the spot employing them to produce heads.

1860-1870 Establishing the Business

For the next ten years — 1860-1870 — Steiner's address is rue de Saintonge. Until 1862 he is to be found at number 11, from then onwards at number 25. This will be a decade of activity and establishing the business. In an enterprising spirit he is amongst the first toy makers to make use of the newly created specific heading of "Toymaker" in the Commercial Directory. He changes the terms of his publicity in 1864 to *fabrique spéciale de poupées et bébés parlants, mécaniques et articulés* (specialized maker of talking, mechanical and articulated dolls and babies.) Here he seems to be ahead of his epoch; notwithstanding the conciseness of the wording he covers the entire span of doll making combining techniques, mechanics and form. His 1863 patent incorporating a pull string talking mechanism is in the kid body of the "traditional" lady doll: *poupée parlante*.

The newly founded rubric "Toymaker" will itself be split up in 1862 to mark the difference between toy and doll makers, up to that time intermingled. Steiner some four years after this separation takes advantage of the division and his name also appears under the specialized heading of "Dollmaker." Brief as the words may be, it establishes him as a professional doll maker, pushing into the background the maker of mechanical and musical toys and display items.

This is not only significant for Jules Nicolas Steiner, it also demonstrates how much it was necessary to establish the doll makers as a separate trade entity. This fact alone is full of meaning, acting as a barometer showing the degree of interest and effervescence in the doll making world.

11

Steiner was granted six patents in France, plus their addendas and a registered trademark during this period. However, only two patents directly concern dolls; the others were taken out for a mechanical toy horse, a magic optical box, perfecting the construction of velocipedes (also taken out in England) and ô surprise the improvement of an indispensable article of hygenic sanitation. Jules Nicolas was not a dreamer, but a down-to-earth man in contact with the reality of everyday life. The object of his patent is called euphemistically in French *garde-robe à cuvette inodore*. One would never guess...

In 1867 for the second time the International Exhibition was held in Paris. Jules Nicolas Steiner, although not directly present as an exhibitor under his own name, was implied in several ways. Pierre François Jumeau was awarded a silver medal for his "articulated dolls with porcelain heads, dressed dolls and talking babies" — *bébés parlants*. Printed paper labels bearing the name Jumeau handwritten have been found on both the kicking-crying baby and the waltzing doll produced by Steiner. Henri Nicolle, in the series of articles written about the Exhibition for the newspaper *l'Etendard* and subsequently published in book form in 1868, names Steiner explicitly in connection with a mechanical horse and a crying baby. Here he reveals that if the cost price of the horse and baby is expensive, the reason is that Steiner gets his parts from a small town near Dieppe specialized in supplying the mechanical parts of clocks and watches. It is Nicolle who taxes Steiner directly with not being the real inventor of the *bébé volontaire* as he aptly describes the kicking-crying baby, the initial idea came from Cruchet...

Of this period, the mechanical waltzing doll and the kicking-crying Steiner baby have both been found with those half-printed, half-handwritten paper labels which furnish two important clues to Steiner's activities at this epoch. First, it is difficult to ignore Steiner's primary profession of *horloger-mécanicien* as his patents and the dolls that he made during this period were almost exclusively mechanical. Secondly, these labels prove to what extent he supplied others. Although the consignees differ: Jumeau, Terrène, Fontaine, Garibareli (?), Voblock (?) (see *Doll News*, February 1969; these last two names are given under caution, no trace of them has been found in the directories corresponding to that period; have they been correctly deciphered?), the year 1867 is constant with a slight variation of month. Does that mean the dolls were new for this year?

If Steiner went to the trouble of having labels specially printed with a blank for the name, it is an indication that his market had developed. This is corroborated by the five different names mentioned above. There must be others. Madame Terrène, like P.F. Jumeau in the 1867 Exhibition, probably won her silver medal in the 1868 Le Havre exhibition for her display of mechanical babies made by Steiner. Jules Nicolas Steiner was a wholesaler, not only supplying toy shops but also his fellow doll makers who were not producing the same line of goods as he, mechanician that he was. The theory that Steiner only supplied them with the bodies, although not to be completely rejected, does not seem to apply. These dolls all have an identical kind of bisque head.

The open-mouth bisque heads with two well-furnished rows of tiny teeth are most probably an invention of this era due to another toy maker, George Most, who describes in an 1860 patent how the teeth could be either molded in the half open-mouth or put in separately. These early Steiner heads have a familiar resemblance; they probably came from the same source. Blampoix? Barrois? Gaultier, in business since 1860?

1870 - 1880 In the Ascendant

The troubled times in the beginning of this decade would not make life easy for anyone living in Paris and least of all the toy makers whose role is not essential in ordinary day-to-day existence. The Emperor Louis-Napoléon Bonaparte is discredited; it is the inglorious end of the Second Empire. A new wavering Republic, the third, is set up. France is at war with Prussia and Paris is besieged, encircled, cannoned by the enemy. The 1870-1871 winter was a particularly hard cold one and Parisians suffered famine and want. Even Castor and Pollux, the elephants of the Jardin d'Acclimatation were bought by a butcher's shop...

These hard and difficult months were followed by an insurrection in Paris and from March to May 1871 the "Commune" struggles to retain control of the town. Whole quarters of Paris are ransacked and burned, thousands of communards are executed summarily by the regular army who eventually gains control and squashes the revolt. It was not really the time for proclaiming your wares and Steiner's publicity when the new directory appears in 1872 is discreet.

Under Napoléon III's reign, Paris had been the setting for two International Exhibitions, Garnier had designed the Opera which was being built and the woods on either side of the capital had been transformed in likeness to the London parks that Napoléon had so much admired. Haussmann, the prefect, had terminated a number of outstanding unfinished works and pulled down many buildings bordering the maze of small twisted streets, making way for the large thoroughfares that cut across Paris, making it of easier access and still more important, less possible for the complaining common folk to set up barricades.

The financial tycoons had developed their riches. The accrued flow of wealth influenced fashion and spending, which in turn had a favorable impact on commerce and helped in the development of a new form of shop and way of selling. There was a visible increase of shops, from the Bazar to the *Magasin de nouveautés*, some of which were expanding into the new form of department stores selling all kinds of wares from lace cuffs to toys. Bon Marché was one of the first to emerge; the Printemps, Trois Quartiers, and the Louvre are of this epoch. Some have not survived the 20th century but they remain in the memories of collectors because of the catalogs in which toys were present, for example le Petit Saint-Thomas which sold Steiner dolls, Aux Deux Magots, le Tapis Rouge, Pygmalion...

For Jules Nicolas Steiner this is a decade of change and movement; he leaves rue de Saintonge for rue de Turbigo where he will be located according to the Commercial Directory from 1872 to 1874 at two numbers, for two years at 42, then at 62. He is not listed in 1875, reappearing a year later, 1876, in a completely different district, the 20th arrondissement. The six previous addresses were all located in what is now known as the 3rd arrondissement. The whole district was the site of toy makers and Steiner could probably not step out from one or the other of his workrooms without bumping into Jumeau, Theroude, Blampoix, Vichy, Maltête,

Roullet, and the myriad of toy makers that he knew but whose names have not been passed on.

If Lafosse, one of his successors, later states in the Commercial Directory that Steiner was the creator in 1873 of the *bébé incassable*, it was probably with hindsight because at no time during this decade did Steiner expand and develop his commercial spiel. The nearest to it would be when in 1870 he leaves out the word *poupée* and it now reads *fabrique spéciale de bébés parlants, mécaniques et articulés* (specialized maker of talking, mechanical and articulated babies.) It is doubtful that the later utilization of bébé — meaning *bébé incassable* — can be implied here.

In 1872 he does advertise *poupées articulées* — articulated dolls. Could they be the ancestors of the bébés? He will drop the word mechanical in 1873. When he again appears at his new and final venue, Steiner is still very economical with the wording, but mechanical has been reinstated. It now reads in 1876 "mechanical and talking babies, articulated dolls and babies" — Bébés? Possible. It can be noted in the Louvre catalog of 1876 the term *bébé incassable*. In the directory Jumeau seems to be the very first to use these two words together whilst Schmitt and Son have it in a different order before proudly announcing in 1879 that they are the "founders of a special workshop making *bébés incassables*."

At this epoch these semantical considerations do not seem to concern Jules Nicolas Steiner. He continues to advertise under the two headings of "Toymaker" and "Dollmaker" in his usual concise manner. He has supplied for the last 10 to 15 years many Parisian doll makers and toy shops with mechanical dolls and talking babies, his own invention and creation. Reflecting on the medals that several had received in the trade exhibitions for his dolls probably jolted Steiner to be present in the forthcoming 1878 International Exhibition under his own name. Even so, he never voyaged far afield like Jumeau and Bru, whose names were on the lists of such places as Vienna, Philadelphia, Melbourne, and so forth.

Moving his business three times in such a short and difficult period did not leave Steiner with much time for inventions and they appear to be absent in this decade. It is important to note that even though he and his wife had purchased as early as 1864 a major portion of 60 rue d'Avron — new name for rue de Montreuil, not to be confused with the suburb of Montreuil — it is only in 1876, more than ten years later, that he gives it as his business address. The Steiner firm is well and truly established as a small factory capable of employing a number of on-the-spot workmen and women. Is it from here that the French doll in one of the forms of an articulated bébé originated? The seeds were already latent waiting to be developed.

Jules Nicolas Steiner had had the time to study the body of his kicking-crying baby, to realize that it could not really be put into position for some kinds of play. Similarly, the Japanese form of soft and rigid parts suffered from the same defect and was especially fragile due to the members being of bisque. Was this doll, composed of alternate bisque and soft parts, his *poupée articulée* advertised in 1872? Was this the same doll which is in the Louvre catalog as a "talking baby (*bébé parlant*) made in Paris, bisque arms and legs, enamel eyes, curly wig" with four sizes ranging from 40 to 52 centimeters and advertised in 1877? It was on sale at the same price as an identical size *bébé incassable*. Here *bébé parlant* (two

voice strings hanging from its side are visible) certainly comes under the new connotation of the word bébé.

Who invented the molded carton body of the first *bébés incassables* with its articulated limbs? Several makers from the late 1850s and 60s were preoccupied by the problem of articulations and ways of attaching limbs and torsos; the patents attest to it. But who took the first steps of putting into production this new line of dolls? Steiner? As in all fields at a given period, ideas are in the air and identical research is common. Steiner, although very active, was not alone in the doll making industry which was rapidly developing. It is known that he produced bodies and that he even sold them to other makers (text P. du Maroussem 1894), but this could have been from the late 1880s onwards, following Steiner's patent of 1884 for a machine actioned by compressed air for making dolls, bodies and toys in molded carton.

His new enlarged working premises could have given him, as early as 1875-1876, the scope and incentive necessary to put into production a new line of dolls. A change takes place in 1875. Steiner demolishes and makes additions to rue d'Avron, for from this year to the next his taxes augment. Following the old law, proprietors were taxed prorata to the number of apertures — doors and windows — that the building contained. The total surface of the Steiner property, grounds included, measured some 2000 square meters; the layout of the buildings correspond to that of a much later schematic floor plan drawn to accompany an insurance policy. From this date to the beginning of the 20th century the general aspect of 60 rue d'Avron will remain identical. Only minor changes will occur and an addition wrought about by Bourgoin between 1880 and 1882 who constructs an extra floor on one of the existing ground floor buildings. As an anecdote, the building bordering the street, situated to the right of the main entry gates, was leased from 1876 for 12 consecutive years to the police who established a police station there. Later this becomes the guardian's quarters.

Up to 1875-1876 we know definitely that Jules Nicolas Steiner made and sold three types of dolls: the kicking-crying mechanical baby, the waltzing lady and a kind of articulated doll with opposing bisque and soft parts. He is firmly established, apparently successful and prosperous. He supplies a number of his fellow doll makers with a special line of dolls that only he produces; he is known. His business has so developed that it is logical he must go ahead with the times and extend his range. In the last four or five years of the 1870s this is without a doubt what he is doing. As a highly successful modern French doll maker says, "you must progress or disappear."

The progress could have been that Steiner began to produce his own heads for the new type of doll called *bébé incassable*. Stimulated by the incentive of the Jumeau firm who in the early 1870s established their new workshops in Montreuil with the necessary kiln and process of making their own bisque heads, Steiner may have followed their example several years later. Like Jumeau, J.N. Steiner had been in the doll making business for many years. He was experienced. He had watched it develop; he had even been an integral part of its development. There was still scope for further evolution and 60 rue d'Avron was large enough to accommodate a change in working methods. It is conceivable that it was Steiner himself who undertook the necessary alterations and had built a firing apparatus that still existed right up to the beginning of the 20th century. Several years later when Bourgoin took over, he was given permission in the lease hold to make certain changes. As the muffle furnace, an important addition it would seem, was not mentioned in the lease, can it be assumed that this was not part of the additional changes and already existed as such? Was J.N. Steiner already producing his own heads on the premises before Bourgoin took over? Or did this occur during Bourgoin's reign? Then who was Steiner's supplier? Gaultier most probably.

Another form of progress was the first time that Steiner was present in an industrial exhibition under his own name. He was one of the 21 French doll makers exhibiting their wares in the 1878 International Exhibition. Competition must have been stiff; six medals were awarded as well as twelve honorable mentions in this section. Steiner won a silver medal for his display of talking mechanical babies. Bru, Gaultier and Schmitt were the other three awarded the same high grade, and Emile Jumeau carried off the coveted gold medal.

It was in this much visited exhibition that parents could also take their children to admire the novelty of Elie Martin's swimming doll *Ondine* as well as the recent pocket size all-bisque *mignonnette* — a tiny doll usually measuring no more than 20 centimeters. Children's playthings are beginning to take on an importance that will increase steadily with the coming years.

During this decade a tangible evolution of the doll — in general — occurred. In a relatively short number of years, three or four definite types materialized or became stabilized. *La poupée*, the lady doll on various kinds of bodies, was holding its own; in the next decade this body tends to be unified and almost exclusively kid. The *bébé incassable* was emerging from its nascent cocoon; it will not change much in the next ten years. The *mignonnette* or pocket size doll will remain identical to its primary form for many long years; only the materials in which it is made will vary. Mechanical babies and dolls — excluding automaton — were still popular as seen by Steiner's silver medal. Will this be the continuation and new beginning of the series of mechanical bébés very much in vogue towards the end of the century and be Steiner's indirect influence and work?

1880-1890 Success: Series, Figures and Bourgoin

This period of the next ten years will see the firm at its summit; 1880 to 1890 can be considered as the golden age of Steiner dolls. At the beginning of the decade Jules Nicolas is in the prime of his life, not yet fifty. He has been working as a toy maker for more than 20 years, gaining experience and acquiring fame. His business is thriving; he is the proprietor of a small factory. The silver medal awarded in 1878 for a first time entry in an international industrial exhibition is of consequence. It placed him immediately in the front line, but his entries in the Commercial Directory are still rather spartan, especially if they are compared with Bru's eye-catching 50 lines of bold type and thick tall titles. Even Jumeau is modest in comparison.

Steiner like his counterparts in the doll making world was preoccupied with improving the doll's appearance and giving it life and character. All through this epoch numerous patents are granted for inventions and improvements concerning the doll and its various mediums, its articulations, assembly, eyes,

wigs, hair insertion as well as mechanical systems to resemble human movement. It will develop into a major battleground agitating the four or five main doll makers as the years draw the century to an end.

Of this era, Steiner's six patents in France with their many addendas can be considered a cross section of the whole body of patents for this ten-year period. Two concern eyes (one was also granted in Germany in 1880), their movement and way of making them. One, in 1884, is for a machine producing dolls in molded carton, denoting his interest in the mechanization of doll making. As a true entrepreneur, he was moving with the era, industrializing and economizing on a process which had previously been achieved on a large scale by outworkers. Another is for unbreakable bisque heads and, lastly, excluding a patent about the landing of hot-air ships, is the patent granted for *Bébé Premier Pas*, a walking bébé.

As the recent innovation of a new type of doll — *le bébé incassable* — gained in popularity over the lady doll, the Steiner firm developed to the utmost its fabrication of a different series of heads for its bébés endowing them with varied physiognomies. Jules Nicolas Steiner was the only one to go so far ahead in this field. Emile Jumeau essayed his hand in this domain and brought out the E.J.A. mold and the long face, more poetically named in French *Jumeau triste*. They seem to be the beginning and the end of his experiment for this epoch. Steiner and/or Bourgoin made this difference their Trojan horse. Was it a concerted pre-determined tactic?

When in the spring of 1880 Monsieur and Madame Steiner rented out 60 rue d'Avron to Monsieur and Madame Bourgoin, on a twelve-year lease, it was stipulated that they could only exploit it as a *fabrique de bébés*. This gives credence to the supposition that J.N. Steiner had already commenced manufacturing the series bébés and his own bisque heads, produced on the premises. Added to the clause that Bourgoin could build an additional floor to one of the buildings was another, stating that a portion of the living quarters situated on the first floor of the building set back in the grounds and parallel to the street could be transformed into workrooms. Steiner was obviously aware of the immediate necessity of expanding the working capacity of rue d'Avron, and thus allowed Bourgoin the possibility of doing so.

It is not known exactly how long Bourgoin remained there. His leasehold was divided into three-year periods with a six month's notification prior to quitting. He did not finish the lease of the twelve-year term for by autumn 1890 J.N. Steiner was in the process of leasing 60 rue d'Avron to Lafosse with a promise of sale. Bourgoin's name disappeared from the Commercial Directory in 1888, nor was he cited in the awards of the 1889 Exhibition. It is possible that he left after the end of his second three-year term in 1886; however, it must have been sometime between 1886 and 1888. Corroborating this is a legal document dated January 1887 and another October 1890 where Steiner is named as respectively *fabricant de jouets* — toy maker and *fabricant de bébés*, whereas in 1882 and 1883 he is cited as *ancien fabricant* — former toy maker.

Was Bourgoin, the first of the successors in the Steiner firm, experienced in this line of business? Robert Capia in *Les Poupées Françaises* published in 1979 states that in 1880 Bourgoin was a *fabricant de poupées en tous genres* — maker of dolls of all kinds at 41 faubourg du Temple. It was during his time spent as the successor to J.N. Steiner (1880 to 1886-87) that the firm produced some of its most appealing dolls. His name is irrevocably linked to the dolls marked "Sie" — serie. These are often clearly stamped with his name as well as carrying that of Steiner, contrary to the later successors whose dolls are not explicitly marked with their own name. It may never be known precisely the role he played in developing this line of bébé. Many blanks need to be filled in to determine his influence. A puzzling question arises: although Steiner had rented out his business, he appears to be ever present, hovering in the background. What part did he still have in it? Questions that are unanswered and will probably remain so. It is significant that J.N. Steiner no longer thinks of himself as a toy maker but as a "proprietor" — fulfillment of childhood desires?

He was granted patents concerning dolls during Bourgoin's era and these were put into use under Bourgoin's management; the eyes and eye system made during this period attest to it. They were advertised in 1882. During this period one can sometimes find stamped on the bodies of the dolls a trademark which is a simplified version of the caduceus, Steiner's early trademark registered in 1869. Originally this was to be an oval shaped metal plaque embossed with this emblem and fixed to toy velocipedes. Steiner's profession was given as a constructor. The new utilization of the symbol reduced in size, altered slightly, used to mark dolls, was probably not registered. It was discarded around 1888, being superseded by the mark "Le Petit Parisien."

The early years of the 1880s were probably not easy ones for J.N. Steiner personal-wise. He demands a legal separation from his wife, Marie Anne Laurent, which is granted in the beginning of 1881. The divorce is pronounced and registered some four years later in November 1885. In December of the same year he marries Augustine Adelaide Tremblay; for both it is the second time. J.N. Steiner is almost 54 years old. To cover the legal partition of the property between him and his first wife, Steiner is obliged to sell 60 rue d'Avron — to himself — in 1882. (As an anecdote Marie Anne, his first wife, some years later returns to the district of her early married life, rue Vieille du Temple, where at another lower number she runs a butcher's shop.)

Steiner comes back on the scene in 1888 in force under the recently founded heading of "Bébé Incassable," another division in the rubrics of the Commercial Directory. This new title started in 1881 with the sole name of Emile Jumeau listed. By 1888 there were 26 doll makers claiming to make the now extremely popular *bébé incassable*. This year Steiner is listed with 17 lines of publicity, proclaiming that he is the inventor of the bébé in France (if not the exact truth, his work and inventions would entitle him to this claim more than any of the other doll makers of this period), that the firm was founded in 1855 (the date of his first patent), that his *bébé incassable* called *le Petit Parisien* has moving eyes, articulated wrists and articulations without ball joints. The trademark concerning *le Petit Parisien* was registered much later, in October 1889, just before the World Exhibition closed. If be taken into account that this publicity was necessarily submitted to the printers of the Commercial Directory before the end of 1887, it would signify that he was employing the term, *le Petit Parisien*, but not necessarily the drawing, long before being granted the rights to its use, a not uncommon

procedure. The fact that he deems it necessary to stipulate at this date "impossible to confuse with German fabrication" is evidence of German importations and a supplementary reason for his appellation *le Petit Parisien*.

The next year J.N. Steiner's life-time work of more than 30 years as a doll maker will be crowned and the firm Steiner is at its zenith; he is awarded a gold medal for his mechanical babies and talking and ordinary *bébés incassables* called *le Petit Parisien*. The four other gold medals were won by various toy making firms, one of which was Gustave Vichy, the famous automaton maker. Jumeau was *hors concours*, being one of the judges. Chevrot (Bru firm), Falck-Roussel, Gaultier and son, and Rabery were given silver medals.

Each exhibition has its landmarks and this 1889 International Exhibition, celebrating the centennial of the 1789 Revolution, was characterized by an important feat of engineering skill. This was the work of Gustave Eiffel; his 300 meter's high metal tower will remain the highest building in the world for the next 40 years.

These industrial exhibitions last for approximately 200 days, from May to November, and are much visited by all classes of the French population as well as foreign visitors. Confirming its importance, the toy section, situated adjacent to jewelry, was one of the most visited sections of the whole 1889 exhibition. This interest, nascent at the end of the last decade, is more overtly visible in this exhibition. The toy makers abetted by the stores will cater to the needs of children more and more, creating desires, opening new technical domains and processes of marketing. The owners of the large department stores are quick to realize the importance of this new market and the commercial gains to be won., They will influence children directly by publishing specialized catalogs at Christmastime. The first catalogs containing a few toys and dolls on their pages appear in the beginning of the 1870s. Less than ten years later all the stores and some of the specialized toy shops are bringing out a special edition at Christmas destined to whet the appetite of children.

The proprietors of the department stores will also oblige the doll makers who sell to them to submit to certain conditions, often unfavorable, such as delayed payment for the goods delivered, low prices and stockage of the merchandise, until the store is ready to display it in December. This policy is very much to the advantage of the store keepers who have their share of responsibility in bringing down prices, fomenting competition and a general decrease in the standards of quality of the doll itself. Now begins the battle which, combined with other factors, will end with the demise of all but the strongest doll makers, and the amalgamation of the main body of them.

1890-1900 — Steiner's Last Years: New Successors Lafosse

For a short period following the laurels of the 1889 exhibition, Steiner continues to manage his business. According to a license that was issued to him in 1890, he has working under him 35 workmen and women. His warehouse is situated in the second arrondissement in rue St. Denis. He is still active and his patent for a walking doll called *Bébé Premier Pas* proves that he is as always mechanically minded. Even when he has retired and is no longer living in Paris, he continues inventing and he registers in 1894 a patent for a mechanical toy; he is at that time sixty-two.

In October 1890 a new lease is signed giving Monsieur

Amédée Onésime Lafosse leasehold for 15 years beginning 1st January 1891, combined with a commitment of sale. If in 1890 prospects held a promise, before the end of the decade doll making was becoming a difficult business, especially for those who had known it in its halcyon days, and this sale never took place. However, J.N. Steiner does not disappear completely. His name is still foremost in the publicity of this period and will remain so into the 20th century.

In a study of the Parisian toy and doll industry published in 1894, Pierre du Maroussem writes that toys should become "an inexpensive luxury" accessible to all; that the large scale low-priced manufacture should take precedence over the expensive small-scale productions. This was already becoming a reality but low prices were generally synonymous to low standards in quality and would continue to be so more and more. According to this study, fabrication of dolls could be divided into three types of production: those made on a very small scale, those produced entirely from assembling the different parts bought from various sources and those manufactured industrially. In this last category he cites Jumeau, Danel and Steiner. The Steiner firm could even supply the bodies and limbs completely assembled. As from 1890 Steiner is listed under four separate headings in the directory: dolls, bébés incassables, toys and wholesale toys. This impulsion was given by Steiner himself for he was still in charge at that date. His warehouse (did he have one before?) was situated in another district.

The firm under Lafosse's direction was still foremost on the scene and Steiner's name still shining bright. The new leaseholders were active and enterprising. Amédée Lafosse was a member of the *Chambre Syndicale des Fabricants de Jouets et Jeux* and spent a term as official secretary to this organization. From 1891 to 1898 six patents were granted, two trademarks registered, the firm was awarded a *Hors Concours* in a Parisian exhibition and the publicity was lengthy and explicit.

Amédée Lafosse died between autumn 1892 and spring 1893. However, his widow continued running the business, even taking out patents, for five of the six were deposited under her name. These concerned principally the mechanical devices activating the dolls, for this is a decade of walking, talking, breathing, kiss-throwing bébés and Widow Lafosse followed the trends of the moment, developing this line. Was this vogue for mechanical dolls part of Steiner's heritage and the mark that he left on the doll industry?

One of his dolls, the mechanical baby or kicking-crying Steiner, was still being manufactured in the 1890s. In the 1880s and early 1890s it could still be purchased from one of the large specialized toy shops: Au Nain Bleu, A la Récompense or Maison Nadaud, or the Magasin des Enfants. Steiner dolls bearing a toy shop label seem to occur with greater frequency than do those of other French doll makers. The list of these establishments is long and includes the Maison Bail, Maison Simonne, Au Bébé Incassable, Aux Enfants Sages and the lesser known A la Petite Amazone, one of the early shops of the 1870s which also sold well constructed, elegant lady as well as kicking-crying Steiners. Terrène labels have been found on both the early production of mechanical waltzing lady dolls as well as the cumbersome mechanical baby, but it seems to be those marked the Nain Bleu and the Magasin des Enfants that come up with greater

regularity. From these shops came marked Bourgoins, Series, Figures, *le Petit Parisien*, *Le Parisien*, wire-eyed bébés and *Bébé Premier Pas*, a complete range of the Steiner production.

Most of these stores would have bought the dolls unclad, then had them dressed according to their taste and various price range. The best dressed could cost almost twice as much as those merely clad in a simple chemise.

Contrary to Jumeau, whose dolls were always sold under his own name in the department stores or were stated as fabrication Jumeau when sold under a department store's name, Steiner, like many of his contemporaries, remained anonymous in the catalogs, except for several occasions in the 1890s. From the beginning, Steiner's outlet was the specialized toy shop, large or small. His dolls were sold under various shop names other than his own.

Small and medium sized Steiner bébés can often be found dressed in traditional French regional costume, or sometimes that of foreign countries or the French protectorate. This was very much in evidence during this last decade under Lafosse's management. In 1895 *Bébés nègres et mulatres* were advertised in keeping with the general trend. This vogue for dolls in costume lasted many years; they were not considered as souvenir dolls but as legitimate playthings. Steiner bébés are found more often than others so dressed.

The trademark "Le Parisien" was registered in August 1892 by Amédée Lafosse and that of "Bébé Phénix" in May 1895 by Marie Lafosse, his widow. This name had been used previously by Henri Alexandre in the 1880s for a series of bébés; apparently it had not been registered. Alexandre was amongst the 115 French participants in the 1889 International Exhibition; he was awarded an Honorable Mention for his articulated and mechanical toys, dressed and undressed articulated *Bébé Phénix*. His time as a manufacturer or large scale assembler was shortlived. In 1886 he was granted a trademark consisting of his initials "H A" placed on either side of a schematized drawing of a paper cock; this mark was to be used on toys — dolls were not mentioned. By 1892 Tourrel was his successor. Then he, too, is absent from the listing. A supposition: was Steiner a or the supplier of parts for Alexandre's *Bébé Phénix*? Did Widow Lafosse legally register *Bébé Phénix* as a trademark to be able to continue its diffusion? This bébé is still on the market in 1901.

Due to growing economic difficulties in France and competition, running a business was becoming increasingly problematic for all concerned. The successful years of the late 1870s and 1880s when small affairs could develop and flourish on a tiny capital investment were over. It was not sufficient to have ideas, be hard working and produce quality goods; each manufacturer was part of a large system and was obliged to contend with extraneous factors. Very few were strong enough to resist a slump in trade. After the golden years, the market had reached its summit.

The consortium S.F.B.J. was formed in 1899 but the seeds of this evolution were apparent from the mid 1890s. The Steiner firm was not one of the ten Parisian toy and doll makers who united their forces. It continued to exist as an independent entity, with a change of direction. Widow Lafosse's name disappears in 1899. Jules Mettais takes over. Jules Nicolas Steiner's trace is lost after 1894 when he was granted his last patent. The final chapter in the history of the

Steiner firm is about to commence, inglorious and tumultuous.

1899-1908 Mettais and Daspres — Decline and End of an Epic.

The tenant-hold of 60 rue d'Avron was transferred in May 1899 to Jules Mettais. In October he had already registered three trademarks: "Baby," "Bébé Liège" and "Phénix Baby." (The English word — baby — was in fashion and this anglicism could be found in many French texts of this period.) Two more trademarks follow in 1900 and 1901: "Poupée Merveilleuse" and "Bébé Modéle." Whereas Steiner and Lafosse took out relatively few trademarks, they were granted many patents. Jules Mettais, on the contrary, during the short time he was managing the business registered as many as five trademarks. Patents denote inventiveness, reflection and concern about improving or innovating. Trademarks are tuned to publicity and protection of a name, image of product. Perhaps Mettais with a more modern approach to selling and marketing conceived the idea than an *image de marque* would help promote his dolls. Certainly he was aware, as were many of the other manufacturers, of the need to protect their commercial interests. Toy and doll makers had associated in the late 1870s and formed a syndical chamber, which in 1897 had reregistered the trademark of 1886, having the form of a triangle and inscribed *article français* and *marque déposée*. Each adhering member could use this mark together with his alloted number. Many old established firms used it. More and more makers adhered to this movement; Mettais (identified by his number which is 84) was one of them, as Lafosse was before him. This concept of "buy French" was redeveloped in a slightly different form during the First World War when it became UNIS FRANCE.

The grouping together of a number of manufacturers having a common denominator is not an isolated economical phenomenon, specific to doll makers alone. Two other consortiums formed within several years at the turn of the century, one concentrating together the makers of tin toys, trains, vehicles, and so forth, the other uniting the manufacturers of all kinds of games and board games. The entire profession was undergoing a profound change of mentality. During this period a large number of the smaller, less solvent firms disappeared completely and many of those that remained would be swept away by the maelstrom of the war years. The end of an era is at hand. Mettais, no exception, will not escape; he, too, will disappear.

From 1899 until spring 1903 Mettais continued to use the name Steiner; (Steiner died in 1902); *le Parisien* is still advertised. Mettais was present at the 1900 World Exhibition held in Paris, exhibiting diverse mechanical bébés, bébés and black and mulatto dolls. For the first time since 1867, Germany is amongst the exhibitors. Specially constructed for this grand event were the Grand and Petit Palais, now museums. Orsay and the Invalides stations had just been completed and visitors could travel to the site of the exhibition — the most visited of all time — using a new means of transport: the metropolitan.

When Mettais took over the lease of 60 rue d'Avron, it was under the same conditions as those accepted by Lafosse. The rent was payable quarterly. In May 1903 the second quarter was a month overdue and legal action was immediately taken against him to conform to the terms of the lease. By the beginning of July all that remained intact on the premises was sold in a public auction. The list is not very detailed and seems to be comprised mainly of different types of molds for heads, bodies, limbs, torsos; some porcelain and plaster (sic) heads were part of it. This sale made 246 francs 50; the overdue rent amounted to 2000 francs.

There is a discrepancy between the type of merchandise found on the premises in 1903 and the declaration of an insurance policy taken out by Steiner himself in 1901 for a duration of ten years. He declared that the tenant was a manufacturer of mechanical babies but that the heads, bodies and limbs were made elsewhere. The establishment only adapted the mechanisms (he does not specify where they came from), decorated and dressed the dolls. Was Steiner minimizing in order to pay a small premium or was this old stock and Mettais really just an assembler? The inventory, preceding the sale, records various types of molds, basins, buckets etc., a bin for plaster. The furnace (*moufle* or *four à porcelaine*) had 18 trays and metal grates containing approximately 80 molds to a tray. If dolls were not made on the spot, why so many molds? The list of the various parts make up a complete doll.

An accumulation of fragments, debris, broken pieces of shelves, workbenches, boxes, dolls' bodies, heads, limbs, molds and the wood from several hangars, all in a state of deterioration, littered 60 rue d'Avron, leaving the impression of a passing tornado. It seems like a vindictive action and that the tenant bore the owner a grudge.

Mettais was never present each time the bailiff called, and he called many times. An interesting piece of information comes from a neighbor who reported that since Mr. Mettais had sold the business (sic), he had moved to 22 rue de la Revolution in Montreuil where he made dolls. A one-time entry in the 1902 Commercial Directory under the suburb of Montreuil gives Edmond Daspres listed as a doll maker at this address. Curious coincidence — were they in connivance? Had Mettais taken refuge with Daspres, a legitimate toy maker? Or was Daspres a figurehead? More unanswered questions!

By September Mettais was evicted; the property at 60 rue d'Avron was put up for sale and in 1904 legal proceedings were going ahead. It was sold. The deeds were signed and transferred; in the early spring 60 rue d'Avron had a new proprietor. Although dolls and bébés were no longer produced there, the name of Steiner would continue to appear for several more years.

Edmond Daspres is the final successor of the Steiner firm. In 1902, before being connected to the name Steiner, he was granted a patent for a walking and talking doll. From 1902 to 1904 his address is in the 10th arrondissement. In 1905 he is listed under three headings in the directory and is then located in rue de Belleville in the 20th arrondissement. As Steiner's successor, he advertises *Le Parisien* under *Bébés Incassables* and under that of *Poupées* (dolls) *La Patricienne*, followed by a subtitle, a fashionable society doll, which does not quite signify the same as patrician, as one of noble birth.

Up to 1914 Edmond Daspres' name still appears under "Toymaker" alone; dolls are not mentioned in his publicity from 1909. An economy, or had he ceased producing dolls? It

17

is almost certain that Daspres was an assembler of parts. With him, the last link in the chain, ends the story of the Steiner firm which just fades into nothingness.

The firm had been in existence from 1855 to 1908. It is very much an essential part in the history of the French doll makers of the 19th century. In reality the vintage period of Steiner dolls can be counted from the 1860s to the time when Lafosse is managing the business and Jules Nicolas Steiner himself is still active in the background.

The dolls and bébés produced in the last epoch will have lost many of the qualities that have endeared the early Steiner dolls to collectors. Nevertheless, they should not be overlooked; they are part of the history and the evolution of a business started more than half a century earlier. This business was the fruit of one man's efforts, developed from his hard work, inventiveness and enterprising spirit. He was actively present for some 35 years.

It is difficult not to draw a parallel with the Jumeau firm when reflecting on Steiner. More is known about Emile Jumeau himself, the factory and his methods of work. But are the two firms comparable? The history of the Steiner firm is more complex; in its later stages of development it implies the participation of many men whom we know nothing about: Bourgoin, Lafosse, Alexandre, Mettais and Daspres. Contrary to Jumeau, who had had the advantage of having two generations in which to build up the business, possessing a more industrialized production line, employing a greater number of workers and manufacturing larger quantities of dolls, Steiner, the artisan, the self-made man, the entrepreneur with a smaller business, achieved comparable results. The dolls produced by him are equal, often superior, to those of his fellow doll maker. They are stamped with character and personality and possess an intrinsic childlike quality of charm and beauty worthy of our admiration.

After 1894, when Jules Nicolas Steiner was granted his last patent, his trace disappears. Apart from a few sketchy facts that fill in a small gap in his personal life, nothing is known of him. He was no longer living in Paris, having moved to a small town in the country some 40 kilometers northwest of Paris.

From both marriages Jules Nicolas Steiner was childless. (His second wife had a grown son living in the United States.) Towards the end of his life, in 1897, Steiner, then aged 65, adopted a young man called Emmanuel Steiner who was 24 years old. He became Jules Eugene Emmanuel Steiner and was made the sole legatee in his adopted father's will. No additional information is known other than the hard facts of these deeds, so no conjectures or extrapolations will be advanced concerning the reasons.

Augustine, his second wife, died in 1901, several months prior to Steiner himself who died just before his 70th birthday in February 1902 in a Parisian hospital. The mystery of his last years is still intact.

A few pieces of the puzzle have been filled in but many details concerning his early life, mature years, the reasons and facts of the succession of the various business managers remain an enigma. The tangibility of Jules Nicolas Steiner is that he was a master doll maker; the quality of his dolls are evidence that the man was of significance and his varied patents prove his inventiveness and intelligence. His name will not be lost; he has earned immortality. 1832-1902.

SELECTED BIBLIOGRAPHY

Annuaires de la Chambre Syndicale des Fabricants de Jouets, Jeux et des Engins Sportifs. Paris: 1892-1922.
Capia, Robert. *Les Poupées Françaises*. Paris: Hachette 1979.
_____ *Poupées*. Paris: Arthaud, 1984.
Catalogues des Grands Magasins. 1875-1910.
Commercial Directories. 1820-1916.
du Maroussem, P. *La Question Ouvriere, le Jouet Parisien*. Paris: A. Rousseau, 1894.
Gerken, J.E. *Wonderful Dolls of Papier Mâché*. Lincoln, Nebraska: Union College Press, 1970.

Guide de l'Acheteur. Paris: January 1882.
Nicolle, H. *Les Jouets, ce qu'il y a dedans*. Paris: Dentu, 1868.
Poisson, F. *Bulletin No 7, CERP*. Courbevoie: n.d.
Rapport du Jury des Produits de l'Industrie Française. Paris: 1844.
Rapports du Jury des Expositions Universelles. 1855, 1867, 1878, 1889, 1900.
Archives de la Ville de Paris.
I.N.P.I. (Patents Office). Paris.
Documents from a private source.

Section One

A STUDY OF DOLLS WITH PATENTED MECHANISMS

and

A LOOK AT
SOME EARLY UNMARKED BÉBÉS

of

Jules Nicolas Steiner

COLOR PLATES — Section One

Plate 1. 20 inch (51cm) wax-over papier-mâché *Bébé Parlant Automatique*. 1862 patent. Bright blue eyes, open mouth with two square upper and lower teeth. Original Scottish tartan outfit. *Courtesy of Elizabeth Pierce.*

Plate 2. Mechanism of 15 inch (38cm) waltzing lady with molded cardboard base showing three wheels and tip of paper label, dated 1867. *Hannah Shrand Collection.*

Plate 3. 15 inch (38cm) shoulder head waltzing lady mechanical, pale coloring, blue narrow almond-shaped eyes, open mouth with two rows of teeth, blonde mohair wig and fine ancestry, paper label on base dated 1867. *Winnie Langley Collection.*

Plate 4. Mechanism of *Bébé Parlant Automatique*, the kicking-crying Steiner. Metal-encased bellows signed: "J. STEINER PARIS." Body of purple papier-mâché, circa 1880s.

Plate 5. Close-up view of three decades of the kicking-crying Steiner: Left: 22 inch (56cm) with oval cobalt eyes, pale bisque, flat ears, circa 1870s. Right front: 17½ inch (45cm) the most typical of the Steiner Whiners, circa 1880s. Right back: 20 inch (51cm) with later higher coloring and heavy eyebrows, circa 1890s. *Wenham Museum Collection, Wenham, Massachusetts.*

Plate 6. Classic 22 inch (56cm) Series C 4 wire-eyed bébé. Pale bisque, blue lever-operated eyes, closed mouth, articulated body, with 3½ inch (9cm) long Steiff Lesser Panda; doll circa 1880s.

Plate 7. Porcelain eye globes of previous doll, incised: "STEINER 3 BTE SGDG."

Plate 8. 22 inch (56cm) Figure A wire-eyed bébé with delicate coloring, closed mouth, brown blown glass eyes with waxed lids, circa 1890s. *Bitterman Collection.*

Plate 9. Blown glass lever-operated eyes of the type shown in previous doll, embossed: "BREVETE L4 SGDG," circa 1890s.

Plate 10. 22 inch (56cm) *Bébé Premier Pas*, 1890 patent. Fully-articulated mechanical walking body. Lushly painted head with blue blown glass eyes, expressive mouth with two rows of teeth. *Constance W. Fielden Collection.*

Plate 11. 22 inch (56cm) kiss-blowing bébé incised: "A-15" with open mouth, single row of teeth, blue blown glass eyes. 1897 Lafosse patent.

Plate 12. 18 inch (46cm) bisque hip or "Motschmann-type" shown full view front and back, naked. Swivel neck version, circa 1870.

Plate 13. Close-up of previous doll, showing narrow blue lined eyes and extremely pale coloring. *Lorna Lieberman Collection.*

Plate 14. Full length view of 15 inch (38cm) bisque hip Steiner in her totally original baby dress of ecru linen with lace and blue silk ribbon trim and wearing a puddin', a baby "crash helmet." Circa 1870.

Plate 15. Close-up of previous doll shows pale blue-gray eyes, rimmed in bright blue.

Plate 16. 18 inch (46cm) unmarked bébé on earliest articulated body with six balls, along with a marked Series A on identical body for comparison, circa 1882.

Plate 1. Wax-over papier-mâché *Bébé Parlant Automatique*, 1862 patent.

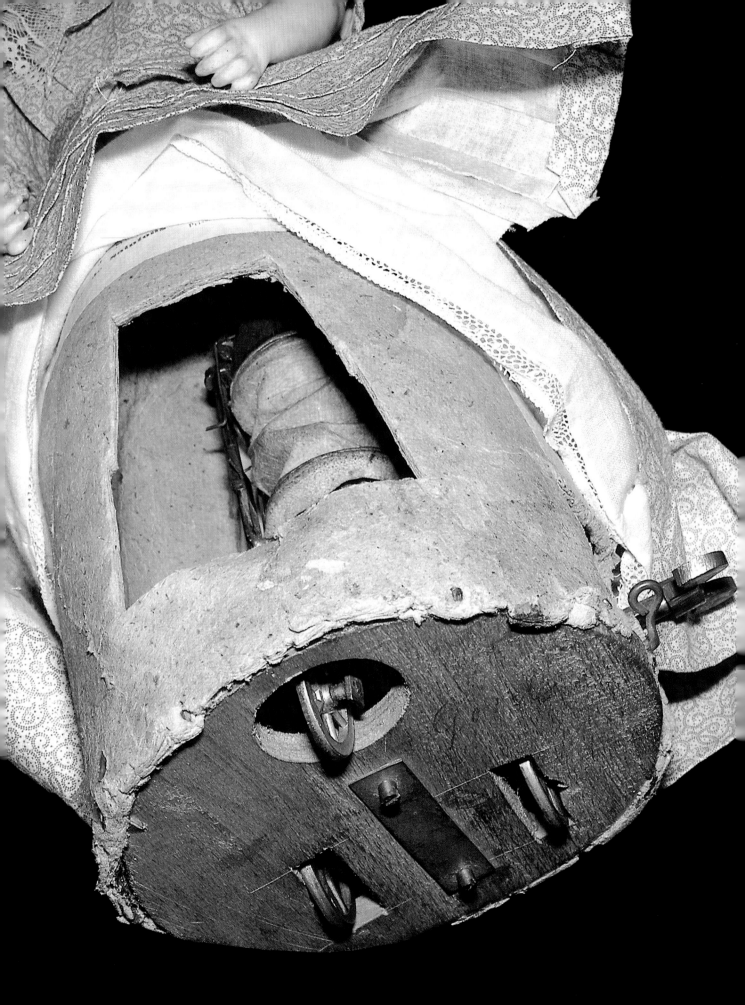

Plate 2. Mechanism waltzing lady, circa 1867.

Plate 3. Waltzing lady, circa 1867.

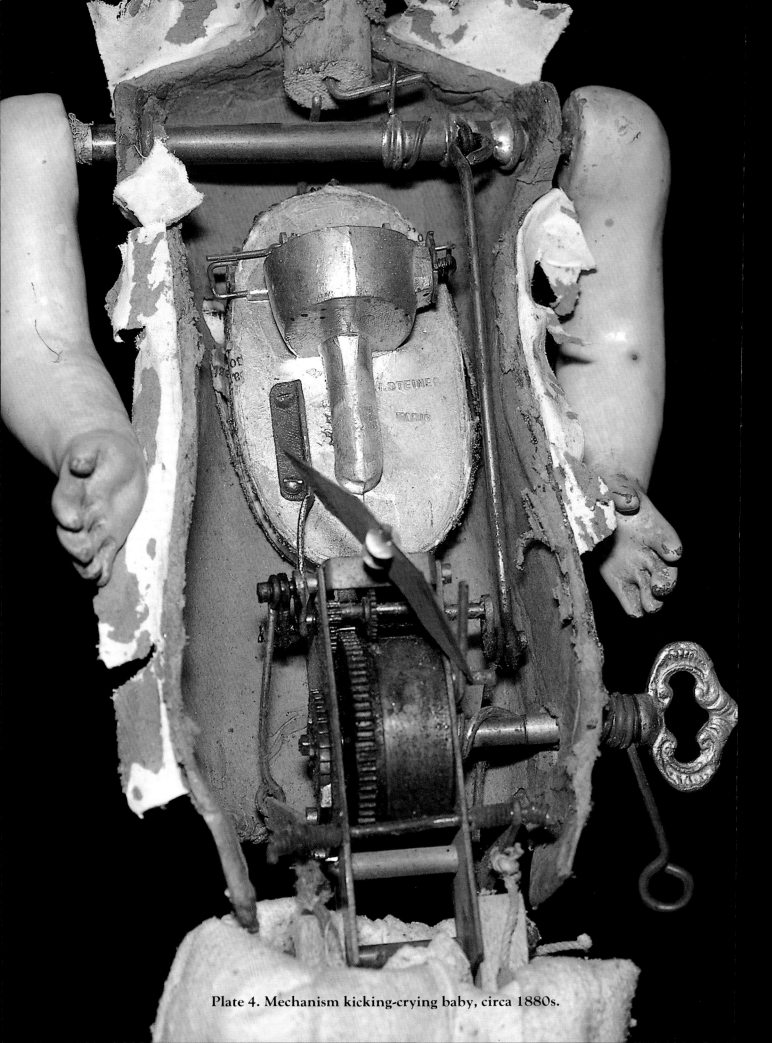

Plate 4. Mechanism kicking-crying baby, circa 1880s.

Plate 5. Three decades of the kicking-crying baby, circa 1870s, 1880s and 1890s.

Plate 6. Classic Series C
wire-eyed bébé, circa 1885.

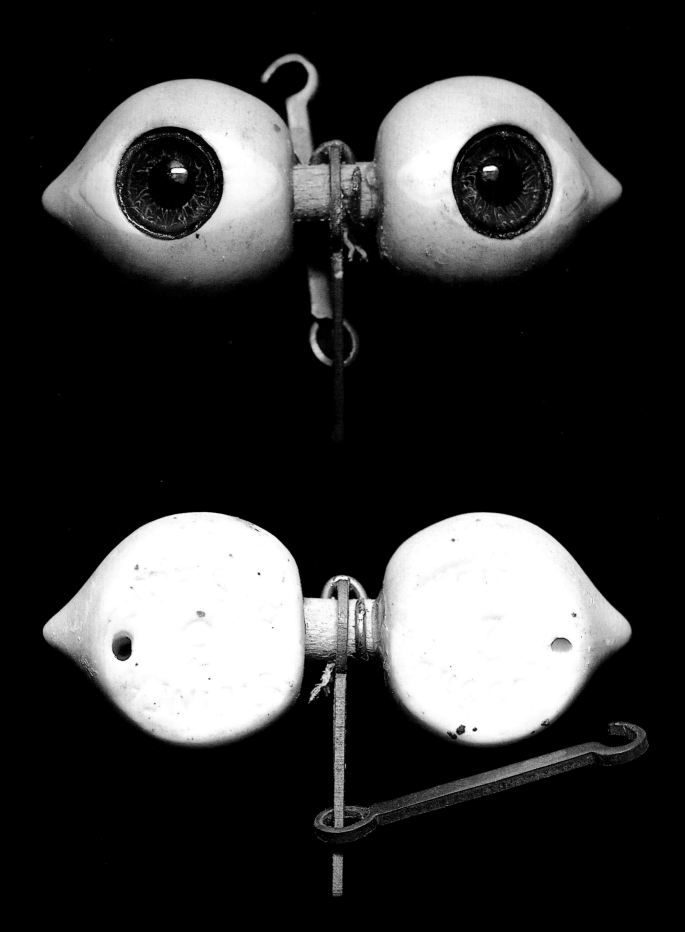

Plate 7. Porcelain globe lever-operated eyes, circa 1885.

Plate 8. Figure A wire-eyed bébé, circa 1890s.

Plate 9. Blown glass lever-operated eye globes, circa 1890s.

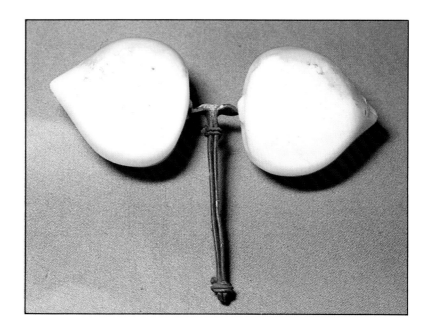

Plate 10. *Bébé Premier Pas*,
1890 patent.

Plate 11. Kiss-blowing bébé, Lafosse patent 1897.

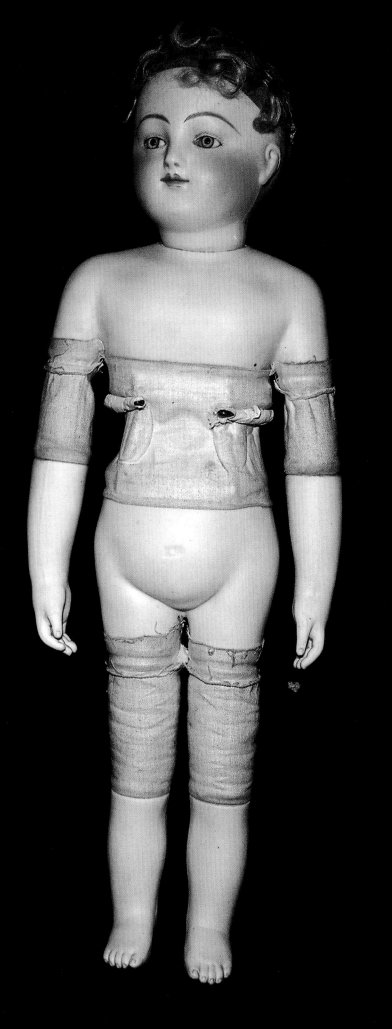
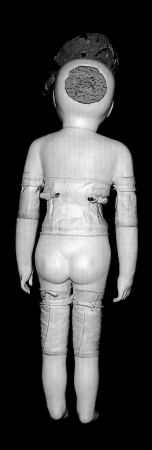

Plate 12. Bisque hip or Motschmann-type, circa 1870.

Plate 13. Bisque hip Steiner, circa 1870.

Plate 14. Bisque hip, circa 1870.

Plate 15. Bisque hip, circa 1870.

Plate 16. Unmarked and Series A bébés on articulated bodies, circa 1880-82.

DOLLS WITH PATENTED MECHANISMS

A study of the dolls of Jules Nicolas Steiner must begin with his patented mechanisms, for that is where his initial steps into the French doll and toy industry were taken, with his first patent in 1855. A consistent theme in Jules Steiner's patents is the use of mechanical devices to impart a "life" to the doll. In the following pages we will examine a number of these patents and dolls. The changes in the mechanics as well as the heads used for various dolls are aids in helping to identify and date these and other Steiner dolls. Not all of his patents will be detailed in this section, but a complete listing with summarized descriptions can be found in the Appendix (page 211.)

While this book concentrates on Jules Steiner, it must also touch on or refer to the patents of his successors, Amédée Onésime Lafosse and the Widow Madame Marie Lafosse. Their patents primarily modify for production purposes those of Jules Steiner and are also contained in the Appendix, along with one obtained in 1902 by Edmond Daspres, the final successor in the Steiner firm.

As we have seen, there had been extensive interest in automatons and action toys over the preceding century. Interesting accounts can be found in both Mary Hillier's *Automata* and Constance Eileen King's *The Collector's History of Dolls*. Chapuis and Droz in *Automata* chronicle the intense interest in creating devices to imitate speech in the late 18th century. Of particular interest is the talking machine of Baron von Kempelen, who adapted and modified the simple age-old rectangular bellows (which produces a cry similar to a bleating sheep) by fitting it with a simulated mouth and nose to recreate human sounds. In 1824, Leonhard Maelzel patented an improved bellows for dolls which, by the use of valves and an intricately notched lever, could say "Mama" and "Papa."

The doll itself as a child's plaything, the very essence of its being, was an emergent idea in the early 19th century as our attitudes toward childhood evolved and machinery made possible mass production in the Western world.

The Edo Period in Japan (1615-1868) had also seen immense enthusiasm for dolls. While many were great ornamental works of art, more sculpture than doll, toward the end of the Edo period a bendable play doll representing a child was developed. This doll felt like a baby when held and had a plump face with small features suggesting the naivety of a child. Called *mitsuore-ningyo*, which literally means three-joint dolls, they could bend at the head, waist and knees by means of dovetail or ball and socket joints. The abdominal joint, significant in representing the Japanese habit of sitting on one's feet, is not common in Western dolls. An outgrowth of this doll, mid-century, was the *Daki-ningyo*, with a fabric middle and floating joints. Daki means "cuddly;" this doll became the everyday play doll of Japanese children. See *Illustration 1*.

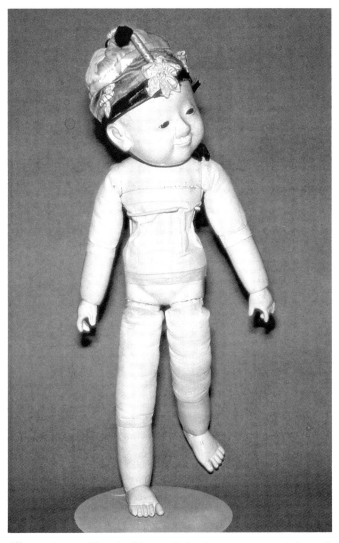

Illustration 1. 20 inch (51cm) "Ti-hee-hee," a Japanese baby with floating joints separated by fabric, predecessor of the German Täufling baby. The composition segments are made of oyster powder and fish glue with a hard paint finish. He has brown glass inset eyes and a generous nose. Late Edo period, circa 1860. *June P. Kibbe Collection.*

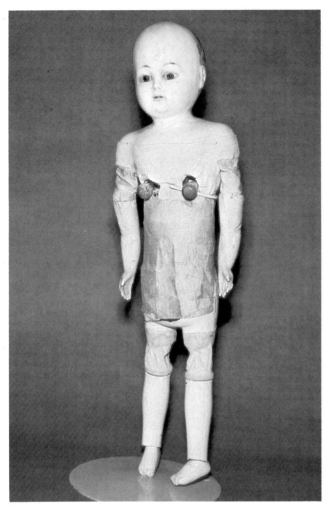

Illustration 2. 20 inch (51cm) German Motschmann-type, copied from the Japanese baby. Body segments are composition or papier-mâché and the head is waxed-over papier-mâché. Blue sleep eyes work by counterweight. The voice box is operated by pushing the knobs; the "Mama-Papa" sounds are not clearly distinguishable. Circa 1860.

Purportedly, this Japanese doll was introduced, perhaps via the Dutch, to the masses at the first International Exhibition held at the Crystal Palace in London in 1851, where it was met with immediate approval. The Germans, quick to manufacture new ideas, produced a great number of these Täuflinge babies in various forms throughout the remainder of the century, a number of which had simple squeak boxes in their torsos. Many of these babies had the so-called Motschmann-type body, an incorrect name which lingers but brings to mind a picture of the baby with separated body parts joined by fabric inserts at the midriff, thighs and upper arm. See *Illustration 2.* It might be more accurate to call this a Japanese-type baby, giving credit where it is due. The influence of this body construction on Jules Steiner and his dolls will be seen both in his bisque and papier-mâché versions discussed later as well as in details of the bodies of Steiner's earliest mechanical bébés, particularly in their lower legs and feet.

Some Täuflinge babies have a solid papier-mâché torso with a cutout area to access the bellows; other examples have a hinged mouth which opens when the bellows is pressed. It is this variant which we also see reflected in Steiner's first patent. These and many other versions are pictured in the *German Doll Encyclopedia 1800-1939* by Jürgen & Marianne Cieslik. The adaptability of this body construction to accept a clockwork mechanism coupled with its popularity and availability must have been a consideration for the young Steiner. As a clock maker, Jules Steiner may have initially been approached by a doll maker to work on such a mechanism for a baby doll, or perhaps he originally intended to sell this patented idea or the mechanism to doll makers.

Whatever the inspiration, on September 17, 1855, Jules Nicolas Steiner registered his first patent, #24828, which describes a "mechanism used to cause the movement of arms, legs, head and mouth of a doll, and of causing it to cry out when laid down." The wording of the patent is for a <u>mechanism</u> and not the production of a doll. It is possible he assembled some examples, though none are known to exist. Note that this first patent details the mechanism for the hinged mouth which would require having the heads assembled as one with the mechanism. This would have been a significant drawback to its production or in selling the mechanism to doll manufacturers. As will be seen, Steiner avoided this complication in his 1862 patent, #57803. It is very likely that in his early years in the toy industry, Steiner was buying available parts, both doll and mechanism, and making adaptations for improved sound and motion. Later, however, he designed or produced both mechanisms and dolls.

Jules Steiner's second patent, #35725, is dated March 8, 1858, and is a 15-year patent for a new system of stopping a wind-up mechanism from unraveling as it is being wound. Accomplished by the use of a gravity or weight-operated lever which releases the mechanism when the toy is set onto a hard surface, this assemblage was for use in almost any wind-up toy, vehicles or animals. The patent also had an adaptation for use in toy boats, a flotation device which would activate the mechanism when the boat was placed in water. (See appendix, page 211.)

The first existing mechanical doll which can be attributed to Jules Steiner is discussed next.

On February 7, 1862, Jules Nicolas Steiner, identified as "toymaker of Paris," requested a 15-year invention patent (#52929) for a *Bébé Parlant Automatique* (automatic talking baby). Its primary characteristics were:

"...the adaptation of a mechanical system which can produce at the same time a movement of the head, the eyelids, the arms and the legs, and in addition provides the bébé with the ability to speak the words 'papa and mama' to a degree never before attained."

Additionally it provided for:

> "...the change in emitted sounds by the mechanism to differentiate the baby's cries, which standing says 'papa and mama' and, lying down, imitates the weeping of a real child."

This patented system contains the basis of the mama-papa crying and kicking mechanism which Jules Steiner used in his long production of the "kicking Steiner" as *Bébé Parlant Automatique* is frequently called. The mechanical parts were changed over the years as improvements were made.

The heads used in these first production dolls are of wax-over papier-mâché and have a look far more German than French. Factories in Sonneberg, Germany, had been producing this type of doll in great numbers over the preceding decade. This doll's round face was designed to represent a baby, just as Steiner's mechanism was meant to imitate one.

With this first production doll, the mouth is not hinged, but the mechanism is attached to the eyes which open and close. Thus, while this is less complicated than his first patent, it is still not as simple (comparatively speaking) as the variant of this patented doll on which

Steiner later settled, the traditional solid-dome bisque-headed kicking Steiner with stationary eyes. (That head is a separate entity which is easily attached to the body as a final step, eliminating some tricky mechanical inter-connections. By the end of the 1860s Steiner was utilizing these bisque heads, but the change to bisque followed his first use of bisque heads for his mechanical lady dolls.)

Color Plate 1 is of a 20 inch (51cm) wax-over papier-mâché *Bébé Parlant Automatique* of the 1862 patent. A study of the remains of the mechanism indicates Steiner had adapted an existing simple rectangular wooden frame and leather bellows for his improved "speech." The acoustical piece is a wooden trumpet, not rubber as the patent states. Frequently, however, an item will differ from his patent description which is customarily very broad. In our example, though, the doll may slightly predate the patent. The springs and levers of this doll's mechanism are basically as they will be in future models, but the attachment of the limbs of this doll is different from those of later models. In this doll the wires come down from the shoulders and are embedded into the composition arms which begin just above the elbows. A similar arrangement attaches the legs. In later versions the arms are full and attach at the shoulder with a compression fitting onto a dowel. The legs of later models are fastened to wooden stakes that go from the hip into the hollow lower leg.

As with all "kicking Steiners," the arms and legs move, the arms simultaneously and the legs alternately, while the head turns from side to side. Additionally, this mechanism is connected from the arms to the eyes which open and close as the arms raise and lower. Sleeping eyes operating by means of a lever protruding from the body were not uncommon in European dolls

LEFT: Illustration 3A. Shapely leg of 20 inch (51cm) wax-over papier-mâché kicking Steiner, 1862 patented *Bébé Parlant Automatique.*

BELOW: Illustration 3B. Note the decidedly separated big toe. The bottom of the foot is very realistic, like a podiatrist's pediatric model.

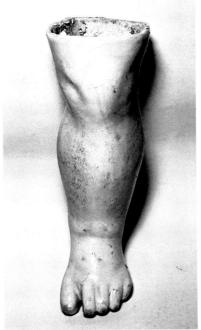

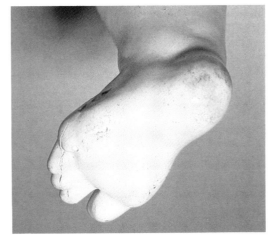

of this period; Jules Steiner's innovative adaptation to clockwork operation was *au courant*, given the day's fascination with mechanical toys that imitated life.

The doll's body is made of gray papier-mâché or cardboard and its boxy shape nicely houses the mechanism. The very round head is of papier-mâché with a wax coating, likely of German manufacture. The eyebrows are single-stroke painted and her mouth is open with two square upper teeth and two lower teeth which appear to be bamboo as found in papier-mâché heads of this period, the 1860s. The eyes, which seem German also, are a bright cobalt blue blown glass. Her composition limbs are very well modeled and of particular interest is her shapely foot with a decidedly separated large toe (*Illustrations 3 and 3A*) indicative of her Japanese heritage. These are feet that can easily wear clogs.

John Noble, in his book *A Treasury of Beautiful Dolls*, describes three well-worn wax dolls as being in a state of "pleasing decay." An architectural term used to describe the natural and mellow weathering of buildings from exposure to the elements over time, it is one which can well be applied to completely loved dolls like this wonderful one. Her skin wig is still thick and her original stylish Scottish costume, though frail, is complete. It consists of a wool Royal Stewart tartan skirt with a nicely fitted black satin jacket, called a doublet, with ecru lace at the wrists and neck. A matching plaid with fringed ends is carried over her shoulder and fastened with a brooch. She also wears dark brown leather ankle length bootines, but her stockings are missing. Were they also tartan? Her hat is a grand little black quilted satin pillbox affair with a flat mauve velvet upturned brim. Perhaps she was originally dressed for export to England, although the influence of Queen Victoria on world fashion is well known. This charming French -German - Japanese - Scottish - English flavored *Bébé Parlant Automatique* long ago traveled to America, perhaps even before our Civil War. Additionally, she is a little boy.

Another example of the early wax-over papier-mâché *Bébé Parlant Automatique* is pictured in Jim and Madeline Selfridge's *Dolls, Images of Love*, Vol. 1, page 43; that mechanism is complete and signed "Steiner." It also bears an 1867 paper label and employs the tubular bellows discussed.

Several of the bisque-headed examples of the *Bébé Parlant Automatique* and the most typical mechanism are seen in *Color Plates 4* and *5*, and discussed on pages 43 through 47. However, for a chronological study of Steiner's patented mechanisms, it is necessary to digress to the mechanical lady doll now, which represents the next step in Jules Nicolas Steiner's production.

While Jules Steiner was at this time producing the wax-over papier-mâché baby — *Bébé Parlant Automatique* — it is important to remember that the 1860s in France was a time which saw a growing demand for lady dolls with bisque heads. Steiner, as an emergent doll and toy maker, saw this demand and sought to enhance his offering with an innovative adaptation of his speaking mechanism, housed in a lady-bodied doll. This represents his earliest use of bisque heads, ones that were available from suppliers in Paris. It is conceivable he assembled and sold ordinary lady dolls as well; if these heads were unmarked (as is typical), it is impossible to verify them as Steiner, although some carry a splendid resemblance to heads Steiner favored. See *Illustration 27*.

On March 13, 1863, Jules Steiner had made application for a patent invention of 15 years for a "mechanical doll with a single pull-string operation." This is his patent #57803. The drawings and description are for a leather-bodied doll with lady proportions having the "advantage of being able to accept pins." It was to house a vertical tubular bellows formed by a spiral spring and covered with leather or rubber. Encased in a metal envelope, it operated by a single pull string which hung from the doll's body. While lady dolls having voice boxes with two pull strings exist, no examples of Steiner's precise description were available to confirm identity. However, in the patent he states:

> "Whatever other uses of the talking mechanism that I plan to use in dolls, their functions will always be the same, that is, a bellows held in place or sprung by means of whatever spring acts to produce the emission of the words 'papa and mama'...I may at my option vary the forms, materials and dimensions of any and all parts used depending on the various applications sought."

Likely it is a variation of this 1863 patented cylindrical bellows that is seen as a part of the mechanisms of some of the very early bébés and "waltzing" ladies. These ladies have molded cardboard bases that house the drive mechanism as well as the bellows. *Color Plate 2* shows the cylindrical mechanism in the cone or skirt-shaped base of one such lady. The earliest examples of this mechanism have rubber bellows which invariably have disintegrated; however, in this example the bellows

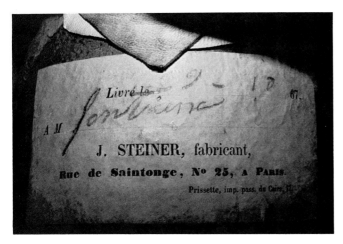

Illustration 4. 1867 paper label from a 15 inch (38cm) waltzing lady with molded cardboard wheeled base. Dated October 29, 1867, it records delivery to a M. Fontaine. *Hannah Shrand Collection.*

is of leather and has thus survived the ravages of time. She bears the 1867 Steiner paper label, partially visible in the plate and shown in *Illustration 4.*

Color Plate 3 is a close-up of an almost identical doll. She, though, had a rubber bellows but all that remains is the marked skeletal framework. See *Illustration 5.* She, too, carries the 1867 paper label in addition to a provenance verifying her age. Her label (also seen in *Illustration 5*) is of particular interest for it reads she was delivered to "Mr Jumeau." Apparently "Mr" was more commonly used in the 19th century as an abbreviation for Monsieur, as many of Jules Steiner's patents carry this abbreviation on the original application. Several labels have been seen marked "Jumeau" which substantiates belief that Jules Steiner was at that point in time selling dolls to Pierre Jumeau for his distribution.

The label on this doll was underneath a muslin covering, indicating the doll was sold naked and the base was covered when she was dressed.

All of these gliding ladies are 15 inches (37cm) tall. On the bottom of the base are three wheels, two rear and one front. The right rear is the drive wheel and the single front wheel can be turned to any angle to make the doll go in left or right circles or roll straight forward. This concept dates back to the 18th century. As with the bébé, the arms raise and lower as the lady rolls around, and on every stroke of the mechanism she cries out "Mama" or "Papa." While a lady in form, she is, alas, a bit childlike in deportment. However, it is the combination of sound and freestanding movement, so appealing to children of all ages, which makes this a triumph and a commercial success. This is an item which Jules Steiner continued to produce for many years, and an examination of the heads and/or bellows will indicate whether an example dates from the 1860s or closer to the end of the century.

Noteworthy, too, is the shape of the cardboard base. In the earlier examples, it is quite cone-shaped with just a hint of gathered shaping at the back of the waist. Also, the bottom of the wood base forms a nearly perfect circle in the early examples. The base of later examples is more oval and the molded cardboard skirt is much more slender and shapely, molded with a bustle effect in keeping with the silhouette of the 1880s. These interesting design improvements are typical of the great care given his products by Jules Steiner.

These waltzing ladies are found either with stationary bisque heads of early manufacture having pale coloring and almond-shaped glass eyes such as found on the doll

BELOW: Illustration 5A. Cylindrical metal framework for bellows marked: "J. STEINER PARIS." The original bellows were rubber but others have been found made of leather. The base of the doll contains the rest of the mechanism which is still intact.

RIGHT: Illustration 5B. Label from this doll records sale to Mr. Jumeau on June 27, 1867. *Winnie Langley Collection.*

41

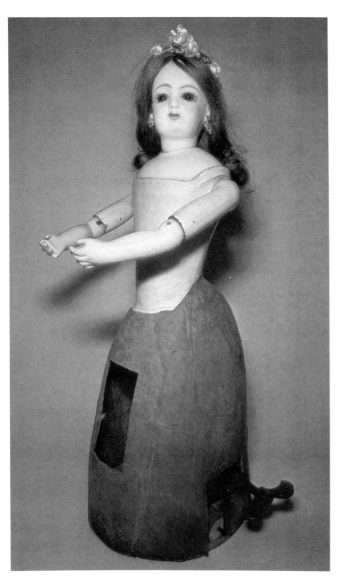

Illustration 6. Late 19th century example of the gliding lady with swivel neck and large blue paperweight eyes. Note the shapely cardboard base with molded-in bustle effect, circa 1880s.

is pictured a marked E. B. head with two rows of tiny teeth, which looks very much like the heads found on the early waltzing ladies. One known example of Steiner's mechanical ladies is herself incised "E.B." (on the lower front edge of the shoulder plate under the kid) which indicates that E. Barrois was a supplier of heads for Jules Steiner. The bisque used is a high quality kaolin paste pressed into the molds. The method of making teeth was one which we see in all but the very latest of Steiner heads. A narrow serrated bisque ribbon or strip is cut to length for the size of the mouth. A separate strip is used for upper and lower teeth which are then fired in the head. In small lady heads only a few teeth show, but in larger bébé heads there are numerous teeth, giving rise to various names such as fish teeth or shark teeth.

Concurrent with or immediately following this first use of standard bisque lady heads are specialized Steiner dolls including the bisque hip or Motschmann-type dolls (see pages 57-59) certainly made especially to Steiner's specifications. It is unlikely Steiner had any kilns at this early point in time, so his bisque parts were probably purchased finished and the dolls assembled in his workshop. During this period, the 1860s, Jules Steiner was located at two small shops on rue de Saintonge, first at #11 and later at #25.

The late 1860s also saw Jules Nicolas Steiner, entrepreneur and inventor, registering patents for other items including a mechanical horse, a magical optical box toy and an "odorless toilet with automatic valve" which did not become the standard we know today. He also registered a patent in 1869 in both France and England, followed by two French additions within the year, for improvements in the drive mechanisms of velocipedes. The popularity of velocipedes and their phenomenal numbers is recorded in an 1869 New York publication, *The Velocipede: Its History, Varieties and Practice:*

in *Color Plate 3*, or with socket heads on bisque shoulder plates. These tend to be later and have Steiner's later flat metal-encased bellows in the mechanism. The later heads usually have higher coloring, heavier eyebrows and larger eyes, typical of other dolls of the later 1880s or 1890s. Such an example is the waltzing lady in *Illustration 6*, who also has the more shapely base.

There are many variations in the arms of these ladies, reflecting both the vogue and the availability of parts at the time. The 1867 doll in *Color Plate 3* has long bisque arms to above the elbow with kid-covered metal upper arms connected to the shoulder pivoting rod. The later doll also has bisque lower arms, but hers are jointed at the elbow. Her upper arms are also metal. The fingers of both are nicely shaped; the fingernails of the later doll are outlined in red.

The similarity between the doll in *Color Plate 3* and heads marked "E.B." is by no means coincidental. In Coleman's *Encyclopedia of Dolls*, Vol. I, page 613, there

"In France, fashion writers and fashion leaders rack their brains for the contrivance of velocipede costumes; velocipede clubs are formed; velocipede championships contested for at velocipede tournaments. There are not less than ten thousand machines running in the streets of Paris. They are used by postmen, government employees, students, messengers, and peddlers; and shopmen send their clerks about on machines covered with flashy advertisements. All velocipedes there are required to carry lanterns in the evening, and though we have no such regulations here, young gentlemen may be seen almost every night, in our cities, riding their velocipedes with head-lights attached.

"In Paris they can be seen driving at breakneck speed along the narrow stone parapet beside the Seine, and even down the hundred steps of the Trocadéro, their riders all the time indulging in gymnastic feats that would seem to invite certain destruction. At Rome, gentlemen practice the bicycle in the courtyards, and are seen riding on the Piazza de Spagna. Country trips are taken upon them in Japan, and they are no longer a novelty in the streets of the larger Chinese cities.

"The patent powers in Washington are literally over-whelmed with applications for patents of different models of these articles. In a large room in the Patent Office, there are some four hundred of these models awaiting investigation. Over eighty models have already been examined and patents for them issued; others are now under examination. Some hundred caveats or notices that patents will be applied for have been lately filed. In one week eighty applications and caveats were received. One single agency in New York city has lately prepared seventy patents for improvements."

Jules Nicolas Steiner's patents described velocipedes for both adults and children and they employed clock-work techniques in their mechanisms. His advertising included mention of velocipedes, and in November of 1869 Steiner registered his first trademark, #3823, seen in *Illustration 7*, which features the caduceus, likely chosen as a symbol of speed, a major concern in his velocipede patents.

Throughout this period of diverse involvements, our Renaissance man was not neglecting his steadily growing doll business. An important factor in its success was the <u>bisque-headed</u> version of *Bébé Parlant Automatique*, discussed next. By the 1870s its time had truly come, its form was defined and it was to remain a standard for the next 30 years.

Illustration 7. Trademark #3823, registered November 9, 1869, by Jules Nicolas Steiner. Stamped in relief on metal placques for mechanical toys and velocipedes, and shown actual size, it is the earliest Steiner usage of the caduceus mark, a version of which is found on Steiner jointed bodies through the 1880s. It is likely that this symbol of Mercury was chosen simply to reflect the speed of the fleet-footed messenger, also known as the Roman God of Commerce and Gain. In the Greek mythology, he is Hermes, known, too, as God of Science and Invention.

--- COLOR PLATES 4 & 5 ---

As noted, Jules Steiner's first use of bisque heads was likely the stock heads for the mechanical gliding lady. Since bisque was fast becoming the material of choice for dolls' heads, it appears Steiner then had the round face of his early wax-over papier-mâché *Bébé Parlant Automatique* specifically adapted for bisque production. One can further imagine that Jules Steiner, a proud Frenchman but with a Germanic name, likely was attuned to anti-Prussian sentiment of the time. A change to the use of Parisian bisque heads would establish his dolls as FRENCH, a proclamation he made in later advertising. The round bisque head of this baby, like its predecessor, has small features; nevertheless, she seems far more related to her lady ancestors than her bébé descendants. These solid dome heads have a wide flange neck; fixing the head in place is a simple last step in the doll's assembly. The mechanism, covered in the 1862 patent, reflects the changes made to accommodate this head.

Color Plate 4 shows the inside of a mechanical or kicking bébé with the bellows and voice box metal-encased, the configuration most usually seen in the Steiner mechanism, and used in all body types, well into the 1890s. (It is only in the very latest mechanisms from the Maison Steiner, under Amédée Onésime Lafosse or the Widow Lafosse, that we see this signed metal framed bellows replaced with a simpler or cheaper version, which is the Amédée Lafosse patent #221582 of May 12, 1892.) In the examples seen here, and in all known bisque-headed kicking babies, the body mechanism is no longer connected to the eyes, which are set stationary. The mechanism is, of course, still clockwork, key wound from a hole on the left side of the lower torso. When activated, the head moves side to side, the arms raise and lower and the legs kick. In France, this doll is sometimes called *"bébé gigoteur,"* a word used to describe these multiple movements of an active baby.

This mechanism is extremely strong and durable. After a hundred years or more, most still work nicely despite often having been stored in dusty or damp cellars and attics. Those not functioning usually require only a cleaning and lubricating. Frequently, though, the strings to the legs are broken, but the springs and moving clockwork parts generally remain solid and strong.

It was for this doll that JNS won the silver medal at the Paris World's Fair of 1878. Jumeau had taken the gold. Rossollin's entries report remarked:

"We must not fail to make mention of the Talking Baby. Its maker, perhaps the only in France to produce this kind of object, has shown models perfect in working order and amazingly lifelike."

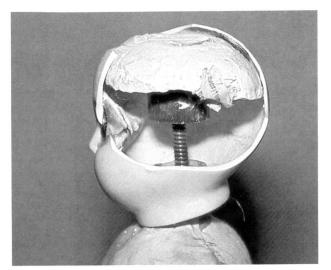

Illustration 8. 17½ inch (44cm) kicking-crying baby with lots of reason to complain. Block of wood from the mechanism was plastered to the top of her bisque head which probably helped save this "Steiner Whiner" from greater damage. Notice the bisque is thinner in places than an American dime. The author wishes to assure those concerned that she did not break the doll to provide this cross-section view.

A look at *Illustration* 8 will show how the mechanism is attached to the head. The flanged neck opening of the head is large enough to accommodate the main pivoting rod from the torso mechanism which has a wooden block attached to it. This is fastened to the top of the inside of the head, usually with a wad of glue-saturated paper, but sometimes with plaster. This secures the head and effects the side to side movement when wound.

These dolls have been found in three sizes. The most common is 17½ inches (44cm), give or take a little. The other sizes are 20 and 22 inches (52 and 56cm). The mechanism, however, is the same in all. While these heads are not usually marked for size, the three sizes are in accord with the heads marked 1, 2 and 3 of Steiner's early bébés on jointed bodies, but their lengths are more in line with sizes 2, 3 and 4.

Another significant Steiner characteristic is noticeable in *Color Plate 4* — the intensely purple papier-mâché. Sometimes called a purple wash, it is obvious from this photograph that the purple color is saturated through the entire mâché used in some of the bodies. Study of dolls that can be positively dated has determined that purple papier-mâché was used during the 1880s, coinciding with the years J. Bourgoin was managing the Steiner firm. It is likely the use of a new paper occurred in conjunction with the use of compressed air in the manufacture of the bodies (patent #162061 of May 15, 1884), and that is was purple when

purchased from the supplier rather than soaked in a purple solution at the Steiner factory. One of the pates in *Illustration* 15 shows a combination of separate purple and gray papers; it would seem if the purple were done at the factory, it would have bled into the gray.

There are numerous chemicals which would impart a purple hue, a number of which could have been used as a disinfectant in the manufacturing process or as an insecticide to counter the vermin problem rampant in Europe at that time. Elemental analysis by electron dispersion has eliminated inorganic or metallic compounds as the source of the color; these chemicals were used as disinfectants.

Organgic agents are more difficult to determine, but a possibility is gentian violet, also used as a germicide. A content of gypsum or like material — plaster of Paris — was found, probably a binding agent in the processing which would contribute to the strength of the papier-mâché. The mâché appears to be a chemically pulped wood product, a conifer not a hardwood. By contrast, an 1870s sample showed no evidence of gymnosperm (conifer) wood pulp.

——————— COLOR PLATE 5 ———————

Because the bisque-headed *Bebe Parlant Automatique* was made during three decades, many detail differences can be noted in the dolls. For example, while the heads are all made from a two-part mold with the join through the middle of the ear, in the earlier dolls the ears are quite flat and unpierced, while later examples have well-formed or applied ears with pierced lobes. The coloring and painting of features tends to echo the fashion of the moment. *Color Plate 5* is a close-up view of three kicking Steiners which illustrate these differences in their long production. The doll in the lower left (and in *Illustration 9*) is 22 inches (56cm) tall. She has all of the characteristics of an early doll, including very pale bisque, flat unpierced ears and extremely finely painted eyebrows which are a delicate light brown in color and are carefully matched to each other. Her eyes, also, are a deep blue, typical of early dolls, and are more oval than the other examples. Her eyelashes are finely painted and rather short. The quality of the painting is like that of the 1860s lady in *Color Plate 3*. This bébé has, as does the vast majority, an open mouth with two rows of teeth, but her rather small lips are particularly

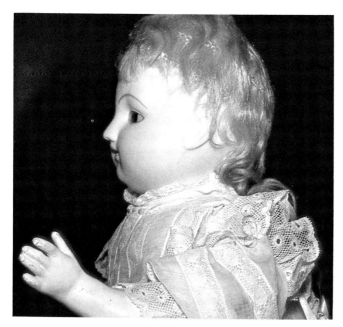

Illustration 9. Exquisite 22 inch (56cm) kicking Steiner. Note the flat ear with the mold line going through the center and the sharp, almost Romanesque nose and well-defined mouth. Unusual, too, are the joined third and fourth fingers of both hands, generally seen on early examples such as this.

well-painted. She has discriminate mauve shading over her eyes and on her chin. Her cheeks are slightly rosy, the bisque is fine and thin and she still has her original very soft blonde mohair wig. The overall effect of this large doll is one of delicacy.

Her torso is of gray cardboard or carton, covered with a white muslin, as found in 1870s and 1890s examples. Her limbs are composition with a lightly waxed finish. As indicated before, the limbs of these bébés vary slightly from the earlier wax-over papier-mâché example. In these dolls the arms are complete from the shoulder, while in the previous version the arm is composition to just above the elbow where a wire from the mechanism is imbedded. Also, the big toe is not quite as separated as on the wax-over, but more so than on a late 1890s example. A curiosity of this 1870s doll's hand is that her third and fourth fingers are joined together, while in later examples each finger is separated. Her fingernails and toenails are painted white and outlined in red, a technique we will see often on Steiner's dolls, particularly those sold through the wonderful Parisian toy shop, *Au Nain Bleu*. Everything about this doll says "early" except the blue stamp on the back of her torso which says:

Le Petit Parisien
BÉBÉ STEINER
Médaille d'Or
PARIS 1889

Surely this head was made long before 1889! Here we have one of the Steiner anomalies, which is usually answered with a theory such as the doll was "old stock" discovered in a move or that the head had previously been rejected because of a few tiny pepper spots. Whatever the reasons, anachronisms such as this do exist in undeniably original dolls. Two other wonderful early examples are seen in *Illustrations 10* and *11*.

Illustration 10. 17½ inch (44cm) kicking-crying baby of great charm. Totally original in white organdy, ruffles, lace and pink bows, she is every inch the pampered baby. Sleeveless in order to allow the arms to move freely, the dress is a style which succeeds magnificently here. She is like an 1870s powder puff. *Pearl D. Morley Collection.*

The second doll of this trio, in the lower right, is interesting both for her painting, which appears to be later, and because of her original box and shop labels, as seen in *Illustration 12*. She carries a Maison Bail shop sticker both on her back and on the inside of her box lid. The numeral 2 is stenciled on the box end which is otherwise unmarked. The box is made of white cardboard on the top and bottom with paper-covered wood sides. A strip of wood reinforces the bottom and traps a pink fabric tie for securing the doll. It is a very serious box, which may have been made in one of the "ateliers" — workshops — at the Steiner complex at 60 rue

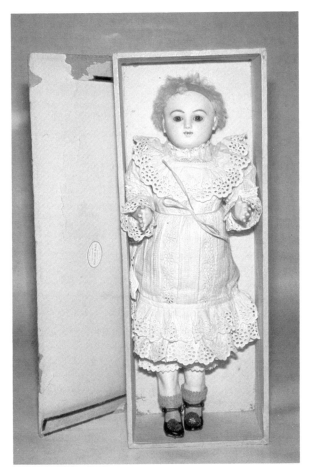

Illustration 12A. 17½ inch (44cm) *Bébé Parlant Automatique* or kicking Steiner in original Maison Bail box from 1882. Her costume is detailed in the description of *Plate 5*.

Illustration 11. Another special kicking Steiner is this from the Simonne toy shop in Paris. Her label, a paper sticker on her torso, is seen in the inset. While her dress is remarkably similar in fabric and effect to the beauty in **Illustration 10**, this elegant *Bébé Parlant Automatique* seems much more the young lady than infant. The pert pink trimmed hat is both original and the frosting on the frosting!

d'Avron. According to the 1901 insurance plot plan, several of the rooms were designated as workshops, box or wrapping rooms.

The doll herself is 17½ inches (44cm) tall, the most common size. She has higher basic coloring, but is very nicely painted, with rosy cheeks and shading on her chin, ears and over her eyes. Her eyes are bright blue and lined, but quite different from the other two dolls. Indeed, Steiner eyes are very inconsistent; many different types of stationary eyes are found in Steiner heads — lined, feathered or clear color, flat or deeply paperweight. This suggests he had a number of sources of paperweight eyes.

The clothing of this doll is completely original, as is her skin wig which, sadly, at some time in her past was visited by moths. The dress is of white eyelet lace on lawn in strips inserted between strips of embroidered piqué which are all sewn together to create the total fabric. The dress has a dropped waist with two eyelet ruffles and a squared neckline, which is eyelet ruffled

Illustration 12B. Detail of Maison Bail shop label.

and lace-trimmed. The lawn underpants have matching eyelet trim and a bound cutout like a giant buttonhole on the left hip to accommodate the keywind and stop-start lever. The soles of her shoes are unfortunately missing, but the remaining ribbon rosettes have a decorative metal star also seen on what appear to be other original Steiner shoes. The socks are short aqua cotton knit, not unlike those of many French dolls of the 1880s.

Her head had been affixed to the wooden block with a wad of glue-saturated newspaper which had come loose. This was carefully removed and softened in water in hopes of obtaining a date, which was successful

46

— December 1881. As the body of this bébé is bright purple, it is all consistent with the newspaper date.

Another fanciful example, likely dressed as she came from the factory is seen in *Illustrations 13A and 13B*.

The third doll appears to be a very late bébé but she bears no marks. Her overall coloring is much pinker, consistent with coloring of the 1890s. Her eyebrows are heavy and dark and they nearly meet in the center. Her mouth coloring is also very dark. She is 20½ inches (52cm) tall. Her eyes are also blue, but more feathered and crystalline than the other two. While she has two rows of teeth, an occasional doll from the later 1890s will have but one row. She nicely contrasts with the others to clearly demonstrate the differences in painting which underscore the long-lived success of this model.

A curious, probably experimental, model is pictured in "Three More Steiners," an article by Betty Lou Weicksel, *Doll News*, February 1969, showing the solid dome head cut open in the back to accept the wire-eyed sleep mechanism which Steiner patented in 1882. Not present now, it is impossible to confirm if that self-contained mechanism had ever been installed although indications are that it had been.

A final example, and an unusual one, is seen in *Illustration 14*. The body and mechanism are the standard Steiner configuration but the doll's head is of poured bisque with an open crown and a rim at the top. The doll's unoutlined open mouth has one row of teeth. The eyebrow painting follows the later Steiner feathered style. The face and head shape is like that of the traditional Steiner and the flange cut of the neck shows the head was made for a use such as this. It appears to have been made from a Steiner mold, after the turn of the century, and hints at German manufacture. It likely represents efforts to complete dolls by one of the final successors of the Steiner firm, Jules Mettais or Edmond Daspres.

During its long years of production, the *Bébé Parlant Automatique* remained a constant, undergoing relatively minor changes. The feet illustrate an interesting progression of being modeled and finished with less detail and less separation of the large toe; three examples are seen in Section V, FEET, page 200. While not the most popular of Jules Steiner's dolls today, the kicking-crying Steiner is nonetheless a very significant doll, one which makes both a beginning and continuing statement of ingenuity combined with quality and durability.

LEFT: Illustration 13A. 17½ inch (44cm) totally original kicking-crying baby overdressed in fashionable knee-length burgundy satin ruched and box-pleated walking (or kicking) dress, circa 1885.

BELOW: Illustration 13B. Bronze kid shoes of this doll marked: "1 PARIS DEPOSE," a mark found on shoes of several originally-dressed Steiner dolls.

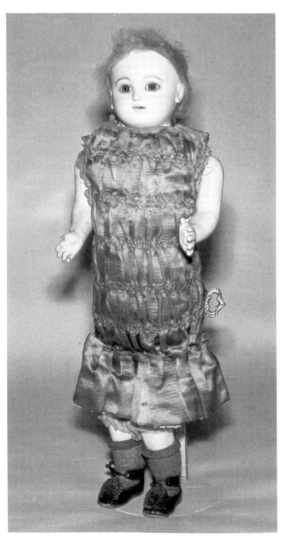

COLOR PLATES 6 & 7

The period of the 1870s was marked by the Franco-Prussian War and its aftermath. The spirit of regrowth included the birth and enthusiastic reception of the bébé, a doll with a jointed composition body with childlike proportions and large exquisite French enamel paperweight eyes. By the end of the decade, all the major Parisian doll makers were claiming both its invention and the superiority of their product, including Jules Nicolas Steiner. He, though, by his manufacture of *Bébé Parlant Automatique* shows his early interest in a doll representing a child and was surely a frontrunner in the articulated bébé race.

Jules Nicolas Steiner, ever the skilled inventor, in wanting to make the bébé more lifelike combined his mechanical abilities with a radical departure from the French paperweight eye. On June 18, 1880, he registered his next patent, #137333, and during the ensuing year he obtained three additions to it as well as a second patent, #140916, and an addition to that as well. All of these concern the very significant and special "wire eyes," the lever-operated system found on many of the

Illustration 14A, B, C. Full face and side views of unusual poured bisque head of kicking-crying Steiner with open dome and rim at the top. The rod and block from the body attaches to the pate. The flange neck and head shape are like that of the solid dome Steiner heads, indicating adaptation of a traditional Steiner mold for this doll. *John Diamond Collection.*

Steiner bébés. These patents richly detail the multitude of materials and processes he might employ to produce these eyes. The initial patent primarily concerns the lever-operated framework for opening and closing the eyes at will. The eyes themselves are described only as being of Parisian enamel, wired together to keep them properly positioned. A serious drawback with this use of a paperweight eye would have been the need for deep spacing from the socket in order to allow the eye to move, a factor which surely contributed to the development of the porcelain eye globe described in the second patent (May 1881), which is the basis of the 1880s system as we know it. This invention also allowed him to manufacture his own eyes, rather than be dependent on other suppliers. *Color Plates* 6 and 7 show a classic Series C bébé with this type of eye and the eye itself. This flawless 22in (56cm) closed-mouth beauty seen also in *Illustration 45* is incised "Sie C 4," carries the Bourgoin stamp and epitomizes early Steiner wire-eyed elegance.

The porcelain eye globe is actually a cup into which the colored iris is set. This can be made by a variety of techniques including chromo-ceramic paint with an overlay of crystal or with a chromolithographed paper iris (decal) glued to the back of a clear half-round crystal lens which is then set into the porcelain cup with gutta-percha or wax. Often a rim of black is visible around the iris where it has been set into the porcelain eye globe. This is the gutta-percha which is white when fresh and which turns black as it ages. The white of the porcelain eye is china glazed and the eyelid tinted pink before it is fired so there is complete stability of the eye material — neither heat nor cold can affect the eyes as with waxed lids. The back of the eye cup is incised:

The two eye globes are securely joined by a piece of wood and the eyes can then be set beautifully close to the eye opening with plaster. Steiner's June 1881 patent addition is partly to protect his proprietary rights to the eye framework utilized in this system. This is a high quality arrangement operated by a series of brass wires and linkages. See *Illustration 16*. A brass wire protrudes from the doll's head behind her left ear (for easy operation by a right-handed person). It is imbedded in the wooden bar inside the head, makes a 90° turn in the center of the head and attaches to a second brass connection from the eyes. The wooden bar rests on and is glued into the square cutouts at the rim of the head. The movement of this mechanism is very smooth and, unlike weighted eyes, these can be opened or shut with the doll in either a vertical or horizontal position.

With the use of chromo-lithography, beautiful eyes of many colors were possible, while the use of crystal dropped onto the iris provided a depth that imitated the

Illustration 15. Two molded cardboard pates for Steiner bébés. Note the applied piece forming a lip with cutouts to fit around the wooden bar for the wire eye mechanism. The pates are impressed with a size number on top (note #4 on larger pate) and are either purple or gray, depending on date of production. Smaller pate is a combination gray and purple. Circa 1888.

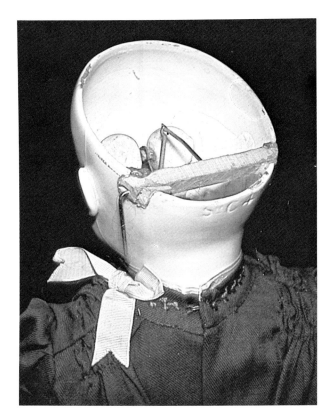

Illustration 16. Lever-operated "wire eyes" of Series C Steiner with Bourgoin stamp, which have enameled lids. Note square cutouts for bar of mechanism. Purple cardboard pate has matching cutouts to fit around wooden bar. Circa 1885.

human eye. Additionally, allowing the child to open and close the eyes at will lent an active involvement with a special toy.

It is interesting to note also that Steiner in his patent touted the self-contained aspect of this system as an advantage, though few dolls at this time were employing the old-fashioned levered or pull-string eye system which operated through the body to which he was apparently referring.

This porcelain eye and lever operated mechanism was used in a great many of Steiner's dolls throughout the 1880s, the same period that J. Bourgoin was manager of the Steiner firm, which has led this to sometimes erroneously be called the "Bourgoin system."

───────── COLOR PLATES 8 & 9 ─────────

Color Plates 8 and 9 show a second version of the Steiner lever-operated eye. While the mechanism remains basically the same, in this eye the globe is made entirely of glass. The embossed markings on the back of the eye are:

Note that it no longer includes the name Steiner; perhaps this is a change instituted by Amedee Onesime Lafosse who took over management of the Steiner firm in 1890. A pair of glass eyes of this type have been recently noted embossed LEGRAND BREVETE S.G.D.G. A search of patent records may provide further details and document the association with Steiner. The eye itself has the advantage of being smooth, with the iris and eye-white on one plane, as if an ordinary beautiful glass eye were placed onto a molten glass globe, or blown into a glass mold. However, with this method, the lids now required waxing for color and in time most eyes examined have lost some of this colored waxy lid. The production costs were probably considerably lower and the open eye is very naturalistic, so this method had both advantages and disadvantages.

These eyes have been found in numerous Figure A heads dating from the early 1890s, dolls which often have the 1889 Steiner paper label on their bodies. With these heads, also, another modification has been made. Instead of the square cutouts in the bisque into which the wooden bar with the inserted lever sets, there is a small round hole in the bisque behind the left ear near the crown. This hole receives the brass wire which is still encased in a wooden bar. This method more effectively traps the mechanism lower inside the head. Simpler and less costly than making two square cutouts, this method

also increased the strength of the head rim. These eyes are seen in the handsome closed-mouth bébé in *Color Plate 8* and *Illustration 17*. Of superior quality, she is 22in (56cm), incised "J. STEINER//BTE S.G.D.G.// PARIS//FIRE A 15" and is an exquisite early 1890s example very similar to those seen in *Color Plate 36*, Section III.

By way of reassurance, Steiner dolls with cutouts or holes in the bisque but with stationary set paperweight eyes are often found and are legitimate.

The eyes were a major concern of Jules Nicolas Steiner and his lever-operated system was truly a triumph of mechanical engineering and production. This production was continued by the Lafosses and was later modified by her patent #229995 of May 10, 1893, for a combination counterweight/wire-lever system.

Illustration 17. Lever-operated all glass "wire eyes" of Figure A Steiner. This type of eye has waxed and painted lids from which wax worn away is visible. Note single hole by left ear and uncut rim, a modification made in early 1890s. *Bitterman Collection.*

───────── COLOR PLATE 10 ─────────

Two patents will be considered in an examination of this bébé. Overlooking for the moment the mechanism involved, we see an articulated bébé body of a composition material.

The Maison Steiner's advertising, in 1891, stated that Steiner was the creator, in 1873, of the articulated bébé without balls. This is another anomaly, for his earliest known articulated bodies have six balls. Only the upper legs are "sans boules." Perhaps he or Lafosse's advertising man misremembered.

We must remember that the toy and doll business was very competitive, and Jules Nicolas Steiner was a man of his time, a man intrigued by the widespread application of machinery that had become available through the Industrial Revolution. This interest extended beyond the toy industry into other phases of modern-day living as evidenced by his many other patented inventions; he was a man proud of his inventions and his products, ever ready to improve on them, a man very aware of what was going on around him. Thus, it is worth mentioning here that Steiner was surely well aware that in 1867 Pierre Victor Clément had received a patent for lady bodies of embossed leather or blown kid, and that Clément's widow had continued this production through the 1870s. These admirably lightweight but durable, handsome bodies may have inspired Steiner to develop his method of using compressed air to improve his papier-mâché bodies. Further, it is conceivable that the embossed leather lady bodies which continued to be made into the 1880s but which are marked only "brevete" were made by Steiner, for his patent is, as usual, very broad, including both "bébés and poupées." However, it would seem to be out of character for Jules Steiner not to have marked these with his name if he did indeed make them.

The visionary Jules Steiner had seen several advantages in the use of compressed air for the mass production of doll bodies. Not only could this method create lighter, stronger, smoother bodies of uniform size, it would produce them more rapidly than molds pressed by hand. Hence, his patent #162061 of May 15, 1884, detailed the machinery involved

"to take advantage of compressed air to mold objects made of paper, pasteboard or other material, generally used in the manufacture of bébés, dolls and other children's toys, statuettes (figurines) etc."

The resulting new articulated body was a fine simplification of the earliest bébé bodies and a genuine improvement, for its production both cut costs and produced a superior product. For instance, the early, handmade and somewhat lumpy Steiner bodies with six balls (detailed in *Color Plate 16*) are awkward to pose, while the new articulated body offered a range of movement not possible with most other dolls. Note that the modeling at the elbow of the doll in *Color Plate 10* allows the doll's arms to bend in any natural position, even to realistically

touching her face with her hands as a child might. This is careful, thoughtful design at its best.

Additionally, Steiner's use of compressed air did definitely result in composition bodies considerably lighter and stronger than previous ones. The earlier papier-mâché was thick and quite porous or fibrous, while the compressed air method appears to have used a finer paper. This could account for the change to purple papier-mâché, perhaps from a different supplier. The new refined bodies required very little gesso filler to smooth the surface and the parts fit and work together perfectly. Further, this firmly compressed mâché enabled the redesign of the hand. The hands of Steiner's early bodies had short stubby fingers, and while this mold was not abandoned, by the end of the 1880s we see longer, more slender fingers, a shapely and delicate hand made possible by the use of compressed air in this molding process. It is noteworthy that these fingers have stood the test of time and play well, proving Jules Steiner's vision correct in his desire to "bring to perfection the elegance and quality of the products produced."

The second patent represented by this bébé is #206131, dated June 4, 1890. This is Jules Steiner's patent entitled "Bébé Marcheur dit 'Bébé Premier Pas,'" which translates "Walking Baby called Baby First Step." There are times when the French name should be maintained, and this is one of them. A patent name or registered trademark should not be translated.

Illustration 18. View looking into torso of mechanism of *Bébé Premier Pas*, 1892 patent.

51

four limbs and head, they function especially well. The mechanism to the legs produces a back-and-forth movement as well as an up-and-down one, alternating left and right. Hence the bébé moves in a natural way, placing one leg in front of the other. In the patent Steiner asserts that throwing back the foot of one leg will cause the doll to hop and that lifting both legs allows the bébé to sit and shuts off the motor.

Note that the mechanism is placed into the torso in the reverse way of the earlier kicking and crying baby, whose key and start-stop lever is on the doll's left hip because the child would have held the doll facing her. A child walking *Bébé Premier Pas* would likely do so from behind the doll, therefore the clockwise-turning key to wind the mechanism would want to be on the doll's right hip for a right-handed person, as it is. As any left-handed person can attest, ours is a right-handed world!

Instructions which have been found dated 1890 can apply to all of Jules Steiner's keywound mechanisms: *Bébé Premier Pas*, *Bébé Parlant Automatique* and the gliding lady dolls. They were printed in four languages, French, English, German and Spanish. The English reads:

> "To make the mecanism (sic) work it is sufficient to wind up with the brass key attached to the baby, turning to the right, just as one winds up a watch or clock.
> "When the movement is wound up, one must, to obtain the work, push behind the iron wire which is near the key; one can stop the movement, as one whises (sic) in pulling to one's self the iron wire.
> "When the baby is wound up, not to forget to lift up the arms like those of a child who calls, holding out his arms.
> "Even children can wind up themselves this mecanism (sic) without danger.
>
> J. St., breveté s.g.d.g., Paris"

It appears most likely these instructions are for the kicking-crying baby, but since they only concern the winding and stop-start, they cover all uses. However, instructions for *Bébé Premier Pas* might have been more complicated since her walking movement required more involvement from the child playing with her.

A certificate of addition to the patent was registered October 7, 1890, which added a talking mechanism (the standard metal-frame bellows) which this doll has, as well as a walker to support the doll. (See patent drawing in the appendix.)

Bébé Premier Pas, seen in *Color Plate 10*, has a Figure A head incised: "J. STEINER//BTE S.G.D.G.// PARIS//FIRE A 15." Her ears are pierced and she has a beautiful, expressive open mouth with two rows of teeth. Her eyebrow and eyelash painting is thick and lush, a time-consuming technique used on these dolls or at least by one artist who had the opportunity to paint the high quality heads of *Bébé Premier Pas*. A close-up of a brown-eyed example which must have been painted by the same person is shown in Section III, *Color Plate 34*.

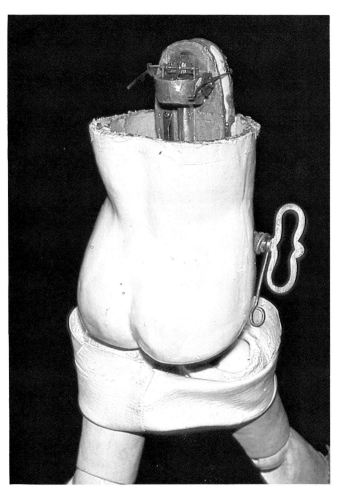

Illustration 19. The body of *Bébé Premier Pas* is completely finished. (Note thigh.) It could have been assembled without mechanism as an ordinary jointed doll.

Bébé Premier Pas is unique in that her body is actually a complete jointed bébé body, although the patent indicates that a variety of articulations of limbs were possible, as with non-mechanical dolls. The torso is made in two sections and joined together after the mechanism is inserted, as seen in *Illustration 18*. The Steiner bébé torsos are made in two halves regardless of whether or not a mechanism or voice box is used. The lower section of the torso is itself made in two parts; a U-shaped join is sometimes visible on the lower back. While the form and the finish of the body indicate it was made under compressed air, the papier-mâché used is an ordinary gray, not the purple seen during the 1880s. The doll measures 22 inches (56cm) tall and apparently was made in just this one size. The thighs are completely finished and a pair of not-too-loosely fitted kid pants are attached to her thighs and cover her to her waist. See *Illustration 19*. This doll utilized existing body parts and combines the features of a jointed bébé, capable of sitting down, with a walking doll.

The bellows is white metal encased and marked "J. STEINER PARIS." The trumpet is also metal and seems to be cast in one piece. The clockwork and gears are heavy duty and since they only drive the legs and not all

52

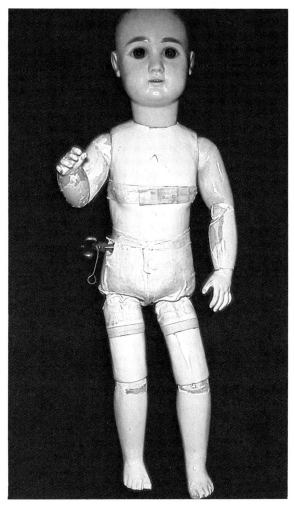

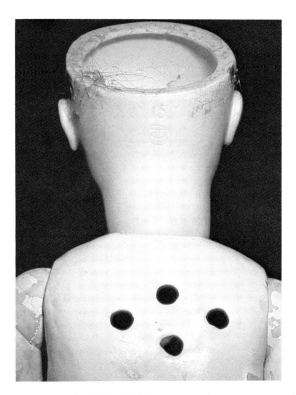

Illustration 20A & B. 22 inch (56cm) early 20th century walking doll. Direct descendent of *Bébé Premier Pas*, her body form and the key for her mechanism are almost identical to Steiner's bébé. Paint finish is not of Steiner quality, but doll was greatly loved and endured two generations of active play. Note hand retains excellent finish and nail outlining. Head of late edition walking doll is of poured bisque, German manufacture and is incised with an anvil and the number 15, the same size number as *Bébé Premier Pas* in *Plate 10. Lynn Eckhardt Collection.*

Shortly after *Bébé Premier Pas* was released, Amédée Lafosse took over the Steiner firm. This bébé must have been an expensive doll to produce, for although it continued to be made, in 1893 and 1894 the Widow Lafosse registered two patents for a much simpler walking doll as well as for modifications for its assembly. These were:

> #234713 December 11, 1893, and an addition
> March 24, 1894
> #238710 May 22, 1894

Additionally, the final successor, Edmond Daspres, in keeping with the walking tradition, had also registered a patent #323175 on July 21, 1902. While this was a few months after the death of Jules Nicolas Steiner on February 4, 1902, and prior to Daspres' acquisition of the Steiner firm, that patent is also included in the appendix.

It may also have been under Daspres that the doll seen in *Illustration 20* was marketed, although it is possible that it was a post-Steiner firm production, using remaining Steiner parts. She is a very late version of *Bébé Premier Pas*. Her body has the identical form, except that her wrists are jointed. Some of her body parts are wooden. The shape of her hands and feet are Steiner-like, the key for the mechanism is identical and the operation is the same. The poured bisque head is

incised with an anvil and the number 15, the same size as is on the head of *Bébé Premier Pas*. The anvil symbol is reported to be a trademark of Franz Schmidt & Co of Thüringia (Germany) who specialized in wood and papier-mâché parts as well as doll heads. Several other anvil-marked heads have been found on Steiner-marked bodies; if these were released through the Steiner firm, it would verify their purchasing heads from Germany in the 20th century, as did many French doll firms. It is a very interesting example which poses some very interesting questions.

——————— COLOR PLATE 11 ———————

Several patents will be considered with this doll. The first falls into the area of speculation. On June 20, 1889, Jules Nicolas Steiner registered patent #199084 for

53

unbreakable heads made of porcelain. (Appendix page 211.) The patent reads in part:

"My invention is intended to, as much as possible, make these porcelain or biscuit heads unbreakable, or at the least to make them in such a way that, in the case of a fall followed by a crack where the pieces don't become detached, they will not separate; thus the accidental fall results in cracks which do not require an immediate repair, causing separation of the doll from its clumsy owner. Additionally, no accident will be a dread one for the child no matter how severe the break.

"To accomplish this goal, the porcelain, biscuit, etc. heads are made in the ordinary manner, then I coat the inside with glue and apply onto this coating a resistant and suitable fabric such as buckram, linen, marli or other more or less tight material. I let it dry and these products have the qualities mentioned above. One can drop the head from a great height or knock them vigorously; either way, if a crack results, all the material remains intact, still attached to the lining and the accident produces but traces of cracks or star-shaped dents. One may repeat this experiment, and no fragment falls loose; a child cannot be injured from a break of this kind.

"In the course of my experiments, I have obtained good results from using both strong glue or paste glue, using any and all of the fabrics mentioned, and whatsmore, using hide pieces or felt, even nap or oakum Fabric made of rubber may be used as well..."

No examples of heads lined in this manner are known, yet for many years J. Steiner's advertisements in the Didot-Bottin, the commercial directory, listed

"Tete biscuit doublée presque incassable" or

Nearly unbreakable lined bisque heads as one of his claims.

At a time when most manufacturers were pouring their heads, a more efficient method, Steiner's heads appear to be of pressed bisque, just as the early bisque heads had been made. It seems anachronistic for a visionary, pragmatic and innovative businessman such as Jules Steiner to have continued making his heads in the old way, yet they _do_ have the characteristics of pressed bisque. However, the patent resume refers to the lining being applied to the interior surface of the head, "which itself is constructed by means already widely known," possibly a reference to the pouring of bisque heads. Questioning this led to pondering the possibility that instead of lining with one of the broad choices of fabric noted in his patent, which must have been a very time-consuming process, that perhaps Steiner "lined" a thin poured bisque head with a paste of bisque. This would likely have been in the greenware stage prior to firing or as part of the lower temperature secondary firing of the painted heads. However, as porcelain manufacturers also sold heads "in the white," after the first firing, it is conceivable only the secondary firings occurred at the rue d'Avron Steiner factory.

Inside the head of this doll with the arm mechanism, at the neck opening, there is a lump of bisque, yet the edge of the opening is very smooth as in heads that have

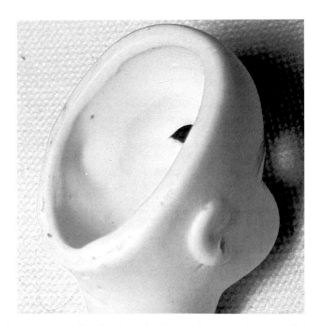

Illustration 21. 8 inch (21cm) head incised: "A 1" which is made from poured bisque. Note rim and indentation at ear.

been poured. Occasionally an obviously poured bisque Steiner head from the 1890s turns up, noticeable by a rim at the crown and an indentation at the ear as in _Illustration 21_, but most Steiner heads, even the very latest, appear to be of pressed bisque. See _Illustration 22_. It is worth considering that these heads may simply have a secondary porcelain wash for reinforcement, and that the obviously poured ones simply missed the second step in the process. Though "pressed" will continue to be used in describing heads throughout this book, with this possibility in mind, the descriptions could read "apparently pressed."

This patent concerning the lining of heads was filed shortly after Jules Steiner returned to active leadership of his company. The 1890s saw a number of changes, including a succession of "successors;" however, it is known that Jules Steiner retained ownership of his firm throughout his lifetime.

The second patent under consideration also involves a lining process. As observed, the Lafosse patents generally modify for production purposes those of Steiner. A viable example is patent #276458 registered on March 29, 1898, by the Widow Lafosse. Very similar to Jules Steiner's patent of 1889, it reads in part:

"My invention's purpose is for a manufacturing method for the heads and members of bébés so as to make them lighter...

A process...characterized by the application in the mold of the piece to be made first of a sheet of thin jointing paper...

...and finally, of pieces or strips of fabric coated with strong glue to consolidate the piece, while producing a great lightness, an elasticity, and a remarkable fineness, the decasted piece being then finished in the usual way."

As a process for making heads of papier-mâché, this seems to have a great merit. _Illustration 23_ shows a

54

LEFT: Illustration 22A. 22 inch (56cm) head marked: "A - 15 Le PARISIEN." Head of kiss-blowing bébé, Lafosse 1897 patent. Head is of apparently pressed bisque, but has curious lump of bisque at neck hole with smooth bisque underneath, suggesting a two-layer process.

BELOW: Illustration 22B. Neck hole showing the lump of bisque over a smoother base.

Illustration 23. 14 inch (36cm) papier-mâché head lined for reinforcement, lightness and strength with glue-saturated fabric as detailed in Lafosse 1898 patent #276458.

papier-mâché Steiner head made in this manner. The doll is also seen in Section IV, *Color Plate* 56. She is a lovely, rare and totally original turn-of-the-century papier-mâché bébé.

The primary patent to be studied in conjunction with the doll in *Color Plate 11* was granted to the Widow Madame Lafosse who had succeeeded her husband, Amédée, in the management of the Steiner firm in 1892. Her maiden name was Marie Lambert; it is undetermined if she was related to Leopold Lambert, the automaton manufacturer.

On February 26, 1897, the Widow Lafosse registered patent #264464 for a bébé with a single pull-string mechanism for speaking, crying and blowing kisses. The pull string from the hip causes the bellows to, rather familiarly, "alternately utter 'Papa' and 'Mama' when the doll is standing and to cry or weep when lying down." (*Déja vu!*) This is controlled by a notched lever as in earlier Steiner examples. Additionally, the bellows has a string which goes through a pulley in the shoulder to a pulley in the elbow (*Illustration 24*), which causes the forearm to move towards her face when the pull string is drawn. According to the patent this is achieved by:

> "arranging the jointing of the arm on the forearm obliquely to the horizontal plane, so that during the movement which simulates the blowing of a kiss the hand comes exactly to the height of the lips instead of reaching to just below the chin, as is the case in known arrangements."

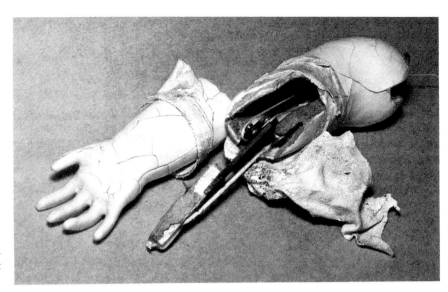

Illustration 24. Mechanism in arm of kiss-blowing bébé, Mme. Lafosse 1897 patent #264464.

This could be a reference to examples on the market made by Bru. Two serious test reactions to this example, after reading this patent description, were: "if you say so" and "more or less." This doll has also been observed saluting, grabbing her stomach and beating her breast, a versatility previously untouted.

"Walking" is, however, mentioned as an optional ability of this doll, but this is afforded not by a keywind mechanism, but by providing the bébé with a pair of

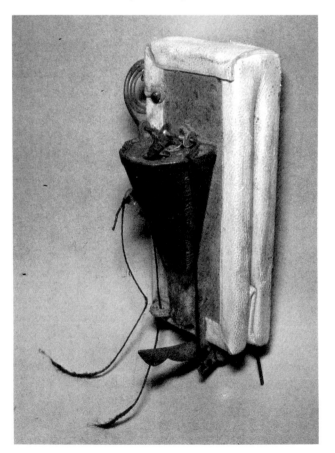

Illustration 25. Rectangular bellows of kid-covered wood is from a Steiner bébé body of early to mid 1890's. Metal trumpet is marked: "J. STEINER PARIS."

straight (unjointed) legs attached to an axle which alternate as the doll is pushed along.

The new improved bellows employed here is the "old-fashioned" or standard rectangular wooden frame with kid covering, much the type of bellows Jules Nicolas Steiner used in the 1862 wax-over papier-mâché *Bébé Parlant Automatique*, except that here the sounding trumpet is of metal. Neither mechanism is marked, but the configuration is like the marked bellows seen in *Illustration 25*, which was in a body marked: "Le Petit Parisien//BÉBÉ STEINER//Médaille d'or//PARIS 1889" dating from the early to mid 1890s.

This kiss-throwing doll is 22 inches (56cm) tall. Her body is made of gray papier-mâché and there is a heavier coat of gesso and paint on the limbs which has cracked over the years. The coloring is a bright pink, quite unlike the previous dolls. Her fingers are long, slender and shapely but the nails are not outlined nor are the feet as well defined as in earlier dolls. There is a purple stamp on her left hip: "BÉBÉ 'LE PARISIEN'//Médaille d'or//PARIS." Note that enough time has passed that the date is no longer given. Her head is incised: "A-15//PARIS" with a red stamped "LE PARISIEN," as was seen in *Illustration 22*. She has good quality bisque of an even color with gentle cheek coloring. Her multistroke eyebrows are medium brown and quite restrained although they nearly meet in the center. Her nose and nostrils are sharply defined and her open mouth is well painted. She has only an upper row of teeth and it is still the bisque ribbon used from Steiner's earliest days. The head is of far better quality than the body, but with this doll we can see the reign of Jules Nicolas Steiner passing — time and competition have begun taking their toll.

However, during the decades represented by these dolls with patented mechanisms, a number of "ordinary" play dolls were also made. An examination of them begins now, first with a look at some early unmarked dolls of Jules Nicolas Steiner.

UNMARKED DOLLS
BISQUE HIP STEINER
———————— COLOR PLATES 12 - 13 - 14 - 15 ————————

The wonderful dolls pictured in these four color plates are two Motschmann-type or bisque hip Steiners. The problem of what to call this type of early body has plagued collectors and researchers alike. Most often referred to as a Motschmann-type because of the papier-mâché example which was discovered and published that had "Ch. Motschmann" stamped on its body, it has since been realized that he was involved only with the voice mechanism of what was simply a Täufling baby. However, the terminology is now in our vernacular, and it works. Täufling baby does not really apply to these Steiner dolls as that is German for infant. Japanese-type baby is perhaps too broad. "Bisque hip" is simple, and while it does not completely describe the doll, it does certainly bring to mind the image of this unique body, so it is a good term. (We run into trouble again, however, when we meet the papier-mâché version of this doll.)

Color Plate 12 shows the naked 18 inch (46cm) doll both front and back. Here we clearly see the influence of the Japanese baby dolls on the doll industry and on Jules Steiner. The mold for this doll could have been taken directly from a Japanese example, except that the big toe is not separated, although they are not always separated on the Japanese dolls. The toe here is, however, one of the smallest big toes found on any of Jules Steiner's dolls; it angles toward the other toes as though the separated-toe foot mold had been adapted for this bisque version. The bisque sections are all joined together by twill. The limbs are beautifully formed. The arms are long and shapely and the hands have nice finger detail, with the nails outlined and lightly tinted. Dolls 12 to 20 inches (31 to 51cm) have been noted.

The doll is produced in two versions, shoulder head or swivel neck on a bisque shoulder plate. Actually, in both cases, the modeling of the upper torso is a complete bust, not a shoulder plate. The shoulders are wonderful, soft and round, and the upper arms are fully formed with a bisque armpit dividing the arms from the rib cage. The detail of the hip section is also remarkable — not exactly anatomically correct, but noteworthy! Sometimes this body is found with a hole in the bisque of the upper back and a hole on the left hip which is for a pull string voice box. The cylindrical midriff of the pull string version is firm, reminiscent of the description in Steiner's March 13, 1863, patent #57803. However, that patent describes a single pull string bellows, while the bisque hip bellows has been noted with two pull strings. The midriff bellows area of the Motschmann-type with pull string voice box varies in length depending on the type of bellows it contains, which was likely a function of what was in production at the time. Of course, Jules Steiner did consistently reserve the right to modify his plans...

Most of the bodies examined which have a hole at the hip and the back of the shoulder plate have contained a push-squeak mechanism which is a simple metal reed embedded in an oval wooden disk, as seen in *Illustration* 6 in Section II. The disk is the same size as the outside perimeter of the bisque torso, and a similar wooden disk is matched to the lower torso. These are joined by a coiled spring and covered with leather to form a cylindrical bellows. The tubular midriff bellows segment is then tied into place through sew holes in the bisque parts. Afterwards, it is covered with fabric which is glued and tied on through grooves in the bisque edges. See *Illustration 26.*

Of special interest in the swivel neck (socket head) version is the very small opening at the back of the head for the insertion of the eyes. A tiny cork pate covers the opening. The shoulder head Motschmann-type has a solid dome head shaped much like the head of the kicking-crying baby, but that head terminates at the neck in a wide flange which also allows room for the insertion of the eyes and teeth. Occasionally a socket

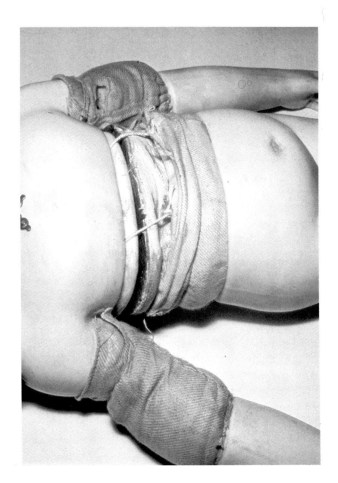

LEFT: Illustration 26. Midsection of Motschmann-type or bisque hip Steiner showing leather-covered cylindrical bellows affixed to bisque parts before being covered with fabric.

head with a tiny opening such as is seen here is found on a jointed composition body. With these dolls, we see the first of the <u>closed-mouth bébés.</u> The face is just as round, the nose broad and the mouth, small and pert, is tucked right up close to the nose. The eyes tend to be almond-shaped.

Color Plate 13 shows this exquisite doll close-up. She has a serene expression, perhaps accentuated by her narrow eyes which are a luscious vivid blue and evenly lined. The narrow eyes are typical of these early unmarked heads and reflect the dominance of the lady doll in the 1870s. While this doll represents a child, and similar heads are found on jointed bébé bodies, this elegant head is transitional between the ladies and the wide-eyed children to come. Her eyebrows are evenly painted with very fine short multiple strokes. Her nose looks broader than it is because her small, nicely defined mouth is placed very close to the nose. Most examples studied have a closed mouth, though the doll has been found with an open mouth and two rows of teeth as well.

A characteristic which we will see in many of the Steiner doll mouths is a well modeled upper lip that dips in the center; the shape is like a flattened M. This shape

Illustration 27. 30 inch (76cm) unmarked young lady of great charm, but with characteristics and coloring of early Steiner dolls. The wideset eyes and "M" mouth line are particularly Steiner-like, but being totally unmarked she can only be called a Steiner-type. Circa 1870.

is often in the mold and is frequently accented by being painted as a red line. In many open mouth versions the cut follows the mold line giving a deep dip to the center of the upper lip. In early dolls the mouth is nicely outlined and consists of two or three shades of color.

Another facial characteristic which we will consider particularly in studying the later models is the groove between the nose and mouth, called the <u>philtrum</u>. A subtle characteristic which varies considerably on Jules Steiner's dolls, its treatment contributes to the differing looks of the faces. In these early dolls, the philtrum is a simple circular indentation.

The basic face shape is very round, as was the bisque head of *Bébé Parlant Automatique*. Her ears are unpierced and quite flat. Her wig is of blonde mohair as delicate as she is herself. She is wearing a soft red plaid wool jumper and a lacy white lawn guimpe and bonnet. Judging from the quality of the head and its pale coloring, this doll was likely made in the very early 1870s or even the late 1860s.

Another doll from this time period to look at for comparison here is an unmarked young lady on a long-limbed cloth body. Seen in *Illustration 27*, she has a swivel neck on a deep shoulder plate and is totally unmarked, but her quality of bisque, modeling and painting suggest Jules Steiner. As he was likely purchasing his bisque — available to others as well — in these early years, it is presumptuous to label such heads Steiner. However, "Charlotte" is the type of young lady whom Jules Steiner could have embraced.

——————— COLOR PLATES 14 & 15 ———————

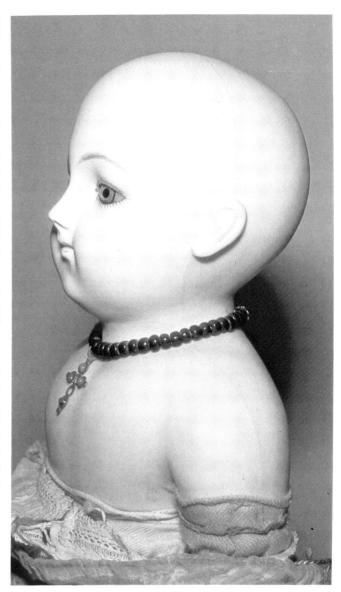

Illustration 28. Shoulder head version of bisque hip Steiner showing her solid dome head, crisp features, unpierced ears and tiny mouth placed right up under her nose. Note also the mold line goes through the ear and across the shoulder. Even though the doll has much detailed modeling, only a two-part mold, front and back, was needed.

Shown here is a second example of the bisque hip Steiner, a rigid neck version, with pale blue-gray unlined eyes outlined in a bright blue, and wearing a totally original and wonderful baby outfit. She measures 15 inches (38cm) tall. Her head is a solid dome and her ears are also unpierced but are not quite as flat as those of the previous doll. Her shoulders and chest are nicely modeled and her facial features are very much like the other doll's. See *Illustration 28*. Her rosy cheek coloring and eye shadowing is a little deeper than her big sister's and her eyebrows are a little less tightly painted. She is a wonderful example of the bisque hip or Motschmann-type Steiner particularly because she is so totally original. She also dates from about 1870.

Color Plate 14 shows her in all her splendor! This hunky child is wearing an ecru linen box-pleated dress trimmed with needlepoint lace. It has an attached balayeuse at the hem. The dress falls from a square lace yoke and a wide blue watered silk sash creates a dropped waist effect. An attached organdy chemisette and matching undersleeves complete the dress. Silk ribbon bows (called choux) adorn the sleeves and a turquoise necklace with a gold cross is worn around her neck. The baby is also wearing a woven baleen hat, called a puddin', a rare example of a 19th century infant crash helmet. She also has her original delicately curled blonde mohair wig and an appealing pair of scuffed brown leather boots; from the top of her head to the tip of her little bisque toes, she is special!

FIRST ARTICULATED BÉBÉS

The birth of the bébé on a jointed composition body was one of the remarkable events of the 1870s in the doll industry. While Jules Steiner's advertising of the late 1880s, as noted, claimed he was the "true creator of the bébé without balls" in 1873, a study of the early dolls seems to contradict quite this early a date. At any rate, the first of his articulated bébé bodies had separate balls at all joints except the upper thigh. That body, as seen in *Color Plate 16* and in *Illustration 29* is very interesting. Curiously rough and lumpy and full of somewhat inaccurate anatomical detail, it is unquestionably a chunky child's body. The detail of the thigh modeling is wonderful; the rolls of fat tell us this is a child who is going to have to watch the bon-bon consumption.

The shape of the foot is very like that of the bisque hip, with the small unseparated big toe. The lower torso shows modeling similar to the Motschmann-type; it is as though that body were remodeled into this fully-articulated body.

The fingers of this body are also quite interesting. They have a spidery appearance, which is not part of the mold but which occurred simply because the hands, after they were painted, were hung to dry fingers down. A hand from which some paint had chipped (*Illustration 30*) shows the short, evenly-shaped papier-mâché fingers and the paint collected between them. The result looks like a five-icicle hand. The hands of later bodies were probably simply dried fingers up, creating the familiar "short stubby fingers." It is not until the later 1880s that we see the long slender fingers which are also "typical" Steiner hands. This early, hand-pressed body is a far cry from the streamlined body we usually associate with Jules Nicolas Steiner, the body produced by the compressed air machine process of the 1880s. This early body type is usually found made totally of a heavy papier-mâché or composition, but occasionally of wood or with wooden limbs. Sometimes a combination such

Illustration 29. 10 inch (26cm) bébé marked only "3/0" at top edge of crown. She has the early articulated body with separate balls at the joints. Note various lengths of fingers. They were not broken; red fingernail outlining remains on all! This the first of Steiner's petite sized dolls, circa 1880.

as wooden upper arms and lower legs is used. At other times, a turned wooden lower arm has a papier-mâché hand securely fixed to it at the wrist. Variables such as these are fascinating and show a curiosity in exploring methods of production.

With this early jointed body, we see Steiner producing tiny dolls, something that was to become a specialty. It is likely the earliest efforts were of wood,

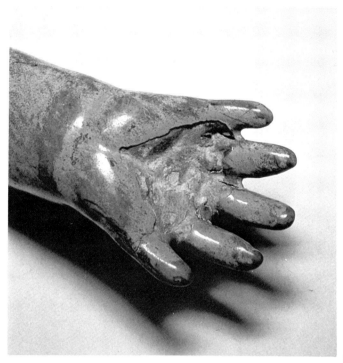

Illustration 30. Hand of early articulated body with fingers like icicles. Chipped paint shows how the paint collected between evenly shaped papier-mâché fingers when the hand was hung to dry.

typical of these bébés, as is the narrow cut of the eye. The doll in *Illustration 32* is an excellent example.

Narrow eyes are characteristic of the <u>earliest</u> unmarked heads; the eyes became progressively rounder as the bébé evolved into the 1880s. Again, the tiny doll in *Illustration 29* is a good example. Her rounder eye cuts give an alert, wide-eyed childlike look that changes her visage without having changed the mold. In this small size the mouth modeling is not deeply defined, but is carefully painted and shaded.

The same mold, treated differently, can go from the sublime to the almost silly. The charming boy with the hat in *Color Plate 16* is such a case. While not the finest bisque, he has sufficient charm to enable him to slip through any quality control check. He is 18 inches (46cm) tall and incised simply "2" at the crown. His medium brown eyebrows have an underwash which is more in keeping with the later dolls while retaining the very fine short strokes which are typical of early examples. He does not have blushing on his chin or

lathe-turned and carved, although molds for making these small bodies in papier-mâché were soon employed. The 10 inch (26cm) in *Illustration 29* is a good example. Her body is made completely of papier-mâché, poses awkwardly, has fingers of uneven length and more charm per centimeter than most dolls because she is such a faithful miniature version of her larger siblings, such as the boy in *Color Plate 16*. Her head is incised "3/0," a marking that reflects her reduction from a larger sized head mold:

	size	- 16 inches	41cm
size	1	- 16 inches	41cm
	0	- 14	36
	2/0	- 12	31
	3/0	- 10	26
	4/0	- 8	21

A size 1 socket head is the same size as his smallest bisque-headed kicking-crying baby, which might, logically, have been considered size 1. A complete size chart can be found on page 201, and a concentration on the petite dolls in Section V.

Another charming, small, unmarked Steiner is seen in *Illustration 31*. She is unusual in that she looks very much like the Bru Brevete with her full cheeks and chins. Is this a coincidence or a case of imitation being the most sincere form of flattery?

The heads of the earliest unmarked bébés are of exquisite quality. Usually found in larger sizes, 16 to 24 inches (41 to 61cm), the bisque is the finest to be found and the painting is precisely detailed, just as it is in the two bisque hip dolls shown. The whiteness of the bisque with contrasting rosy cheeks and eye shadowing is

Illustration 31. 11 inch (28cm) unmarked Steiner bébé with very full cheeks and chins giving her a strong resemblance to a Bru Brevete. *Courtesy Maurine S. Popp.*

61

above his eyes and his ears are larger and pierced through the lobes. His mouth has three shadings, from very dark in the center to lighter on the edges with darker outlining — a lot of detail painting for a small mouth. His rounder eyes are blue, lined and rimmed in darker blue and are about a size too small for his head, giving him a cross-eyed devilish charm. Or, to quote an admirer of his, "one eye is so beautiful the other can't stop looking at it!" He seems to be a late early bébé. Could he be the work of an apprentice? an "irregular?" or a later doll done in the early style? These are unanswerable questions. Nevertheless, he is the kind of delightful doll that one cannot help but love — just looking at him makes you happy.

His body is a combination of papier-mâché and wood. The torso and thighs are papier-mâché; the upper arms are completely wood. The lower arms are wood to the wrist and the lower legs wood to the ankles with composition hands and feet attached to them. The fairly coarse papier-mâché is a gray-brown in color, predating the purple used later.

He is not wearing his wonderful red wool jacket and pants with blue soutache braid trim, but that does not matter. Nothing bothers him.

Nothing, that is, except the trespasser on the right in *Color Plate 16* who has nicer bisque, wonderful eye shadowing and large, luminous violet-blue lined eyes. This interloper does not belong in this section on unmarked bébés because his head is incised: "Sie A 2." He is here to provide a comparison between the early unmarked heads and the Series A, the first of Jules Steiner's marked heads. There can be no doubt the molds are nearly the same; we will examine this doll in the next section, Section II, a study of dolls marked: "Series."

Illustration 32. Magnificent 22 inch (56cm) early Steiner bébé with very narrow blue-lined eyes, small beautiful closed mouth and exquisite painting. On a fully-articulated bébé body, she is one of the finest, most elegant of the dolls of Jules Nicolas Steiner. *Louise Lund Collection.*

Section Two

A STUDY OF THE
DOLLS MARKED "SERIES"

from

A to G

Plate 17. Three petite Series A bébés, all size 3/0, all from *Au Nain Bleu:* 10¼ inch (26cm) on fully-articulated body, in red. *Sylvia MacNeil Collection.* 9½ inch (24cm) boy with papier-mâché "Motschmann-type" body. *Beulah Franklin Collection.* 9½ inch (24cm) little girl with label on tummy. *Nancy A. Smith Collection.*

Plate 18. Sie A 5, open mouth 24 inch (61cm) on articulated body. *Courtesy of Chantal Dagommer.*

Plate 19. Sie A 5, closed mouth, 24 inch (61cm), on articulated body. *Courtesy of Claude Detave.*

Plates 20 & 21. Sie B 2, 18 inch (46cm) with unusual facial features, delicate coloring and great appeal seen in close-up and in side view in *Color Plate 21. The Strong Museum, Rochester, New York.*

Plate 22. Sie C 6, 28 inch (71cm) bébé with big brown eyes, closed mouth and very pale coloring. *Mary Thomas Justice Collection.*

Plate 23. Sie C 4, 24 inch (61cm) open mouth with two rows of teeth holding two Series C 3/0 bébés, all with fully-articulated bodies. Inset: Sie C 3 with unusual GREEN wire-operated eyes. *Mary Christie Collection.*

Plate 24. Sie C 3/0 in totally original clothing as she came from the Steiner factory.

Plate 25. Sie C 5, 25 inch (61cm) with brown wire-operated eyes, open mouth and two rows of teeth. *Constance W. Fielden Collection.*

Plate 26. Sie E 2/0, 12 inch (31cm) closed mouth Series E of winsome appeal. *Ferné Young Collection.*

Plate 27. Sie E 3/0 closed mouth 10¼ inch (26cm) with Sie E 1, 16 inch (41cm) open mouth version, both with very white bisque coloring.

Plate 28. Sie F 2/0, 15 inch (38cm) young lady on long slender body with molded bosom, marked: "La Patricienne," with unusual mouth modeling.

Plate 29. Sie F 2/0 seen in previous plate with Sie F 3/0 a 10 inch (26cm) white faced clown of great originality and rarity. *Yvonne L. Baird Collection.*

Plates 30 & 31. Sie G 6, 28 inch (71cm) handsome and rare Steiner of superior quality and magnificent detail. *The Strong Museum, Rochester, New York.*

Plate 32. Sie G 3/0, 10¼ inch (26cm) tiny size with wonderful depth of modeling, blue paperweight eyes, fully-articulated body. *Gail Cook Collection.*

Plate 17. Three Sie A 3/0 bébés, circa 1880-85.

Plate 18. Sie A 5, circa 1880-82.

Plate 19. Sie A 5, circa 1880-82.

Plate 20. Sie B 2, circa 1890.

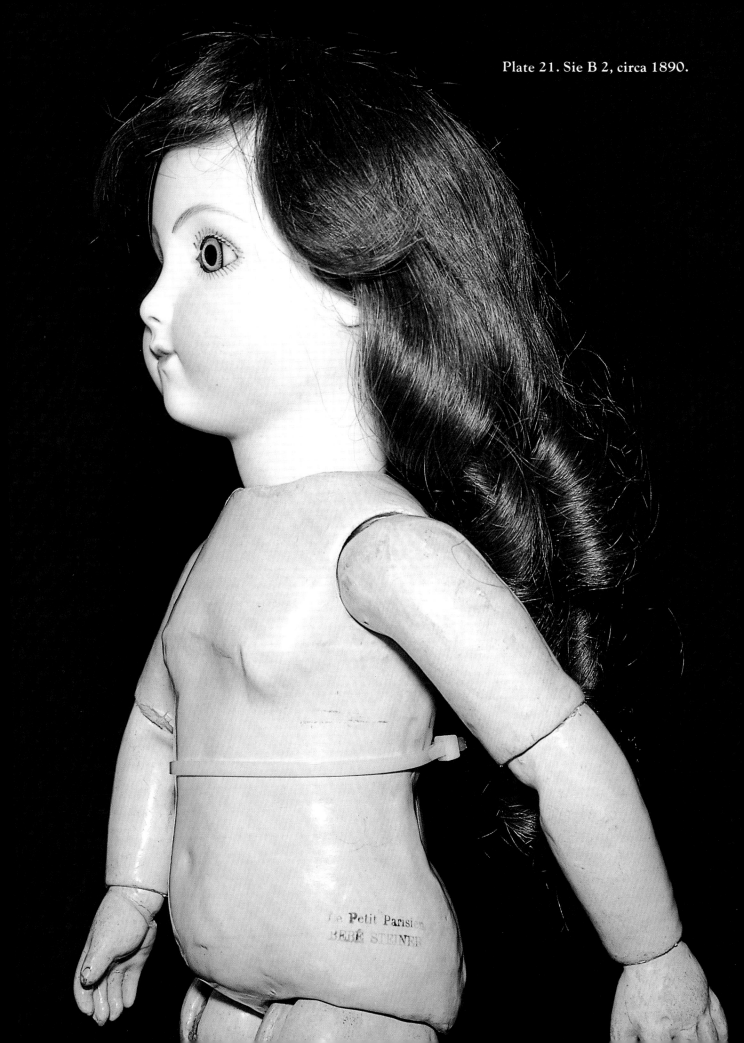

Plate 21. Sie B 2, circa 1890.

Plate 22, Sie C 6, circa 1885.

Plate 23. Sie C 4 with two Sie C 3/0 bébés. Inset: Sie C 3, all circa 1885-90.

Plate 24. Sie C 3/0, circa 1885.

Plate 25. Sie C 5, circa 1885-88.

Plate 26. Sie E 2/0, circa 1885.

Plate 27. Sie E 3/0 and Sie E 1, circa 1885.

Plate 28. Sie F 2/0, circa 1905.

Plate 29. Sie F 2/0 and
Sie F 3/0, circa 1895, 1905.

Plate 30. Sie G 6, circa 1885.

Plate 31. Sie G 6, circa 1885.

Plate 32. Sie G 3/0, circa 1885.

A STUDY OF THE DOLLS MARKED "SERIES"

The first of the dolls of Jules Nicolas Steiner with marked heads were those marked "Sie," the abbreviation of the French word "serie" (series). Thus it is correct to call only dolls marked in this way "Series" Steiners. This mark is often incorrectly recorded as Ste. Most of the Series heads originate in the 1880s while J. Bourgoin was leasing the Steiner firm from Jules Steiner, details of which are found in the *Historical Perspective*. The Series A head seems to be the first to appear, but this logical beginning does not continue as the other letters do not follow in clear-cut alphabetical order. It is possible these marked heads, or some of them, were the first to be made in Steiner's factory, as the kilns may have been present at that early date, even if Steiner himself was not.

While this grand collection of faces and their initial time-frame within the decade varies, the Series heads do have some consistent characteristics, which include:

1. All are of very fine quality pressed bisque.
2. All are incised at the crown as shown in the following example: **S<u>IE</u> A·2**

   Sometimes the "IE" is not underlined or so faintly underlined that it is hard to detect.
3. Some heads also have a written or stamped Bourgoin mark.

4. The "old size" numbering system is used, as follows:

INCHES	CM	SIZE
8¼	21	4/0
10¼	26	3/0
12¼	31	2/0
14¼	36	0
16¼	41	1
18	46	2
20	51	3
22	56	4
24	61	5
28	71	6
32	84	7
38	96	8

5. Series heads are most commonly found on light-weight fully-jointed bébé bodies, usually of purple papier-mâché, most often with straight wrists and short fat fingers. Exceptions include early body with balls, separate bisque hands or composition hands with large curved "banana" fingers.
6. Bodies are generally unmarked or have the caduceus stamp. Later 1880s examples may be marked "Le Petit Parisien," a trademark registered in 1889 but first used slightly earlier.

Illustration 33. A row of Steiner bébés which will be studied in this section show variations in head shapes. From left to right: Unmarked (3/0), Series A, Series B, Series C, Series E and Series F.

While these generalities have some exceptions, the group of dolls marked "Figure," studied in Section Three, will show a much wider range of treatment and of quality.

It may never be known who sculpted the Series heads or if they were all done at one time. A possibility is that when the unmarked Steiner heads were modified and softened to better represent a child, the **entire** Series of heads was sculpted. The A was most like the unmarked head, B much more avant-garde, C more moderate, and so forth. The faces could then have been chosen for production as desired or as appropriate.

Curiously, the bisque of some of the Series heads such as B, E and F tends to be left quite white with very rosy cheek coloring in substantial contrast, an 1870s effect, but with techniques for painting features generally used in the later 1880s or 1890s. Other molds, such as C and G, usually have a more evenly overall soft pale pink bisque color.

It is not always possible to ascertain if a body is original, which complicates dating some of these dolls. However, it is apparent that the vast majority were produced or released in the 1880s. Three factors which contribute to this dating are the use of purple papier-mâché for most of the bodies, the finding of the Bourgoin stamp on many of the heads and of the caduceus mark on a number of the bodies, all indicative of 1880s production.

By the end of the decade, a number of additional different Steiner heads, marked "Figure," were being made. With this in mind, it is difficult to understand the exact meaning of the Steiner advertising of 1889, as reported by Robert Capia in *Les Poupées Françaises:*

> "...le seul fabricant qui puisse offrir une collection de cent cinquante modeles et quatre physionomies..."
> "The only maker who can offer a collection of 150 models and four faces."

Considering all the different molds, in the multitude of sizes, plus the mechanical and novelty items, the 150 models is quite comprehensible. Less clear is what is meant by the four physionomies — faces — for after studying the Series faces alone, it is certain there are more than four different looks. A provocative article by François Theimer discussing symbolism in Steiner's marks appeared in *Polichinelle* Vol. 20, October 1985. But perhaps "four physionomies" was simply a very general reference to face shape: round, heart-shaped, oval or square!

Illustration 33 shows several, but not all of the Series heads and one unmarked Steiner, revealing their different face shapes. They will be looked at individually. A study of all the molds, Series then Figure, shows the myriad variations in the dolls of Jules Nicolas Steiner.

SERIES A

COLOR PLATES 17 - 18 - 19

Some of the Series A heads are so similar to the unmarked bébé heads that it is worth another look back at *Color Plate 16* in Section One for comparison. Both the unmarked and Series A faces were used for many years and have an overlapping time frame. Both are found either open or closed mouth and both have very round faces. They have a very similar head sculpture but with changes that significantly alter the look of the doll.

The eye sockets of the Series A are cut larger and more open than those of the unmarked heads. These eyes are also more deeply inset and there is more definition of bone structure at the eyebrow. They additionally are set slightly wider apart, further accentuating them and making a round face seem even rounder, while also broadening the bridge of the nose. See *Illustration 34* for a view of an unmarked and a Series A head at three-quarter angle. Note that the Series head is cut with less forehead, but this does not affect the doll's look when a wig is in place.

One of the endearing characteristics of all French bébés of this period is their large luminous eyes, so it is reasonable to expect to see this change in Jules Steiner's bébés at this time as well. The handsome boy in *Color Plate 16* is no exception; his eyes are, however, exceptional. Intensely deep in color, a rich violet-blue, they are darkly lined and outlined. Not only is the actual eye cut larger, but the iris fills more of the opening than in the unmarked head. Further, this larger eye is framed by upper and lower lashes that are both long and close together. There are nearly twice as many eyelashes on this Series A head as on the unmarked companion. A deep rosy eye shadow further draws attention to his eyes and his eyebrows are quite lushly painted. They are medium brown with a darker undercolor over which numerous longer, curved, eyebrow strokes are painted. Series A is also found with wire operated eyes, as seen in *Illustration 35*.

Another interesting aspect of the eye in some Series A (and unmarked) heads is that the inner corner of the eye has an additional little cut suggesting a tear duct. A

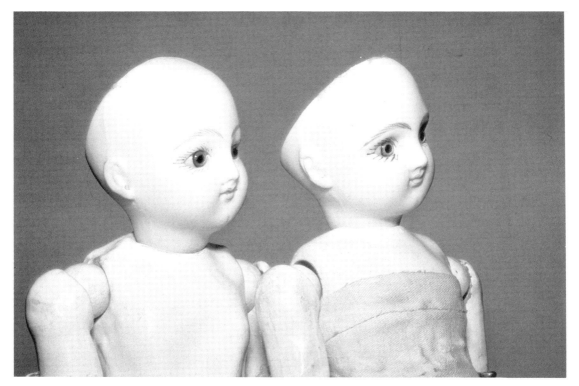

Illustration 34. Comparison of unmarked head and Series A head. Note modeling of bone structure of eyebrow on Series A.

Illustration 35. Alert-looking 28 inch (71cm) closed mouth Sie A 6, with blue wire-operated eyes with enameled lids. Her large eyes give her a real bebe look, but a small number of wire-eyed Series A heads have been found on leather lady bodies. This is a face which is close in time and appearance to the lady dolls which preceded her.

small dot of reddish color is found there on the bisque, as on most dolls, but this detail of the eye cut subtly adds to the eye interest. It is no accident that the eyes are the focal point, so to speak, of this doll. This is one of the first of the idealized and sentimentalized bébés of the 1880s, a time when children were themselves adored and pampered.

The other facial details, like those of the unmarked heads, include a generous nose, a small circular indentation for the philtrum and a very small mouth tucked right up under the nose. This boy's mouth, with its several shadings, is more like the mouth of the unmarked boy in the hat than of the other closed mouth Series A dolls shown in *Color Plates 17* and *19*. They have the more usual Series A mouth treatment which tends to be two-color, with a darker outline and the "flattened M" line through the center, and with a substantial projection of the lower lip. It is a distinctive mouth with more than just a suggestion of a smile.

The mark on this delightful child's head is shown in *Illustration 36*. The lovely red script mark reads:

Steiner Bte SGDG
Paris
Bourgoin, Suœr

The Bte is an abbreviation of Brevete, or patented. Sometimes just a "B" appears. SGDG is an abbreviation of *Sans Guarantie du Governmente*, or without the guarantee of the government, which is thereby not protecting the rights of the person or company who registered the patent. In the advertising directories, J.

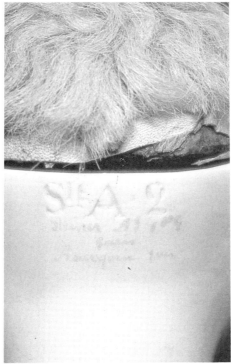

Bourgoin is listed as J. Steiner's successor from 1881 to 1887. Note in *Illustration 37* the uncommonly large advertisement; this was in the 1882 *Annuaire Guide de l' Acheteur*. However, as we have seen, Jules Steiner remained involved during this period and registered several patents. The script mark on heads is found written many different ways, on either side of, below and around the incised marks. In this day and age, it is hard to conceive of each of these heads being individually signed, but labor costs were not what they are today. However, by the end of Bourgoin's years, a block letter stamp was being used — the Industrial Revolution had struck again! The script Bourgoin mark dates this boy about 1881 or shortly thereafter, while the pudgy papier-mâché body confirms he is very much a transitional example. Made of a rather heavy brown stock, the body is in the early style with six balls. Since this head mold was used throughout the decade and perhaps into the 1890s, most examples of Series A have the later, traditional, sleek Steiner body, as does one of the darling trio in *Color Plate 17*.

Illustration 38. Small listing is from the same 1882 publication of the *Annuaire Guide de L'Acheteur* seen in *Illustration 37*. It is more typical of Steiner listings in commercial directories. *Centre du Documentation du Jouet Musée des Arts Décoratifs, Paris.*

——————————COLOR PLATE 17——————————

Shown in *Color Plate 17* are three small Series A bébés, all alert, wide-eyed, happy-faced little jewels. As were many of Jules Steiner's finer dolls, they were probably sold through the wonderful Parisian toy shop, *Au Nain Bleu* (The Blue Dwarf) and were dressed in that shop's completely charming, somewhat fancy style. Similar to our F.A.O. Schwarz, *Au Nain Bleu* catered to a discriminating clientele whose appreciation of beautiful dolls, including Jules Steiner's bébés, has enriched our world.

The heads of all three are incised "Sie A 3/0." The doll in the center is on a typical, fully-articulated body with straight wrists and short fingers. She stands 10¼ inches (26cm) tall. The other two have papier-mâché Motschmann-type or "enigma" bodies, and are 9½ inches (24cm) tall. The modeling of the hip sections and lower legs of these bodies is very much like that of the bisque versions seen in Section One. However, the jointed arms of this papier-mâché version are exactly as found on the fully-articulated body with six balls, also seen in Section One. The chest area is simply the upper torso section of that body. An infrequently found doll, it is invariably in this tiny size. There is a reeded squeak mechanism in the torso as seen in *Illustration 39*.

The *très joli bébé* in red wears her original costume, a red silk and lace confection. It is so well preserved, one

can be certain she was well protected from the elements, particularly dust and sunlight. A style found frequently on dolls from *Au Nain Bleu*, it is sweet eloquence in its illusion of simplicity. Of fine red silk, it has rows of vertical cotton lace insertion from its squared yoke to its dropped waist. The skirt is finely pleated with a gathered overlay of wider lace. A wide red satin ribbon ties in the back. The straw hat is lined in a gathered garnet satin and it retains a tiny *Au Nain Bleu* paper sticker. Little red cotton knit socks and black leather shoes complete a pristine package.

The little boy on the left — be still my heart! It is not simply his serious "A" smile, it is not just the lush skin wig, the natty blue cotton suit, the straw sailor hat with the stretched-out tie, the loose-strung arms and head... It is not just <u>that body</u> or that over a hundred years have not only <u>NOT</u> taken their toll but have somehow <u>improved</u> him, that he survived so intact not because he was not loved, for it is impossible <u>not</u> to love him ... It is all this and more.

Although his clothing and body are not marked, another similarly dressed little Steiner boy still has a paper label inside his hat, so we can assume that this boy's has been lost. His shoes and socks are identical to the doll's in red and his body, seen in *Illustration 40*, is the same as the little girl's on the right who proudly displays her *Au Nain Bleu* label. She needs nothing else to be a more than acceptable member of this elite group! The impish charm of Series A lends itself to these tiny dolls perhaps better than any other of Jules Steiner's models.

Illustration 39. Reeded squeak mechanism contained within torso of doll body as seen in *Illustration 8*.

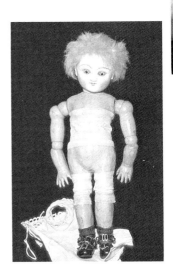

Illustration 40. *"*I love you, Jerome, but I lust after him," 9½ inches (24cm) of beguiling charm, with papier-mâché Motschmann-type body, and a face...seen also in *Color Plates 17* and *70*. *Beulah Franklin Collection.*

Illustration 41. The lusted after Series A 3/0 boy with an 1868 patented manivelle (hand-crank) velocipede. The velocipede is steered by the feet which rest on U-shaped bars at the rear wheels. The arms pump the levers in front with a scissor-like action. The wheels turn freely forward or backward; an inopportune encounter with a rock could suddenly reverse the operator's direction. It would appear that the bicycle helmet came into use at about this time. In 1869 Jules Steiner registered a patent, #85858, for improvements in the construction and drive mechanisms of velocipedes. *Beulah Franklin Collection.*

—————————COLOR PLATE 18———————————   ———————————COLOR PLATE 19—————————

The large bébé in *Color Plate 18* is incised "Sie A 5," and measures 24 inches (61cm). She is the harder-to-find open mouth version of Series A. The mouth treatment here is very much like that of the unmarked heads. There are shadings of color in addition to a sharply pointed cut in the center of the upper lip. The lower lip also seems to be hand shaped after the mouth was cut open, an intriguing attention to detail. She has a small chin dimple, merely a suggestion, and very pale bisque. As with the others, she has incredibly large eyes and a nose as broad as the Champs-Élysées. The Series A is surely a happy face!

The exquisite bébé in *Color Plate 19* is incised "Sie A 5" and measures 24 inches (61cm). A triumph of delicate pink shadowing and cheek color over pale bisque, she exemplifies "A" artistry at its finest; she is a masterpiece! Both of these large dolls (*Color Plates 18* and *19*) are on fully-articulated papier-mâché bébé bodies. They are a wonderful pair.

The Series A dolls examined here have been chosen because they are representative of the various body types and facial paintings one finds with this transitional mark. Some are found on bodies of purple papier-mâché with the caduceus mark. The Series A head with wire-operated eyes has also been found on a kid lady body which appeared original. Most were made during the Bourgoin years, though some less carefully painted examples, or those with grainier bisque and higher coloring, are likely products of the 1890s. All of the molds are, of course, subject to an individual artist's style of facial painting and they also reflect the moment's vogue, thus creating variations in generalities.

86

SERIES B

The Series B head represents a more major departure from the broad-faced heads which we have seen thus far. A rarely found head, its humanly realistic features seem more consistent with dolls of the later 1880s, suggesting that the Series marks were not made or released in alphabetical order. The few examples seen have not carried a Bourgoin stamp; one has a stamp "Le Petit Parisien//BÉBÉ STEINER" on her body, which would indicate she was made in the late 1880s. The trademark was registered in 1889 but was used slightly before then as it appears on other bodies which are also marked "J. Bourgoin." It is curious that other Series molds such as C and G consistently appear with Bourgoin head marks, conclusively dating them in the earlier 1880s.

The modeling of the Series B is very gentle and naturalistic. The forehead is more vertical in profile than the Series A or unmarked heads in which the forehead inclines back. See *Illustration 42*. The nose is longer and the tip is softly rounded. The mouth is not as close to the nose, which in addition to adding to its naturalism, creates a longer and more shapely philtrum, the groove between the nose and mouth. The Series B mouth is quite special, with a suggestion of a content smile. There are little lines molded at the corners of the mouth and a natural dimpled cleft below the lower lip. A lot of care was given in the forming and finishing of this head. While the face is actually surprisingly round, it is the more natural placement of the mouth which better defines the chin and gives the face a longer, more heart-shaped appearance. As in all Series heads, the ears have good detail, but do not have incised canals.

The Series B has so far only been found in a closed mouth version. Two views are seen in *Color Plates 20* and *21*, as well as a straight front view in *Illustration 43A*. This doll, from The Strong Museum in Rochester, New York, is incised "Sie B 2" as seen in *Illustration 43B*. She is 18 inches (46cm) tall. The incised lettering is more curved than in some of the other Series marks.

Her bisque is almost white with rosy cheek coloring. There is an understated quality to this bébé. Her eyebrows are very lightly feathered with a wash under and the eyelashes are by no means excessive. It is her mouth painting, however, in addition to its exquisite modeling, that sets her apart. The softness of the two-tone mouth coloring is created by the omission of outlining, presenting a more "Impressionistic" mouth, a treatment we will encounter in the 1890s, but which succeeds particularly well here because the sculpture itself is so tender and graceful.

A 9½ inch (24cm) Series B, size 3/0 which has a papier-mâché Motschmann-type body is shown in Section Five, *Color Plate 72*. Even in this tiny size, the detailing of the mouth is excellent, although it is of higher color and slightly outlined. While the overall effect may not be as delicately impressionistic as the bébé featured here, it is, nonetheless, very special.

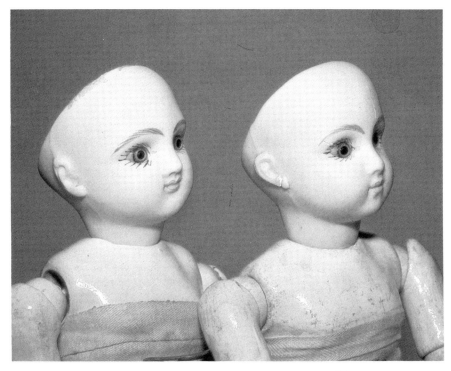

Illustration 42. Series A and Series B 3/0 heads in three-quarter profile to show differences in sculpture. Note the lower placement of the Series B mouth and its delicate detail.

87

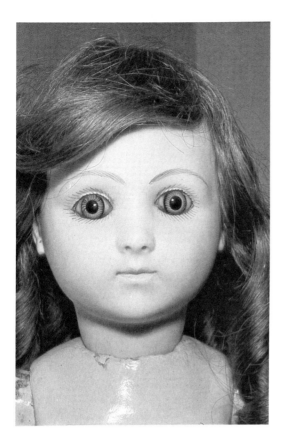

Illustration 43A. 18 inch (46cm) Series B, incised: Sie B 2. Other views of this doll are seen in *Color Plates 20* and *21* with descriptive details in the text.

SERIES C

The "classic" Steiner bébé has to be the Series C Steiner. A softly idealized face, it was made throughout the entire Bourgoin years and beyond, as evidenced by heads without the Bourgoin mark and by original costuming identical to that of later Figure C marked dolls. The Series C was probably the doll most highly competitive with Emile Jumeau's *E.J.*, although she is not at all similar in appearance to that bébé.

The Series C, while basically considered a round face, is actually more square, especially when compared to the Series A. This is mostly because her cheeks are fatter and lower on her face. See *Illustration 44*. There are no lines around the mouth as on the Series B, but the mouth itself is full, almost sensuous, and quite close to the nose. It is lightly outlined, with the upper lip, particularly in the larger sizes, making a definite dip in the center. This actually casts a shadow and accentuates its depth. More tender and much more serious than a Series A, she has an aura of tranquility about her. It is not hard to fathom the longstanding appeal of this sweet bébé.

Illustration 43B. Mark of Series B Steiner. *The Strong Museum Collection, Rochester, New York.*

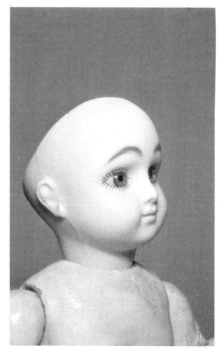

Illustration 44. Series C 3/0 head in three-quarter profile shows softly sculpted facial features.

The Series C is usually painted as softly as she was sculpted, with a more evenly applied pink wash over her entire head and with less contrasting shading at the eyes, cheeks and chin. The philtrum tends to be very slightly oval and not excessively deep; a light touch is seen in almost all aspects of this doll. Even in large sizes, the feeling is generally one of delicacy with a Series C Steiner. It must be remembered that these dolls are hand-painted; they are actually pieces of art, despite being produced in the work place. An individual artist's techniques and flair show in his work, so that variations are the norm. Often, even, a study of the flow of eyelash or eyebrow painting can indicate if an artist were left or right-handed. So, while there are, of course, variations in the painting here, there tends to be a remarkably even and consistently moderate and careful touch in Series C heads.

Series C is found in both open and closed mouth versions. The open mouth has, not surprisingly, a softer look than we have yet seen in an open mouth Steiner. A peculiarity of many open mouth Series C dolls is that shrink lines have formed in the firing at the corners of the mouth. This is likely because the pressed bisque was very thin and perhaps on the dry side for easier handling or because the mouth cuts were stretched to shape the mouth and to facilitate the insertion of the two rows of teeth. The mouth of the Series C is, it seems, always outlined.

A variety of Bourgoin marks, script and block, are found on the Series C heads, though not all are marked with his name. Most have bodies of purple papier-mâché and when marked, it is usually with the caduceus stamp. Generally, they have straight wrists and short stubby fingers, though they have also been found with articulated wrists with bisque hands and composition hands of the large, curved finger type. Additionally, a broad spectrum of eyes are found in the Series C heads. Frequently, they are wire-eyed, with the bisque eye cups as seen in Section One, *Color Plates* 6 and 7.

—————————— COLOR PLATE 22 ——————————

The magnificent bébé featured in *Color Plate 22* is incised "Sie C 6." She is 28 inches (71cm) of absolutely the highest quality bisque and workmanship to be found. Her bisque is flawless, its painting faultless; photographs do not do her justice. Her large brown

paperweight eyes are unusually soft and complement her subtle understated elegance. One picture is worth a thousand words...

—————————— COLOR PLATE 23 ——————————

Featured in *Color Plate 23* is a captivating 22 inch (56cm) open mouth Series C, size 4, holding two perky little 10¼ inch (26cm) charmers. In the inset is seen a 20 inch (51cm) size 3 bébé with lever-operated eyes, but hers have a most unusual green coloring; they appear to be lithographed. The eyes of the other three are blue paperweight and all have identical bodies with straight wrists and short fat fingers — classic Series C bébés. It is particularly nice that these small dolls were as popular as they were, for while they are not wildly plentiful, they do turn up. When they do, it is always a happy experience, but never any more so than when the bewitching brown wire-eyed gem in *Color Plate 24* was first encountered.

—————————— COLOR PLATE 24 ——————————

We, as doll collectors, are in many ways a fortunate generation, for we still occasionally experience the discovery of a doll from the attic. After a hundred years, to have a precious bébé surface, stitched in her high-fashion costume quite as she had left the Steiner factory, albeit a bit soiled and faded, but intact — that is a pleasure that not many generations more will have. Of course, we have now the knowledge to appreciate a century-old treasure in a way that the generations before us could not. If she could but speak...

She wears her original lace-trimmed underpants and a Steiner factory chemise with red ribbon trim. (This style chemise is usually found with red, yellow or blue trim.) Inch (3cm) wide bobbin lace is edged with a row

Illustration 45. 22 inch (56cm) classic Series C bébé seen in *Color Plate 6* is years ahead of herself wearing souvenir hat marked: "Blériot." The first man to fly the English Channel, July 25, 1909, Louis Blériot had made a fortune manufacturing auto head lamps and designing airplanes, among them the famous S.P.A.D. of World War I. Born to good fortune, "Lucky Louis" survived 50 plane crashes.

FAR RIGHT: Illustration 46. 28 inch (71cm) incised: "Sie C 6," "Stephanie Steiner" is unusual in her crisper mouth painting, larger than usual eyes and lower than usual eyebrows, a combination giving her a look strongly hinting of Series A. *Coleman Collection.*

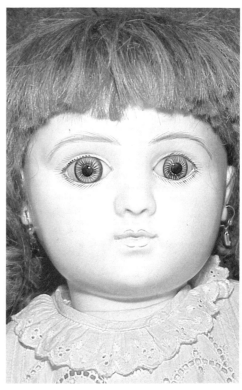

Illustration 47. 20 inch (50cm) wonderful Series C seen in inset of *Color Plate 23.* Her wire eyes are an unusual green and appear to be lithographed. Her mouth painting suggests a little tongue tip, and her bisque is superb, pale with lovely tinting. *Mary Christie Collection.*

FAR RIGHT: Illustration 48. The 18 inch (46cm) blue wire-eyed Series C 2/0 seen here is on a wood articulated lady body marked in an oval in green ink: "AU BENGALI," the shop name. Series C and Series A are occasionally found on various lady bodies. These two molds best reflect their lady doll heritage. *Constance W Fielden Collection.*

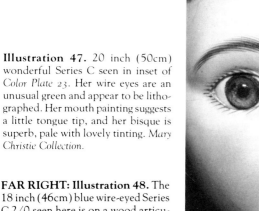

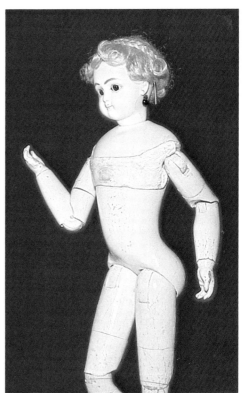

90

FAR LEFT: Illustration 49. 12 inch (31cm) Sie C 2/0 baby with fully-jointed bébé body has totally original, infant clothing, consisting of a buttoned piqué swaddling wrap with a square bib with embroidery and lace trim. A pink satin ribbon is tied around the waist and she carries a glass nursing bottle embossed on the front "BIBERON POMPE" with "MONCHOVAUT" and "A PARIS" embossed along the sides. The nipple of the bottle is wooden. Note that she has her *Au Nain Bleu* label on her stomach. Circa 1885. *Dorothy Dixon Collection.*

Illustration 50. 9¾ inch (25cm) Series C 3 0 in typical *Au Nain Bleu* lacy dress.

Illustration 51. 8¼ inch (21cm) Series C 4/0 bebe with fully-jointed body, bisque hands, blue wired eyes and charm galore — proof positive that good things come in small packages.

of narrow net lace, then gathered and stitched to the chemise. A pink cotton satin pleated skirt is sewn to a buckram waist and carries a balayeuse of wide bobbin lace. All of this is stitched onto and through the chemise and none of it has ever been off! Her coat dress is a bronze windowpane checked taffeta with a pink cotton satin plastron and bustle bow. All of the seams are finely piped and the sleeves are banded at the wrist in the same pink fabric. Inside the folds of the fabric which is now faded to beige, it is astounding to see the vivid pink it was when new. Her hat is of matching pink fabric, wide wire-brimmed, with faded pink satin ribbon trim now likewise beige. Little silver metal stars adorn the hat and dress including the plastron, sleeves and shoulders; time has taken a few. These are stars identical to those on the rosettes of the shoes of the kicking-crying baby in *Illustration 13B*. They are also sewn on a pair of shoes marked "A.T.," an interesting coincidence. Her shoes were missing, however, so she borrowed a pair for the photograph. Can there be any doubt that hers were star-studded slippers?

Additionally, and most specially, she has a curved comb in her skin wig — a wig which words can hardly describe. It is better seen with her hat off, as in *Color Plate 64* in Section Four. Now, if anyone styled a skin wig like that today, people would laugh...but "Felice Delaire" came out of Jules Nicolas Steiner's factory on rue d'Avron in that hairstyle — is that not outrageous!

──────── COLOR PLATE 25 ────────

Color Plate 25 features 25 inches (61cm) of delicate open mouth Series C beauty. She is incised "Sie C 5," and like the petite doll in the previous *Color Plate 24*, she has brown wire-operated eyes and extremely fine mouth painting. She combines quality and a wistful charm in a large but graceful and aesthetically pleasing package. She has very well-formed and tinted ears, but consistent with all Series heads, they do not have incised ear canals.

A sampling of other Series C dolls, from baby to lady, are seen in *Illustrations 45 through 51*. Jules Steiner's Series C is a marvelous blend of simplicity and sophistication.

SERIES D

The Series D head is positively the most elusive of Steiner's marks. It is inconceivable that one does not exist. Perhaps a second printing will find this gap filled.

Frequently the word "Series" is wrongly used to identify all Steiner heads, both "Series" and "Figures." One such example was reported to be a Series D, but further investigation proved it a *Figure D*, also rare. Therefore, this space is reserved:

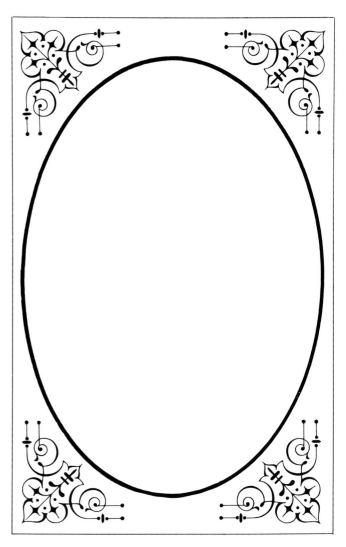

In the meantime:
WANTED: In any condition Sie D 3/0, or any other size: 4/0, 2/0, 0, 1, 2, 3, 4, 5, 6, 7, 8...Contact author or publisher...

SERIES E

COLOR PLATES 26 and 27

One of the more whimsically appealing faces found on Jules Steiner's bébés is his Series E. Similar in basic shape and treatment to a Series B, it differs considerably in the mouth modeling and that the face is more oval in shape. Found in both open and closed mouth versions, the closed mouth Series E is deeply sculpted into a definite smile with a depth between the open-closed lips not found in most other Series molds. A darker center line, again like a flattened "M," is painted for accent and the lips are outlined top and bottom center. The nose is longer and relatively broad, and the eyebrows are multistroke over a light wash. The bisque tends to be vary pale with highly contrasting cheek color.

Two small examples, sizes 3/0 and 2/0, are seen here. Both have six-ball articulated bodies with straight wrists and spidery fingers. Their bodies are of brown papier-mâché and have the caduceus stamp on the left hip. *Color Plate 26* shows the 12 inch (31cm) Sie E 2/0 while the 10¼ inch (26cm) is seen in *Color Plate 27*. These mischievous-looking children have longer faces than the Series A or C, but like the B, the length is partially achieved by a more natural placement of the mouth between the nose and chin, as seen in *Illustrations 52* and *53*. The two dolls are painted so similarly they appear to be the work of the same artisan, and both have brown stationary eyes. The Series E is an enchanting and happy face. Not a doll who can easily wear elaborate silks and satins, she is instead a child whose impish character shows through. It is this appearance that catches one's fancy.

The open mouth version, incised "Sie E 1," seen in *Color Plate 27* and *Illustration 54*, is also very special. She is 16 inches (41cm) tall, and she, too, has almost white bisque with rosy cheek coloring and eye shadowing. Her expressive open mouth has two typical rows of tiny

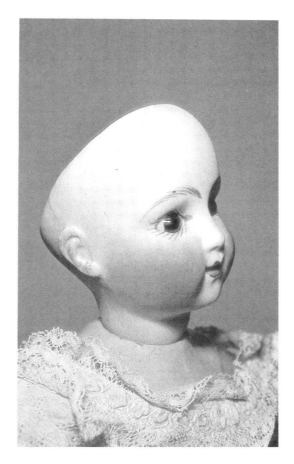

Illustration 52. 10 inch (26cm) Sie E 3/0 without wig in three-quarter profile shows creative depth of modeling around mouth.

teeth. The upper lip is cut with a pronounced drop in the center and is accented by three shadings as in the early unmarked examples. Her body is of purple papier-mâché with straight wrists and short, fat fingers. She has a pull-string Mama-Papa bellows which is the metal-encased variety commonly found in Jules Steiner's dolls from the 1880s. The bellows is signed "J. STEINER PARIS."

She has another "signature," a red paint fingerprint on her neck. Barely visible in the color plate, it is also shown in *Illustration 54C*.

Her blue-gray paperweight eyes have white lines and a darker rim, and her skin wig, though thin, is original. Her red cotton gingham dress is possibly her original homemade one which perfectly suits her "real little child" charm.

53

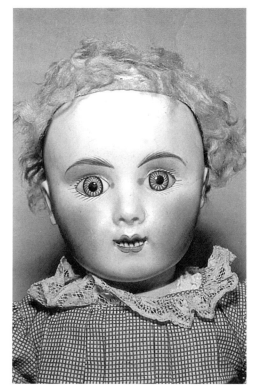

54A

Illustration 53. 12 inch (31cm) Sie
E 2/0, seen in *Color Plate 26*, is an
unusual brown-eyed waif. The Series
E has a longer face and a long-standing
appeal. *Ferne Young Collection.*

Illustrations 54A, 54B and 54C.
16 inch (41cm), the open mouth
Series E has distinctive mouth
detailing. The marks of this Series E
include her incised: "Sie E 1" and a
red fingerprint on her neck which is
as yet unidentified.

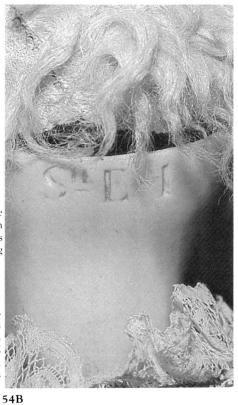

54B

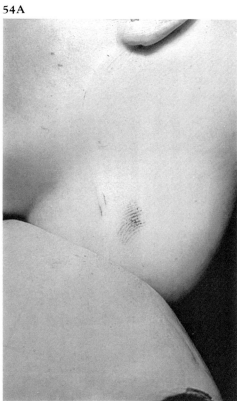

54C

SERIES F

COLOR PLATES 28 and 29

One of the most unusual of Steiner's dolls is the Series F. This face looks so much more like a little German character than a French bébé that one cannot help but be surprised to find that it is a product of Jules Steiner. The face is quite similar in basic shape to the Series E; again, it is the mouth detail that is unusual, for she has a decidedly open-closed mouth with a row of molded teeth, with two little dots for dimples in the cheeks. See *Illustration 55*. This is not a case of rarity and beauty going hand in hand. This is a "cute" doll.

It seems inconsistent that this head sculpture was done at the same time as the other Series molds. One example was noted with a block-letter Bourgoin stamp on the back of the head, however, which would indicate the later 1880s. This still seems to be a date somewhat premature, despite the fact that Steiner and Bourgoin were in the vanguard of the doll industry.

The two examples shown in *Color Plates 28* and *29* are themselves marvelously unusual. The disparity between using this funny-cute head as a clown and as a young lady on a rather elegant body is indeed surprising. They both have, true to form with Series marks, the old sizing. The clown is marked "Sie F 3/0" and is 10½ inches (26cm) tall. His bisque is pressed and is quite thin. The five-piece composition body is typical of those found on novelty-type Steiner dolls, although quite often the heads found on straight limb bodies are of high quality. The fingers are long and slender, as frequently found on heads marked Figure (or one of its many abbreviations) from the 1890s.

Jules Steiner made many clowns but all others noted have been incised with an abbreviation of Figure A, and with the later sizes of 0 to 6; these are 1890s marks. One such example is seen in Section Four, *Color Plate 57*, whose facial markings are identical to the Series F clown examined here. The workmen appear to have had much license in painting clowns for there are a multitude of variations; it would seem that these two examples were made at approximately the same time in the 1890s.

This little Series F clown's original multicolor mohair wig is avant-garde "punk," and his green-red-gray striped silk taffeta suit is original though somewhat torn. It is notable primarily for the appliqued paper stars

Illustration 55. 10 inch (26cm) Sie F 3/0 in three-quarter profile. Note similarities in head shape to Series E, but with major differences in mouth modeling. *Courtesy of Yvonne L. Baird.*

Illustration 56. 15 inch (38cm) Sie F 2/0 and mechanical waltzing lady reveal the changing form in two generations of ladies. It appears the free-spirited daughter is rejecting her mother's Victorian conventions.

95

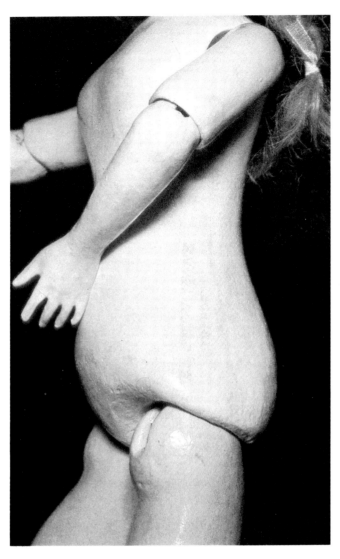

Illustration 57. 15 inch (38cm) Sie F 2/0 showing shapely body which is stamped "LA PATRICIENNE DEPOSE," a mark advertised in 1905 by Edmond Daspres. Note body finish is not as smooth as that of earlier bébés.

on the black velvet vest which are the same eight-pointed shape and size as the metal stars seen on some Steiner shoes and on the doll in *Color Plate 24*.

The other Series F, size 2/0 measures 15 inches (38cm) tall. She is tall because she has a young lady composition body, as seen in *Illustrations 56 and 57*. The body bears two important marks, "LA PATRICIENNE //(DEPOSE)" stamped on her left hip, and, additionally, embossed at the bottommost part of the small of her back are the letters E//D B in a triangle. Edmond Daspres, the final successor of the Steiner firm, used the mark "La Patricienne" in his publicity in 1905. This body has the delicate form of a young lady with a molded bosom, long limbs and long slender fingers in the Steiner tradition. It has been found with an interesting assortment of heads, which include a handsome Simon Halbig 1159 example at The Strong Museum in Rochester, New York, and a lovely A.T. pictured in *Dimples and Sawdust* by Madaline Selfridge and Marlowe Cooper, Vol. II, pages 146 through 148. Then here we have a funny-faced little adolescent girl growing up. As she had her original stringing, there is no doubt she came this way. She wears her wonderful factory original chemise which is embroidered, with a machine chain stitch, "La Patricienne."

Her head is painted not unlike the Series E just seen, with similar lightly stroked eyebrows. She, too, has outlined mouth painting although she has a white space between her lips and faintly molded teeth. Her ears are pierced, tinted and shaped just as found on all small Series heads. Her light brown mohair wig is of excellent quality, very soft and simply styled.

Her eyes are quite unusual, though; they are so remarkably different from each other it is hard to believe they are original, but they are! Perhaps iris coloration is a lesser known change that occurs during adolescence...but it is more likely that all sorts of "old stock" was being used up at this late date.

While not a classic beauty, she is a rare and important doll which documents the transition of the Steiner factory contents to Daspres, and gives us insight into the 20th century workings of the Steiner firm.

SERIES G

 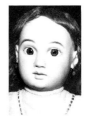 

The step from Series F to Series G is a grand one, for Series G is perhaps the most compelling and the most sublime of the dolls of Jules Nicolas Steiner. This step also takes us right back to the early 1880s. Both bébés examined here have the red script Bourgoin mark.

Color Plates 30 and *31* feature a doll of haunting beauty. Particularly in this large a size, the depth of detail is outstanding. At 28 inches (71cm) tall, she has a commanding presence, with an intensity and impact not unlike a Portrait Jumeau or an A.T. As she has the flatter wire-operated eyes, she lacks the fully-compelling aura that paperweight eyes gives to the others. The modeling of this doll is absolutely extraordinary. The usually broad Steiner nose is instead sharp and quite pointed, the face long and slender, but it is her mouth detail that is so very striking. There is no mere "suggestion" here; the open-closed mouth is dramatic portraiture. There is a lined groove on her lower lip and she looks as though she were about to speak.

Illustration 58. 28 inch (71cm) Sie G 6, handsome and expressive bébé seen in *Color Plates 30* and *31*, she also has the magnificent Steiner bisque hands, as seen here. *The Strong Museum, Rochester, New York.*

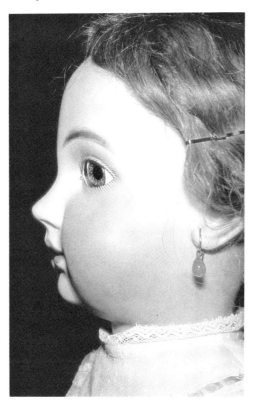 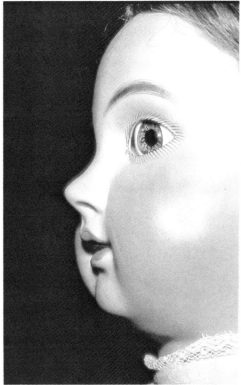

Illustrations 59A and 59B. Two close-up views of Series G. 28 inch (71cm). Note sharp nose and depth of detail around mouth. *The Strong Museum, Rochester, New York.*

The bisque is overall evenly pale with extremely careful cheek coloring and tinting over the eyes. The beautifully shaped nostrils and the oval philtrum are very realistic. This is both a stunning piece of sculpture and an exquisitely finished one. Breathtakingly beautiful, it is impossible to show too many views of her. See *Illustrations 58* and *59*. Her body is fully-articulated and she has the incredibly lovely Steiner bisque hands with magnificently manicured fingernails. Those great hands and that great face are a perfect match! To apply just a few more superlative adjectives: she is majestic, a special spectacular Steiner!

I like her.

But not to be believed is how well this great face is translated to that wonderful 10 inch (26cm) size of which Jules Steiner was such a master, seen in *Color Plate 32* and *Illustration 60*. It is astonishing to know that this is a head the size of a plum! She has a cute pointy little chin, square cutouts for wire eyes but her original very deep blue unlined paperweight eyes, a fully-articulated body and she wears a wonderful gray wool suit of great charm. With so much depth and detail, she packs proportionately as much punch per inch as her big sister.

The Series G is a grand note on which to end a study of Series marks.

By the end of the 1880s, the winds of change were blowing. While the Series heads had strongly carried the Steiner firm, under the management of J. Bourgoin, steadily through the decade, a major event was taking shape. Paris was to be the site of the Universal Exposition of 1889. This may well have contributed to the impetus for Jules Nicolas Steiner's return to his place at the head of his firm. The changes that happen at this time are considered in the following section, a study of the dolls marked "Figure."

Illustration 60. 10 inch (26cm) Sie G 3/0, the favored Steiner petite size with great detail, also seen and detailed in *Color Plate 32. Gail Cook Collection.*

98

Section Three

A STUDY OF THE DOLLS MARKED "FIGURE"

from

A to E

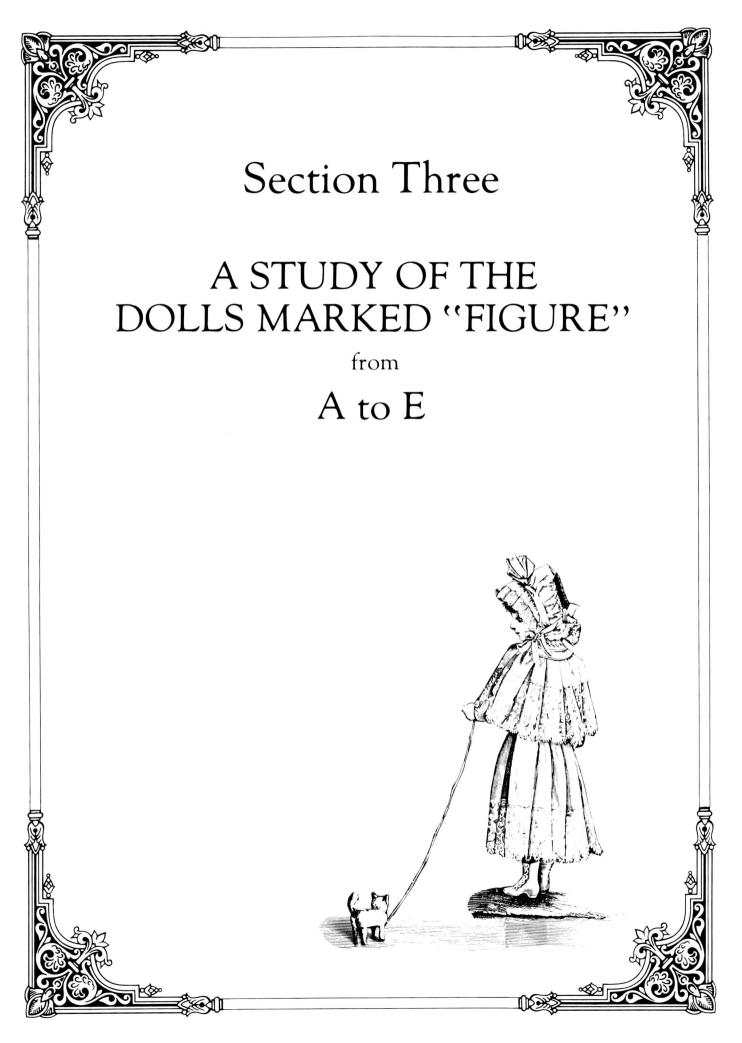

COLOR PLATES — Section Three

Plate 33. Figure A No. 5, 25 inch (63cm), early incised Figure A with blue wire-operated eyes and delicate coloring. *Constance W. Fielden Collection.*

Plate 34. Figure A (FIre A 15) bébé with open mouth, very detailed painting. Doll is *Bébé Premier Pas*, 22 inch (56cm), 1890 patent. *Lorna Lieberman Collection.*

Plate 35. Two mulatto Figure A bébés with fully-articulated bodies, one closed mouth (FIre A 3) and one open (A-5).

Plate 36. 16 inch (41cm) FIre A 9 in totally original *Au Nain Bleu* clothing with blue wire-operated eyes. *Beulah Franklin Collection;* 8¼ inch (21cm) miniature version of larger doll, incised: "Fre A 1."

Plate 37. 10¼ inch (26cm) incised: "A-3," and 12½ inch (32cm) incised: "A 5.6" all-original *Au Nain Bleu* costumed bébés with fully-articulated bodies. *Beulah Franklin Collection.*

Plate 38. 20 inch (51cm) impressionistically painted Fre A 13 with sweet little girl appeal, blue paperweight eyes, closed mouth. *Beulah Franklin Collection.*

Plate 39. Figure B, marked: "B1," classic open mouth bébé with two rows of teeth, fully-articulated body, 16in (41cm), circa 1887-1888.

Plate 40. Figure C No. 4, 22 inch (56cm) with blue wire-operated sleep eyes, closed smiling mouth and crisp painting.

Plate 41. Fre C 15, 22 inch (56cm) with more impressionistic painting, closed mouth, blue paperweight eyes. *Patricia Gallagher Collection.*

Plate 42. Figure C No. 0, 14 inch (36cm), small blue wire-lever eyes, closed mouth, articulated body. *Nancy A. Smith Collection.*

Plate 43. Three Figure C bébés, sizes 2/0, 3/0 and 4/0 from 12¼ inch (31cm) to 8¼ inch (21cm) show precise modeling and painting, variations in body details and eye types.

Plate 44. Figure D Steiner, 22 inch (56cm), incised: "Fre D 15," rare and lovely. *Maurine S. Popp Collection.*

Plate 45. 24in (61cm) *Phénix*, incised: " ☆ 96" shows remarkably similar modeling to Figure D in *Color Plate* 44.

Plates 46, 47 and 48. Very rare Figure E Steiner, incised: "Fre E 3," with full cheeks, overbite pouty mouth and fully-articulated body with metal hands.

Plate 33. Figure A No 5, circa 1890.

Plate 34. Fire A 15, *Bébé
Premier Pas*, 1890 patent.

Plate 35. FIre A 3 and A.5
mulatto bébés, circa 1890-95.

Plate 36. FIre A 9 and Fre A 1, circa 1890.

Plate 37. A 3 and A 5.6 from
Au Nain Bleu, circa 1895.

Plate 38. Fre A 13, circa 1890-95.

Plate 39. B 1, circa 1887-88.

Plate 40. Figure C No 4, circa 1890.

Plate 41. Fre C 15, circa 1895.

Plate 42. Figure C No 0, circa 1890.

Plate 43. Figure C No 2/0, 3/0, 4/0, circa 1890.

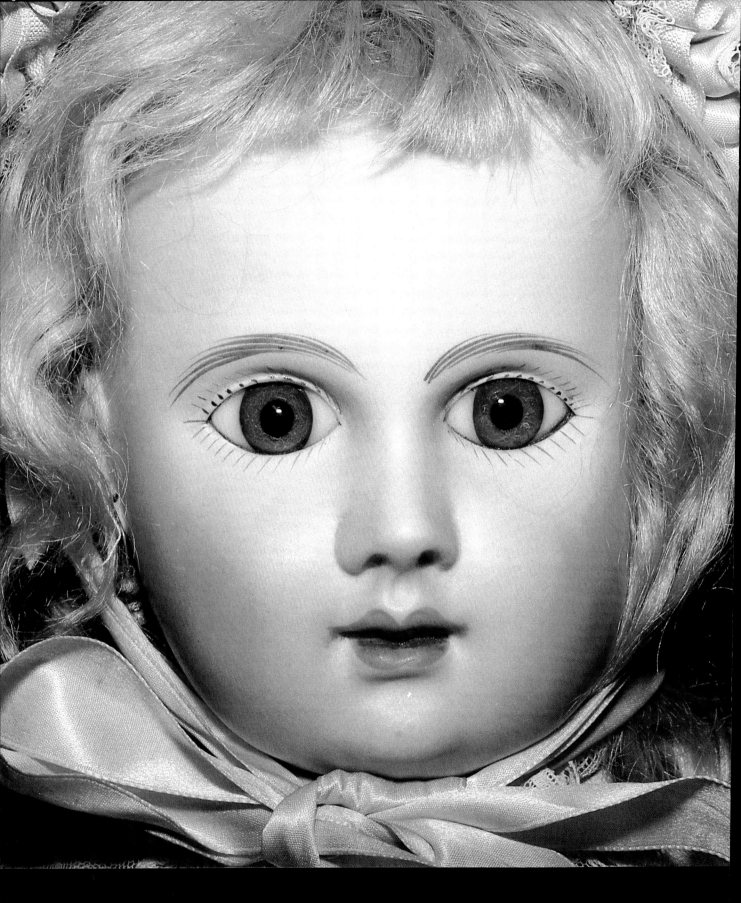

Plate 44. Fre D 15, circa 1895.

Plate 46. Fre E 3, circa 1890.

Plate 47. Fre E 3, circa 1890.

Plate 48. Fre E 3, circa 1890.

A STUDY OF THE DOLLS MARKED "FIGURE"

While a study of the Series heads was relatively straightforward, this is not the case with heads marked Figure. It is at the end of J. Bourgoin's years of managing the Steiner firm, about 1887, that we encounter the first of the Figure marks, the earliest of which are also marked Bourgoin. An ever growing demand for Jules Steiner's dolls, from the exquisite to the simply sweet, had likely created the need for an increased supply. Additionally, Steiner may have wanted a new line of faces to present at the upcoming International Exhibition in Paris in 1889. A different sculptor seems to have been involved in the creation of the Figure heads. While it is evident that the facility for making heads existed at the Steiner factory, it is not known at what point that production commenced or how inclusive it was. It is possible the Figure heads were the first to be produced there, beginning under Bourgoin.

While the standards for the Figure heads remained as high as for the Series heads, there are some interesting changes and modifications in the molds of this new group of heads. Noteworthy differences to consider, some subtle and others obvious, include:

1. The mark. The change from "Series" to "Figure" and starting again at A implies a new beginning, a new line or a new manufacturer. The mark itself is much more complete; but this may have been precipitated by international trade law changes on the horizon. The Figure marked heads also carry the incised name of J. STEINER, this for the first time in over 25 years of Steiner's activity in the doll industry, an interesting change. The crispness of the letters of the Figure marks compared to the generally more curved letters of the Series marks may suggest a change of manufacturer. However, some Series marks, too, have this more block lettering, so this can only be considered a curiosity.

2. The ear. The new ear with the deeply incised canal is only found on Figure marked heads, and only on some of them. As it is never found on Series heads, this suggests the maker of the Figure heads was not the same one who made the Series heads. The ear is a significant change which required a change in the mold, giving rise to the suggestion that another sculptor or mold maker initially approached or was approached by Steiner to produce the new line of heads.

3. The bisque. Both Series and Figure marked heads appear to be of pressed bisque, and both are made from a very fine, translucent kaolin paste. The Figure heads are, however, sometimes more grainy than Series heads, but we must remember there is a decade of increased competition and rising production costs to account for an occasionally flawed finish. The main differences in the heads are in their painting. The basic paint colors are not quite the same on the Series and Figure heads, although this could easily occur within the same factory. The painting of the features, however, differs more from Series to Figure than within either Series or Figure marked heads. While this can be the result of the style of the moment, there is a period in the late 1880s and early 1890s when the heads seem to be concurrent and are painted differently, which is suggestive of two different manufacturers.

4. The size numbers. The Figure heads reflect a change in the size numbers, which encompass an extensive range including some interesting in-between sizes. The very earliest Figure heads have the old Series sizes, but it appears that once they were in full production, the new size system was implemented, although occasionally an old size turns up on a later head. The Series heads, however, never adopt the new sizing, a factor which tends to support there having been a second manufacturer involved.

As is apparent, there are as many questions as answers!

The very first of the Figure marks were not incised, but simply handwritten in black ink or paint. A 10 inch (26cm) bébé was marked " **A⅜** " and " **B1** " was found on a 16 inch (41cm) bébé. These heads were as prototypes; both have old sizing and the new wonderfully sculpted ears with the deeply incised canals synonymous with Steiner, but more accurately, some Steiners. These earliest heads were also stamped in red block letters "J. STEINER B SGDG//J. BOURGOIN, Succr" confirming that the first appearance of the Figure marked heads was in the late 1880s.

The incised marks were soon used. There is no fear of this being logical and consistent, but through the 1890s, the marks tend to follow a pattern of being increasingly abbreviated. Also, in some cases the incised mark is "J. STEINER" while in others it is simply

"STEINER." The latter likely indicates molds made after Amédée Lafosse had succeeded Jules Steiner (1891). Lafosse was operating the Steiner company and using the established Steiner name; the large advertisement seen in *Illustration 61* suggests that Lafosse was an enterprising businessman. Molds marked "J. STEINER" continued to be used throughout the 1890s, so while this marking provides clues, it does not pinpoint a doll's exact date. This multitude of different marks can be seen in the list of Figure marks in Section V. Not all of these variations in marks are found on each of the Figure molds, A through E.

One consistent factor, though, in the Figure marked heads is that they tend to be more evenly overall tinted. The coloring ranges from very soft pale pink or creamy to a deeper dusty rose; only rarely do Figure heads have the sharply contrasting cheek color on whiter bisque that is found on a number of the Series heads. Figure B is consistently painted in a precise manner while C has more variation, although basically the early C mark is more traditionally painted and the later mark is done in a more impressionistic style. Figure A is all-inclusive.

The bodies of the Figure marked bébés usually are of gray-brown papier-mâché, substantiating belief that the purple was used only during Bourgoin's years. The form of the body remained the same as found with the Series heads, but the hands of some of the early Figures with jointed wrists have fat fingers curved inward, all in one plane, somewhat like a bunch of bananas. Some of the later Series bébés have these hands as well. The hands with the graceful long slender fingers, with articulated or straight wrists, were introduced about 1890 and are found consistently, but by no means exclusively, thereafter. The most common body marks are either the paper label showing a jointed doll wearing a bead necklace and carrying a tricolor flag, or the blue stamp of the trademark "Le Petit Parisien//BÉBÉ STEINER."

It does appear that the Series marked heads were used less and less as the Figure marked heads grew in popularity and production. Some of the Series and Figure heads have similar physionomies, and since Figures A and B were initially released at the same time, and quite likely C as well, it further clouds the speculations about the exact meaning of the 1889 Steiner advertising of four physionomies. It is also probable that an early Figure D was part of the four, which, as an ensemble, may have been intended to replace the Series marked heads. It is a continuing and intriguing question.

Nonetheless, the Figure marks and the dolls themselves present a broad and fascinating spectrum. Nowhere is this more apparent than with the most multitudinous of heads, the Figure A, whose many treatments will now be considered.

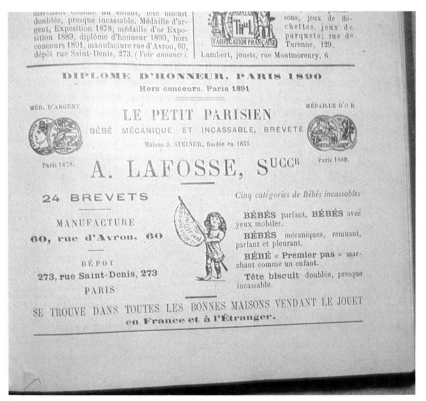

Illustration 61. This large advertisement is from the 1893 *Annuaire Officiel des Jouets et Jeux Français* and lists A. Lafosse as successor. The only mention of Steiner is in the smaller listing above it which says "ancienne" (formerly) maison J. Steiner. Both the 1878 Silver Medal and the 1889 Gold Medal won by Steiner are depicted; mention is also made of the 1890 Diplome d'Honneur and of his being Hors Concours (out of the running) in Paris in 1891. Shown, too, is the trademark #31596 registered October 29, 1889, by Jules Nicolas Steiner picturing a jointed bébé carrying a flag with the words "LE PETIT PARISIEN" and "BÉBÉ STEINER." The advertisement further lists five categories of unbreakable bébés and says they can be found in all the good stores selling toys both in France and abroad. As with the Bourgoin ad seen earlier, it is remarkably large, spanning the entire page. *Centre du Documentation du Jouet, Musée des Arts Décoratifs, Paris.*

THE MANY TREATMENTS OF FIGURE A

It is impossible to conjure up a single picture of a Figure A Steiner because there are so many variants, but its basic head sculpture is a constant. The face shape is more nearly rectangular with no real extremes of modeling. The doll has a soft look, full-cheeked and wide-eyed. The evenly cut eye sockets, while large in proportion to the rest of the face, are no more so than those of other French bébés. It is a face more like that of the bébés of Emile Jumeau than any other of the Steiner faces; the competition between the two doll makers is very apparent here. As with the Jumeau dolls, the nose is more sharply defined. A thinner bridge accents the eyes and leads to a more pointed nose tip which usually has deep oval nostril indentations. The philtrum is well-sculpted in a very slightly teardrop shape. The mouth is naturally and realistically placed between the nose and the chin with deep modeling of the space under the lower lip to the chin. The closed mouth Figure A has open-closed sculpting with the center usually painted in a darker tone. This expressive mouth is very different from several of the Series molds' pert little mouths, notably the "C," with its molded upper lip dropping in the center, giving it, as mentioned before, the "flattened M" shape. However, the open mouth Figure A is often cut with a drop in the center. The open mouth usually has two rows of teeth, but occasionally just one. Later in the 1890s, a single row of upper teeth is more commonly found. The Figure A bébé is very much the look of the moment, reflecting a trend toward realism. This is the basic sculpture, seen in three-quarter view in *Illustration 62*. It is a fine sensitive sculpture, well representing the softness of a pretty Caucasian child.

The influences which change the "look" of dolls are many, just as with fashion. A contributing force may have been the popularity of the Parisian-born actress Sarah Bernhardt, whose long face and heavy eyebrows are reflected in the mode of the 1890s, for both women and dolls, including the Figure A Steiner.

The Figure A head was well-received and became the all-embracing mold, used not only for some of Jules Steiner's loveliest bébés with delicate pink-toned coloring, but for most of Steiner's ethnic dolls as well. These range from light coffee mulatto to jet black in color, and from India to the West Indies in costume. Encompassing, too, the white faced clowns with multi-color facial decoration, the Figure A head was Steiner's universal choice. A number of these special dolls are shown in color in Section IV.

Because these heads were made over a period rampant with change, every style of painting can be found. Sometimes one late 1890s doll will have carefully,

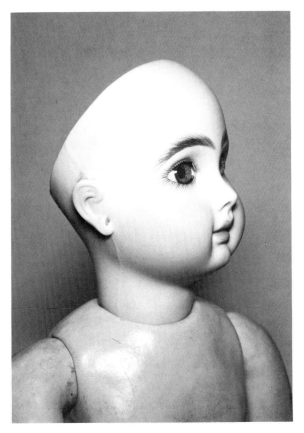

Illustration 62. Figure A head in three-quarter profile shows the basic sculpture, a softened and more natural-looking child's face. Note depth of detail of mouth.

lushly-feathered eyebrows and another will have single-stroke eyebrows; this was likely a factor of the selling price. In addition to the numerous painting techniques and marks found on the Figure A, two types of ears are found. The ear <u>without</u> the deep canal is flatter than the ear found on later Series heads. Eyes of every description, too, are found — both types of wire-operated, blown glass stationary or counterweight sleep.

A list of the various Figure A marks can be seen in Section V. Each mark is, of course, shown only in one size; examples of many of the dolls are seen in *Illustrations 62* through *81*. The pattern of increasing abbreviation may well be the way the marks evolved, as a chronological code. However, models were used for long periods, so that an early mark, as with the word Figure fully written out, can sometimes be found with later treatment, and the later marks, with very diverse treatments. Since the time span involved is primarily the 1890s, it is most interesting to see how much change

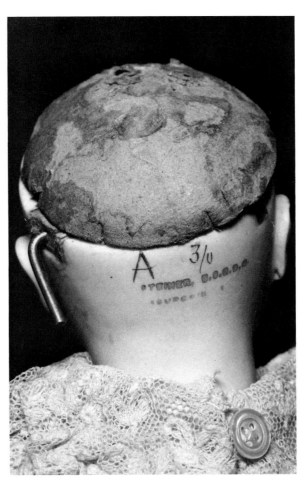

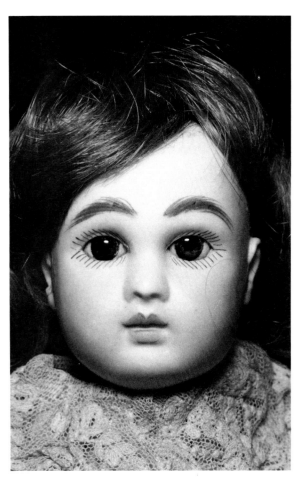

Illustration 63A. 10¼ inch (26cm) earliest Figure A head shows classic, nearly rectangular face. She has blue wire-operated eyes of the early type and the new deeply incised ear.

ABOVE RIGHT: Illustration 63B. Mark of this doll is "A 3/0" hand-written in black and fired into bisque, as is the red Bourgoin stamp.

Illustration 63C. Mold line around ear indicates an adaptation of the mold to accommodate this new ear. Circa 1887. *Arthur and Shelley Fields Collection.*

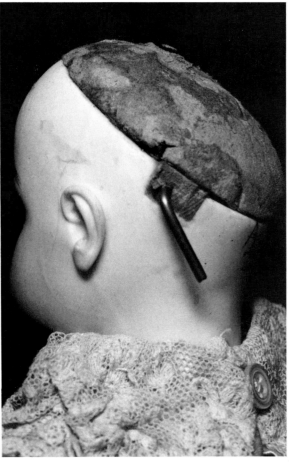

120

occurred in a short period, especially compared to the relative stability of the preceding decade.

A change in the size numbers was effected at this time. While the very earliest heads, those marked in ink "A 3/0," as seen in *Illustration 63B*, and the incised "FIGURE A No 5" in *Color Plate 33* carry the old sizes, the other Figure A marks almost exclusively carry the new sizing. A full chart is found on page 201, but listed below is a portion for easy reference.

INCHES	CM	OLD SIZE #	NEW SIZE #	ADD NEW SIZES	
8¼	21	4/0	1	2	2.3
10¼	26	3/0	3		3.4
12¼	31	2/0	5	4	4.5
14¼	36	0	7	6	5.6
16¼	41	1	9	8	

Note that there is a curious allowance for in-between sizes which, as yet, have been found only on Figure A heads. These incised marks tend to be in the smaller sizes such as A 2.3, A 3.4 or A 5.6. The fractional differences in size are usually a function of body type, not of an in between head size. Usually it is a smaller head on a longer body; this marking may have been an assembly code.

Illustrations 63A, B and *C* feature the 10¼ inch (26cm) earliest Figure A head, marked in black ink "A 3/0." She has the classic Figure A modeling, a rectangular face and naturally placed features. Transitional characteristics also exist, such as the early type of wire-operated eyes with bisque eye globes and square cutouts for their wooden bar. Innovative with this head are, as noted, the wonderfully sculpted ears with deeply incised canals. A distinct half-round mold line appears around the entire ear and onto the cheek, indicating a mold adaptation for these ears. (These mold lines are also visible in the first Figure B head in *Illustration 83B*.) However, most incised-marked heads with these ears show little or no trace of the mold lines so they were, literally, worked out.

The very handsome bébé in *Color Plate 33* is 25 inches (63cm) tall and incised "FIGURE A No 5//J. STEINER BTE S.G.D.G.//PARIS." The first of the incised marks, she has the old sizing and the new look, the gentle countenance of a sweet child. She has excellent bisque and, as can be seen in the plate, the overall creamy but very pale coloring is beautifully accentuated with cheek, ear and eye tinting done with an extremely skilled and delicate hand. Her eyebrows have multiple long feathered strokes over a darker underwash and her eyelash painting is careful and even. Her mouth is two-toned and outlined and her almost circular philtrum is understated, not sharp. She has square cutouts for her blue wire-operated eyes, which are the early variety with the bisque globes and enameled whites. Her ears are, indeed, those wonderful ears sculpted like a medical model, with all the right stuff — helix and antihelix folds and the concha or external canal. The only thing missing is a little wax!

She has a paper label on her hip which dates her in or after 1889, but likely not much after that date. Another similar example is seen in *Illustration 64*. The treatment is almost identical, except for the mold modification of a single hole for the wire lever instead of the square cut outs.

Illustration 64. 25 inch (64cm) Figure A No 5, an early 1890s closed-mouth example. Blue paperweight eyes, but head has single hole for eye mechanism. Fine quality bisque and very even painting. *Karen Copher Collection.*

121

The 22 inch (56cm) bébé shown here is incised "J. STEINER//BTE S.G.D.G.//PARIS//FIre A 15." She is Jules Steiner's *Bébé Premier Pas*, a quality doll and a costly one, deserving of a head given great attention. One can hardly lavish more effort on the painting of a head than has been accorded here. The initial coloring is excellent and the artist obviously had every intention of making her big brown paperweight eyes the center of attention. There is no competition from the flat ears, and while her mouth is carefully and artistically painted and shows two rows of nicely placed teeth, it is almost understated. But the eyes...Her owner calls her "the last doll before lunch," surmising that the artist just kept painting those long curved eyelashes incredibly close together until the lunch whistle blew! Twenty-five lashes below each eye; this bounty of strokes is exceeded only by her eyebrow stroke count. These thick brown feather boa eyebrows arch grandly around the sides of her eyes and yet the total effect is not excessive. Still one wonders if this particular worker might have been paid by the stroke or the hour and not by the piece. It is interesting to note that the *Bébé Premier Pas* in *Color Plate 10* and in *Illustration 65* is painted in an almost identical manner, surely the work of the same hand. These are wonderful heads, not just in quantity but in quality of painting.

Featured here are two small examples of Jules Steiner's black bébés. As mentioned earlier, the introduction of Figure A heads also saw the presentation of Steiner's mulatto and black dolls to an enthusiastic market. Numerous shades of color existed, from light brown to pure black.

The closed mouth bébé on the left is 10¼ inches (26cm) tall, and is incised "J. STEINER//BTE S.G.D.G.//PARIS//Fre A 3." Her fully-articulated

body is marked "Le Petit Parisien//BEBE STEINER." While this trademark was registered in 1889, it was used for many years, making it difficult to pinpoint a date; one can only judge by her quality that she is probably an early example. She has the classic body with jointed wrists, and her long, lovely fingers are painted white and outlined in red. Her original wig is hand tied twisted black wool shirred into curls. She has light coffee coloring with medium brown lashes and delicate multi-

Illustration 65. 22 inch (56cm) *Bébé Premier Pas*, a blue-eyed blonde of great detail, very similar to the bébé in *Color Plate 34*. The heads for this mechanical bébé were of especially fine quality. *Constance W. Fielden Collection.*

Illustration 66. 10½ inch (26cm) A 3.4 totally original mulatto with original box. Her red and white striped cotton dress and box-purse are typical of the Steiner attention to detail. *Tom Bugenhagen Collection.*

Illustration 67. Box end from doll in *Illustration 66* and *Color Plate 60*. Note the stamped "Mulatre" at the bottom right. *Tom Bugenhagen Collection.*

stroke brown eyebrows. As are all the Steiner heads unless otherwise noted, the bisque appears to be pressed, and the head has the single hole for the wire-eyed mechanism, although unlined brown paperweight eyes have been set and are original. She wears a red bead necklace in fine Steiner tradition.

On the right in the plate is a later, open mouth version simply incised "A 5" over which is stamped in black "LE PARISIEN//B S.G.D.G.//A 5." She is 12 inches (31cm) tall. Her articulated body is identical in form to the smaller doll, but her hands are not quite as delicate and their nails are not outlined. The stamp on her body reads "BÉBÉ 'LE PARISIEN'//MÉDAILLE D'OR//PARIS" and she probably dates from the mid to the late 1890s. Her eyebrows are very black and nicely feathered, done with a light touch, as are her eyelashes. Her bisque is a medium brown, but the head and body color match is not as close as with the smaller bébé. Her wig, also original, is of rather coarse curled black human hair. Another mulatto Steiner bébé is seen in *Illustration* 66 and again in Section IV, along with two other choice and very special examples. This doll has its original box; the labeled end is seen in *Illustration 67*.

—————————— COLOR PLATE 36 ——————————

Two fine Figure A Steiner bébés with wire eyes of the later variety are seen here. The small bébé is in the tiniest size, 8¼ inch (21cm) and is incised "J. STEINER//BTE S.G.D.G.//PARIS//Fre A 1." Totally original, she wears an aqua bead necklace with matching earrings and an ecru cotton lace-trimmed chemise over her fully-articulated body. She is seen again in Section V, *Color Plate 71*. As is true of most of Jules Nicolas Steiner's petite dolls, she is a marvelous miniature version of the larger dolls, such as the beauty seen with her.

At 16 inches tall (41cm), the larger bébé carries the same marks except that Figure is incised "FIre" and she is a size nine. Both dolls have precisely outlined closed mouths, classic Figure A modeling, blonde mohair wigs and blue all-glass wire-operated sleep eyes. The larger doll is a vision in her *Au Nain Bleu* signature long gown of lace, ribbons, ruffles and more lace. A style found for many years on dolls from that shop, it has a pink, very pink, cotton sateen underdress trimmed with a row of lace at the hem. The overdress is of fine white organdy

and lace — yards and yards of lace! The bodice is made up entirely of vertical bands of insertion lace covered by a long Bertha collar of ruffled lace. An embroidered band of insertion marks the natural waistline. The skirt is of organdy to the knees where six rows of insertion lace begin and culminate in a double tier of flounced lace on organdy. It is a magnificent construction several inches longer than the doll and worthy of a royal baby, a baptism, or simply a pampered French baby. The matching hat is all lacy ruffles in front and gathered pink satin ribbon in back and is lined in a lightweight buckram. She wears, of course, a complete set of underwear, but the lace-trimmed underpants, chemise and knee-length petticoat, befitting her jointed body, are those of an older child. She is a sumptuous package.

—————————— COLOR PLATE 37 ——————————

Two more lace beribboned confections from *Au Nain Bleu* are seen in *Color Plate 37*. The bébé on the left is in Jules Steiner's favored size 3 (10¼ inch [26cm]) and is incised simply "A 3" with a red stamp "Le PARISIEN//BTE S.G.D.G.//A 3" on the back of her head. She has a blue stamp "Le Petit Parisien//BÉBÉ STEINER" on her left hip. Her body is fully jointed with straight wrists and she has long slender fingers with white nails outlined in red, so typical of dolls sold through *Au Nain Bleu*. Her coloring is even and her painting quite lush. Her eyebrows, dark, heavily feathered and multistroke, arch dramatically around her eyes, a treatment seen in other Figure A examples. Her sleep eyes have the appearance of the all-glass wire eyes, but they are actually counterweight sleep eyes. Unlike many Figure A heads, there is no hole in the bisque for the wire-levered eyes; probably by this time (late 1890s) the cost of manufacturing and inserting the wire eyes had rendered them passé.

Her totally original and wonderful costume consists of a yellow silk underdress again covered by a skirt of fine white organdy and lace, the organdy segment about an inch long from the waist to which are attached three wide bands of lace. The middle row of insertion is beading through which is woven a fine yellow silk grosgrain ribbon. A wider satin ribbon sash circles her waist and is tied in bows, both front and back, with matching bows on her shoulders. The scalloped lace at the hem of her dress is also used for her Bertha collar.

Her hat, too, is of matching lace and ribbons. White socks and leather shoes and a gold and marcasite stickpin complete the ensemble.

The bébé in pink is incised "A 5.6//PARIS" and measures 12½ inches (32cm). Her body is stamped in blue on the left hip "BEBE 'LE PARISIEN'//Medaille d'Or//PARIS" and she retains the typical blue and white *Au Nain Bleu* paper sticker on her stomach. It is interesting to note that while this doll dates from the turn of the century, mention is made again of the gold medal won over a decade earlier, in 1889, by Jules Nicolas Steiner. This could represent some misleading advertising by Jules Mettais, then successor in the Steiner firm. Since there was a Universal Exposition in Paris in 1900, awareness of awards and medals would be high; however, at that exhibition Mettais (Steiner) was awarded a silver medal. While no date is given on this stamped mark, the implication is of a <u>current</u> medal, but it is only an implication.

This bébé represents the next step in the path of progress, for her counterweight sleep eyes have inset lashes while no upper ones are painted on the bisque. Her nicely outlined and shaded mouth is open with one row of teeth and her bisque coloring is pinkish, typical of the period. Her good quality blonde mohair wig shows less detailed styling than earlier examples, but it is full with loose waves down the back. Yet again, it is her wonderful and totally original clothing which is outstanding, coupled with the awareness that she has survived some four score and seven years in a condition not much different from when she graced a shelf at 27 Boulevard des Capucines. Her body paint is flawless, pink-toned with very white nails.

Her pink cotton underdress shows but the slightest of fading; only the silk of her bonnet ties is frail. Her dress is a minor variation on the *Au Nain Bleu* theme. Bands of insertion lace form the overskirt and incorporate a single and a double row of beading with narrow pink satin ribbon. This dress is also accented by a wide satin ribbon sash with bows front and back and matching bows on the shoulders. The wonderfully

Illustration 68A. Full length view of 22 inch (56cm) later 1890s *Bébé Premier Pas* in typical magnificent *Au Nain Bleu* lace and insertion dress.

Illustration 68B. Hat with *Au Nain Bleu* label is large, fancy, frilly and fabulous!

Illustration 68C. Stamped mark on back of head "NAIN BLEU" was likely a caution sign to Steiner factory workers. Probably only the most highly skilled workers were allowed to paint the *Au Nain Bleu* dolls. *Zelda H. Cushner Collection.*

124

detailed hat is much like that of the bébé in *Illustration 68B* and also has a fabric shop label sewn into its cap.

These Jules Steiner/*Au Nain Bleu* petit fours are delectable confections!

Seen in *Illustration 68A, B* and *C* is another impressive example of *Au Nain Bleu* splendor. At 22 inches (56cm), her head is incised "A - 15//PARIS" and it is also stamped in red "NAIN BLEU," surely a two-word directive for a quality finish to the head, as well as for body details such as the characteristic white fingernails. Dolls from other manufacturers, including some marked "DEP" and "Simon Halbig," on typical articulated French bodies bearing *Au Nain Bleu* labels and costuming have been found with the white nails. As noted before, this is also a painting characteristic found on early Steiner dolls, including some carrying other shop labels. This example also has counterweight sleep eyes with waxed lids and inset lashes, no painted upper lashes, and an open mouth with one row of teeth. Her light brown human hair wig has very long curls. She shows superior workmanship in every aspect. Her clothing, also pink, is fabulous — a lace extravaganza! She is unique in that she is also Steiner's *Bébé Premier Pas*. Dating from the end of the 1890s, she also reflects the Lafosse patents for counterweight eyes. Note her wonderful straw hat of silk ruffled ribbon over a straw frame with pink satin ribbon trim matching the dress and crowned with a white ostrich plume, a construction of great detail and magnitude.

——————————COLOR PLATE 38——————————

The 20 inch (51cm) bébé in *Color Plate 38* is a charming, unsophisticated child, reflecting the innocence and wonder of childhood. Incised "STEINER// PARIS//Fre A 13," she has the impressionistic painting which renders a new softness with its gentle treatment. Her overall coloring is pale and creamy with a rosier but natural-looking cheek color in greater contrast than is usually seen on a Figure A. The eyebrows are simply a suggestion with their few long slender strokes. The eyelashes are done with an equally light hand while the eyes themselves are a deep blue-gray feathered paperweight with good depth. But the greatest sense of impressionism is seen in the mouth treatment. Not outlined, the mouth is two-tone, with a splash of darker red color between the lips reminiscent of Renoir.

These color plates have presented but a sampling of the many variations which Figure A takes. Other examples are seen in *Illustrations 62-81*. One example, in *Illustration 70*, carries the distinctive Chambre Syndicale des Fabricants de Jouets et Jeaux trademark. Figure A was well received and became the Steiner firm's basic head throughout the 1890s and into this century. A great many workmen were employed in its production. In addition to changes in the general guidelines for its painting, the individual styles of these artists shine through the bébés' many faces. Just as Figure A delighted many a child of yesterday, she readily delights the collector of today.

Illustration 69. 22 inch (56cm) incised: "J. STEINER//Bte S.G.D.G.//PARIS//FIre A 15," an exquisite bébé with closed mouth, blue wire-levered eyes and bisque hands. She has borrowed the short round wig and hat from the Series C in *Illustration 45* to demonstrate the longer face of Figure A. *Velma J. Ross Collection.*

125

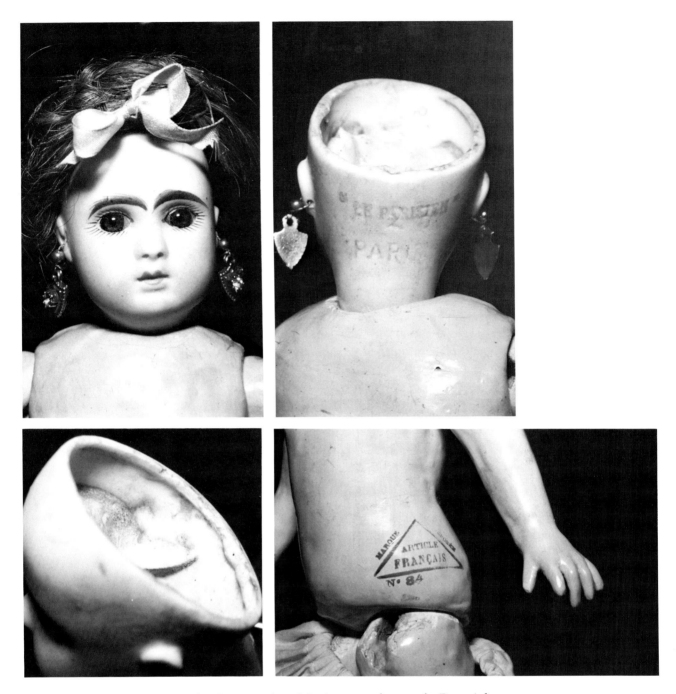

TOP LEFT: Illustration 70A. 9 inch (23cm) incised: "A 2.3" shows typical rectangular Figure A face.

TOP RIGHT: Illustration 70B. Mark of doll.

BOTTOM LEFT: Illustration 70C. Poured bisque head (note indentation at ear and lip at crown) is unusual in Steiner heads. Most appear to be pressed, although it may be a two-part procedure.

BOTTOM RIGHT: Illustration 70D. Body mark of this doll shows symbol of the Chambre Syndicale des Fabricants de Jouets et Jeux, with #84, the number given Jules Mettais. The Syndicale was formed in 1886 as a trade organization composed of a group of French toy manufacturers and continued into the 20th century. *Helen Read Collection.*

ABOVE LEFT: Illustration 71. 21 inch (54cm) incised: "FIGURE A No. 3//J. STEINER Bte S.G.D.G.//PARIS," very early Figure A with deep and expressive mouth. She has "that A.T. look," blue paperweight eyes with large, clear orbs.

ABOVE RIGHT: Illustration 72. Charming 12 inch (31cm) bébé incised only "A-5" and stamped: "Le Parisien." She has a closed mouth, big hat, nice Teddy Bear and a level gaze! *Beulah Franklin Collection.*

Illustration 73. 12 inch (31cm) turn-of-the-century Figure A in complete factory costume of aqua silk, net, lace and ribbons. Her five-piece composition body has unusual mitt-like hands. Lovely blue lined paperweight eyes and single-stroke eyebrows. Marked: "J. STEINER//Bte. S.G.D.G.//PARIS//FIre A 5." *Courtesy of Arthur and Shelley Fields.*

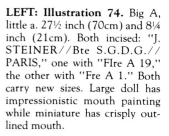

LEFT: Illustration 74. Big A, little a. 27½ inch (70cm) and 8¼ inch (21cm). Both incised: "J. STEINER//Bte S.G.D.G.//PARIS," one with "FIre A 19," the other with "Fre A 1." Both carry new sizes. Large doll has impressionistic mouth painting while miniature has crisply outlined mouth.

RIGHT: Illustration 75. Apprehensive clown incised: "STEINER//PARIS//Fe A 1" is 12½ inch (32cm) tall, has five-piece body, white bisque. *Dorothy Dixon Collection.*

LEFT: Illustration 76. Cute 8¼ inch (21cm) incised "STEINER//PARIS//Fe A 1" has unusual eyebrows composed of four horizontal strokes and five-piece body with mitt hands as in *Illustration 73. The Strong Museum Collection, Rochester, New York.*

RIGHT: Illustration 77. 8¼ inch (21cm) incised: "A - 1" has poured bisque head. Note very full eyebrows compared to small doll in *Illustration 76.*

Illustration 78. 24 inch (61cm) incised: "A-17//PARIS" and stamped in red "LE PARISIEN// Bte S.G.D.G.//A 17." Deep blue paperweight eyes give this classic bébé a pensive quality. The shading between her lips accentuates their depth. Her fully-articulated body has straight wrists and long slender fingers. *Marie Kranich Collection.*

Illustration 79. 16 inch (41cm) bébé is incised: "STEINER// PARIS//Fre A 9." She has the sweet-faced Steiner charm with a delicate unoutlined mouth. Her eyebrow treatment is that of long horizontal strokes. Her seven-piece body is articulated at the elbows. She wears her original pink cotton satin dress with pleated underskirt and simple A-line overdress which is shirred, folded and tacked to create an elegant effect. *Maxine R. Look Collection.*

Illustration 80. This wonderful pair of 9 inch (23cm) Figure A Steiner bébés are both incised: "J STEINER//Bte S.G.D.G.//PARIS//A 2." They both have five-piece bodies, blue paperweight eyes and closed mouths. Their total originality is delightful. The doll on the left celebrates "Le Baptème" and the one on the right "La Confirmation." The baby's outfit is very much like that of the Series C in *Illustration 17*, consisting of a piqué top, buttoned swaddling wrap, buttoned bib and bonnet. The bib has a machine embroidered inset and she carries a bottle with a dropper. The ribbon trim is pink. The confirmand wears a white organdy dress with veil and train. There are three rows of tucks at the hem and tucks in the bodice. She carries a taper, traditional in the rite of confirmation. This pair of turn-of-the-century dolls is special, not only for their condition and originality, but as charming historical documents of customs and tradition. *Private Collection. Photograph courtesy of the owner.*

Illustration 81. This 18 inch (46cm) Steiner bébé is incised: "STEINER// PARIS//F A 11." A lovely combination of classic and unique, she has a definite smile which changes her look. Perhaps softened in the greenware stage, she seems happy to be a Steiner Figure A. She wears a wonderful outfit of navy blue velvet with soutache braid trim. In confidence, charm, costume and quality, she is an A+. *Ann Lloyd Collection.*

129

FIGURE B

The Figure B Steiner may have originally been considered the open mouth version of Figure C (found only closed mouth), because the basic head sculptures are very similar. The differences in the mouth treatment of these two models, however, make for distinctly different dolls.

Indeed, Figure B has an appearance also very much like that of an open mouth Series C. Again, their respective face shapes are very similar, as seen in *Illustration 82*. In both Series C and Figure B the bridge of the nose is wide and the mouth is placed very close up under the nose, giving an overall square look to the face, with the features all quite close together in traditional Steiner fashion. The Figure B appears to have less of an undershot jaw than Series C. Also, Figure B eyebrow painting tends to be placed closer to the eyes than on the Series C. (The higher eyebrows lend an astonished look to Series C.) Nonetheless, the similarities between the two molds are striking.

The differences between Figure B and Figure A are, of course, considerable. In addition to the basic sculptural differences and mouth placements, Figure B lacks the deep modeling under the lower lip so pronounced in Figure A. Also, because B's mouth and lip modeling is not as deep as it is with Figure A, the teeth are set closer to the front of the mouth, which gives the B's open mouth more the look of having "fish teeth." Conversely, the deeper mouth contributed to the naturalistic look of the open mouth Figure A.

The Figure B Steiner is found with far less frequency than other molds, but those examined do show a consistency in the painting, which is a classic crisp Steiner painting. They have been found with both the old and the new sizes, and with the word Figure either fully written out or abbreviated.

The bébé shown in *Color Plate 39* and in *Illustration 83A and B* is the earliest Figure B, marked only in black ink "B 1" and stamped in red on the head "J. STEINER B S.G.D.G.//J. BOURGOIN, Succ.ʳ" She also has a blue stamp on her left hip "LE PETIT PARISIEN//J. ST. Bte S.G.D.G.//J. B. Succʳ PARIS." As with the first Figure A, this would likely be the earliest usage of this trademark. Bourgoin is last listed as

Steiner's successor in advertising for 1887; the trademark registered in 1889. She has old sizing and is 16 inches (41cm) high.

Her classic 1880s body is of bright purple papier-mâché with a very hard paint finish. Of excellent quality, it seems as though extra care was given here to present a superior product. She has jointed wrists and her separate hands are of the large, curved-finger "banana-hand" variety seen on some fine Steiner bébés of this era.

Her head is of very fine translucent bisque with square cutouts for wire eyes, although she has her originally-set blue feathered paperweight eyes with a much greater depth than most of Jules Steiner's eyes. There is a considerable clear crystal orb with a dark pupil deeply recessed. Her mouth is close to her nose, resulting in a smaller, more circular philtrum. The lips are nicely outlined and the upper lip is cut with a slight

Illustration 82. Series C (left) and Figure B (right) in three-quarter profile show basic head sculpture similarities.

dip in the center. Her eyebrow painting is very even, a medium brown with long curved strokes over a brown wash. They are very naturally placed above the eye at the bone structure of the mold.

The wonderfully sculpted ear is also present here; as she is an innovative example, the mold line around the ear is visible, as seen in *Illustration 83B*. The mold line indicates the modification to a mold to accommodate the new ear. Extra care was taken to smooth out the mold line in later examples having this ear. This bébé may well have been introduced for sale at the 1889 Universal Exposition in Paris.

Her outfit was probably made for her by her original owner. Homemade, but well made, it is likely a copy of the child's own dress made in the same fabric. It is a rather heavy creamy yellow velvet dress with a dropped waist and a loosely pleated full skirt which has a little cotton pocket sewn into the seam. A wide ecru silk ribbon sash at the waist is tied in a large bow at the back. Ruffled lace trim at the neck and the wrists of the long sleeves are the only other decoration. She wears a little wire-brimmed hat of the same material trimmed in a narrow ecru ribbon and wears, also, a matching muff adorned with a bow of the wide ecru ribbon. Her wonderful blonde mohair wig has long loose waves in the back with a triple row of tight curls framing her entire face like a halo, accentuating the apparent roundness of her cherubic little face.

Illustration 84A. 33 inch (84cm) Figure B No 7, large and handsome with blue wire-operated eyes, open mouth with two rows of teeth and traditional crisp Steiner painting. She makes an impressive statement.

Illustration 84B. Eyes of 33 inch (84cm) Figure B No 7 are so large they require an extra supporting bar to finely control their movement.

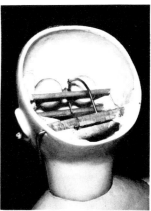

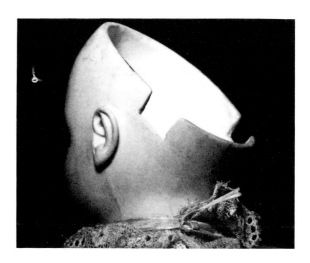

Illustration 83A. 16 inch (41cm) Figure B, marked in black "B 1" and seen in *Color Plate 39*.

Illustration 83B. Deeply sculpted ear of this doll.

131

The large bébé in *Illustrations 84A* and *B* is fully incised "FIGURE B No 7" with the B and 7 written over in red ink or paint. This is quite commonly seen on the Figure marked heads. Painting in the mold and size number would facilitate the handling and proper painting of the various molds. Perhaps this was a practice begun by one worker to sharpen his brush or to aid another whose eyesight was failing! She measures 33 inches (84cm) tall and is on a fully-articulated body with jointed wrists and long slender fingers. The body bears the paper label on the left hip. Her facial painting is typically precise and there is nice shading above the eyes. The eyes are blue lever-operated sleep eyes of the earlier type with the porcelain cups and enameled lids. The head has the hole by the left ear instead of the square cutouts. The large eyes are regulated in the head by an extra wooden bar as seen in *Illustration 84B*. The sweet small version in *Illustration 85A* is similar in treatment.

Both examples discussed have a protruding button at the pull strings for the Mama-Papa voice box, a common characteristic with Figure B. The voice box is probably the metal-encased variety marked "J. STEINER."

Another classic example, a spectacular brown-eyed beauty, is seen in *Illustration 86*. A final Figure B, *Illustration 87*, is a curious mixture of old and new. It has the fully-incised mark without the "J" before "STEINER," <u>new</u> sizing (size 10, 17 inch or 44cm), square cutouts but with wire-type porcelain globe eyes operating by counterweight as detailed in the Widow Lafosse's patent #229995 of May 10, 1893.

Despite these variations, the painting of Figure B remains constant and the doll retains the charm of Jules Steiner's classic open mouth broad-faced bébés.

85B.   **85A.**

Illustration 85A. 16 inch (41cm) Figure B No 1 has fully-incised mark, blue enameled lid wire-operated eyes and almost identical treatment to doll in *Color Plate 39*.

Illustration 85B. Incised mark of doll: "FIGURE B No 1, J. STEINER Bte S.G.D.G., PARIS." *Constance W. Fielden Collection.*

Illustration 86. 25 inch (63cm) incised: "FIGURE B NO 5//J. STEINER Bte. S.G.D.G.//PARIS." This splendid, soft, pretty bébé shows the classic Figure B modeling with especially artistic feature painting. Lush full lips and beautifully feathered eyebrows complement her unusual deep amber paperweight eyes. *Ralph W. Griffith Collection.*

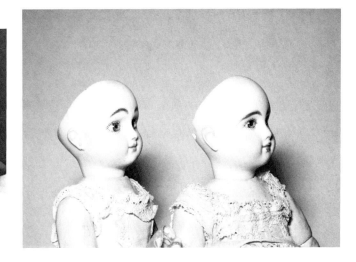

Illustration 87A. 18 inch (46cm) Figure B No 10, traditional Figure B with new sizing, enameled lid wire-lever eyes but operating by counterweight, a Lafosse modification.

Illustration 87B. Note that on this doll's mark there is no "J" before STEINER, another Lafosse change. *Richard Wright Antiques.*

Series C and a Figure C in 3/4 profile for comparison of head sculpture.

The Figure C Steiner was made throughout the 1890s and a variety of painting techniques are found. The heads with the earlier incised mark of Figure fully written out normally have very traditional painting; later examples have an abbreviated mark, frequently without the "J." before "Steiner," and more impressionistic painting. A doll of widespread appeal, four color plates (40 through 43) are given to its study.

Illustration 88. Series C (left) and Figure C (right) show their similar head sculpture. Differences between the two are minor, primarily in the shape and depth of the carving of the mouth.

FIGURE C

─────COLOR PLATES 40 - 41 - 42 - 43─────

The Figure C Steiner is a face with great appeal. She could well be called the smiling Steiner. Found only closed mouth, she, like Figure B, has an overall square face with her features close together in the customary Steiner manner. However, an intensification of the mouth treatment may have been rendered as an "improvement" on the Series C. Surely the Series suggestion of a sweet smile with the upturned corners of the mouth has here evolved into a full-fledged definite deeply molded smile. The modeling around the mouth is usually so deeply cut and the mouth itself so pushed out, that the cheeks seem to protrude in a chipmunk-like response. The mouth's upturned corners are sharply cut, and the center line is deep between the lips. The upper lip is especially well-defined in most examples, as is a deep circular philtrum. The jaw tends to be quite undershot, but this is not unattractive. The appeal of her smile easily conquers the heart. *Illustration 88* shows a

─────COLOR PLATES 40 and 41─────

The two large fascinating bébés featured here nicely show a grand contrast in painting styles. The mold is the same, but the exterior decorators have created two entirely different looks. Both are 22 inches (56cm) tall. The bébé on the left, *Color Plate 40*, is incised "FIGURE C No 4//J.STEINER Bte S.G.D.G.//PARIS" while the sweet faced bébé in *Color Plate 41* is incised "STEINER//PARIS//Fre C 15."

It is obvious that the Figure C in pink has been totally unable to suppress the smile that her predecessor, Series C, contained for nearly a decade. Perhaps the smile expresses the happiness Jules Nicolas Steiner felt on obtaining the coveted Gold Medal at the 1889 Paris Exposition, just as the paper label on her body proudly proclaims this fact. Her modeling is especially sharp; she was very likely early out of the mold. Steiner's molds were not, however, used to extreme; that is, they were not allowed to get too dirty to yield a crisply modeled doll.

Her mouth painting is a delight, accentuating the extra modeling and depth of detail. See *Illustration 89*. The depth of her circular philtrum is exceeded only by the depth of her ears. Her nose is typically broad. Her eye cuts are very large and uniform, and her blue wire-operated sleep eyes have enameled lids. The lever protrudes from a single hole by the left ear. She has lovely overall pink coloring to her smooth fine bisque, with mauve tinting at her eyes, chin and cheeks. Her even dark brown eyebrows are lushly feathered. She is truly greater than the sum of her parts, presenting an air of pleasant self-assurance.

By contrast, the expression of the bébé in *Color Plate 41* is one of impish innocence. A more tentative smile, resulting from an impressionistic style of painting coupled with a lighter touch on the eyelashes and especially the eyebrows gives new meaning to the words "Figure C mold." The choice of moist-looking blue paperweight eyes is harmonious with her simple charm. As with the Figure A in *Color Plate 38*, this bébé has the naive look of a dear and sweet child. Her mark is unusual in that the 15 is raised (embossed), a curiosity found on other examples also painted impressionistically.

Illustration 89. 22 inch (56cm) Figure C No 4, seen in *Color Plate 40*, who looks as though she holds the winning lottery ticket.

Another, still different, Figure C Steiner is the apprehensive little charmer seen in *Color Plate 42*. At 14 inches (36cm), she is incised "FIGURE C No O//J. STEINER Bte S.G.D.G.//PARIS." She is curious in her waif-like appeal, having a very softly contoured finish to her features. Her mouth is particularly interesting as it is not as deeply carved as most Figure C dolls. Indeed, it looks very much like a Series C mouth. Her other painting characteristics are typical of Figure C — the overall even coloring with good cheek tinting and eye shadow. Her dark fully-feathered eyebrows are in good Figure C tradition. However, the eyebrows are placed much higher on her forehead, again reminiscent of the Series C, lending her an uncertain air. Her early type blue wire-levered eyes are quite small, an interesting quality which also adds to her natural appeal.

It is almost as though she were a hybrid, perhaps a Figure C painted by an artist familiar with painting Series C, who did not work this mouth sharply. This would suggest the same factory produced both Series and Figure heads. The corners of this bébé's mouth are not so definitely upturned, and the suggestion of the "flattened M" line between the lips is also seen here as in the Series C. An interesting mixture, the result is a doll of wistful charm and tentative demeanor generally not associated with the confident Figure C bébé.

Shown in *Color Plate 43* are the three smallest sizes of Jules Steiner s bébés. All have the incised word "Figure" fully written out. They are sizes 2/0, 3/0 and 4/0. They all have fully-articulated bodies which are stamped on the left hip "Le Petit Parisien//BÉBÉ STEINER."

The largest doll, size 2/0, stands 12¼ inches (31cm) tall. She has articulated wrists; her hands have long slender fingers. Her facial coloring is lovely and she has realistic brown paperweight eyes which humanize her face. She is gentle despite a nice depth of modeling. Her mouth, in particular, gives her a look suggestive of an A.T., a look seen in other Steiners and a question looking for an answer.

The doll in the middle is also seen in Section V, *Color Plate 75*. She is a size 3/0, totally original, an *Au Nain Bleu* bonbon. Her lace dress with aquamarine ribbon trim is similar to the bébé in red in *Color Plate 17*, as well as to the Series C seen with her in *Illustration 90*. The similarities between these two dolls are many and enhanced by their like clothing. Surely Series C and Figure C were concurrent models, again suggesting that Jules Steiner had two suppliers of heads in the late 1880s and early 1890s.

The 8½ inch (21cm) bébé on the right shows the sharp modeling usually found on the Figure C around the mouth, even in such a tiny size. Her wire-operated eyes are brown and of the early variety. She has the deeply incised ears invariably found on the Figure C, while her little body is fully articulated, including the wrists. Hers are the so-called "banana" hands with fingers which all curve inward. They are less defined in this miniature size than their larger counterparts; this is one of the few instances of Steiner reduction that is not faithful and exquisite. However, slender fingers can be reduced more accurately than chubby ones because of the space between the fingers. In most instances with Steiner dolls, it is impossible to tell in a photograph the size of the doll, but in this case the hands do indicate her small size.

All three are nifty!

Four other Figure C bébés are seen in *Illustrations 91* through *94*. The first is a charming 18 inch (46cm) marked "Fre C 11," painted in an impressionistic style similar to the girl in *Color Plate 41*. Her mouth is perhaps a little more sensuous, but the overall effect is still one of innocence. A curiosity peculiar to a number of Steiner's 1890s bébés is that one eyebrow is painted higher than the other. It lends a slightly skeptical look — this doll looks innocent and naive, but not totally gullible. On the other hand, she <u>could</u> be convinced that "gullible" is not in the dictionary.

The second doll, in *Illustration 92*, is a tiny example. 8 inches (21cm) tall and marked "Fre C 4/0," she curiously shows the old sizing. Probably from the latter half of the 1890s, she still has remarkably fine quality bisque and good detail, despite simple one-stroke eyebrows. The other two dolls are wonderful factory original bébés, one with a five-piece body, the other fully-jointed and with her original box!

The Figure C was a popular doll and it is easy to appreciate her appeal. Like Figure A, this model underwent many painting variations but the integrity of the mold holds firm.

Illustration 90. Series C 3/0 and Figure C 3/0 have almost identical dresses. The Figure C is marked: "Au Nain Bleu;" it is likely the dress on the Series C is also from that shop. Both are from the late 1880s.

Illustration 91. 18 inch (46cm) Steiner bébé incised: "Fre C 11." As described in text, she has impressionistic painting and a skeptical eyebrow. *Dolores Gilbert Collection.*

Illustration 92. 8 inch (21cm) incised: "Fre C 4/0," this late 1890s bébé has unusual early sizing. Her eyelashes and eyebrows total 18 strokes — not par for the Steiner course! *The Strong Museum Collection, Rochester, New York.*

Illustration 93. 11 inch (28cm) incised: "STEINER//PARIS//C 3."
Her mark excludes the "F" for Figure, but follows the Figure abbreviation
pattern. From the later 1890s, this charming bebe has a five-piece
composition body with mitt-like hands, closed mouth, stationary blue
eyes and single stroke eyebrows. Her wonderful factory original outfit is
of ecru silk with lace overlay. An elaborately trimmed matching straw hat
tops off a complete and sassy little package. *Photograph courtesy of Marvin
Cohen Auctions.*

Illustration 94A. 11 inch (28cm) incised: "STEINER//PARIS//Fre C
3" with her original box from the mid 1890s. Her body is marked: "Le
Petit Parisien//BEBE STEINER" as is her box label. Her feature details
are like the bébé in *Illustration 32*, but her body is fully articulated. Note
her original chemise and bead necklace.

Illustration 94B. Box label reads: "the only one which cannot be
confused with those from Germany" and remarks on its lightness and
strength. The price of 3 francs 50 converts to about 70 cents, equivalent
to under $10 in 1988. Copyright *7th Blue Book of Dolls & Values* by Jan
Foulke. Used by permission. *Photograph by Howard Foulke.*

137

FIGURE D

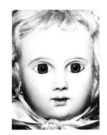

If the group of Figure marked heads were presented to Jules Nicolas Steiner by another head manufacturer or supplier for his approval, Figure A would have represented the "new look," Figures B and C updated versions of Steiner's favored Series C, and Figure D...a mystery.

Only a few Figure D Steiners have been examined, hardly enough for any meaningful generalities, but it is this bébé's rarity as well as her beauty which is of great significance.

One example, shown in *Illustration 95*, reveals again a more rectangular face, effected by the more natural mouth placement. The mouth itself is open-closed and treated with precise painting and outlining as are some of the early exquisite Figure A bébés. However, the Figure D nose is not as pinched and upturned as the Figure A, which intensifies the D's long full face. This modeling and the expressive mouth recall also the Series G Steiner with its haunting impact. The higher eyebrows give her a more apprehensive look; this Figure D is a child who seems about to speak, and people will listen, for she has captured their attention.

Illustration 95. Figure D 19: Rare bébé of great beauty and superb quality. Expressive closed mouth is exquisitely painted and nicely feathered eyebrows frame her deep blue paperweight eyes. Her body is fully articulated, including the wrists. Circa 1890. *Photograph by Doumic, courtesy of François Theimer.*

OPPOSITE PAGE TOP RIGHT: Illustration 96A. 22 inch (56cm) very rare "Fre D 15."

ABOVE: Illustration 96B. A second view of the doll shown in *Illustration 96A* with her face in 3/4 angle show her beautifully sculpted and deep features. Doll is detailed in *Color Plate 44. Maurine S. Popp Collection.*

The second example of Figure D is seen in *Color Plate 44* and in *Illustration 96A, B* and *C*. She is incised "STEINER//PARIS//F^re D 15." She is likely a later example, and while the mold seems to be basically the same as the previous doll, the painting is quite different. Most notably, the eyebrow treatment is different; here it is several long strokes painted close to the eyes with no underwash, while the previous Figure D had higher, fuller eyebrows. This bébé also has fewer and shorter eyelashes. Consistencies within the basic mold include a very natural oval-shaped philtrum with the edges forming it being quite raised, and that both dolls seem to have a nose which is wider by the right nostril, a curious phenomenon. The eye cuts of both dolls are extremely symetrical, and the mouths are modeled with careful attention to detail, including a slightly grooved effect in the lower lip as had been seen in the Series G. While this doll's mouth is not crisply outlined, there are molded edges to the lips giving it a sharp definition while the two-tone coloring gives depth to the open-closed effect. Note also the intensely blue feathered paperweight eyes of great clarity.

A last example, a petite bébé, is seen in *Illustration 97*. Only 12 inches (31cm), her mark is the same as the previous doll's, but she is a size 5. She, too, has a good depth of modeling around her mouth, the longer face shape and sparkling blue paperweight eyes. Her single-stroke eyebrows and higher coloring give her an informal look — she is a delightful little number (and letter!). The bodies of all three are fully articulated, including the wrists; the hands are the so-called "banana" variety.

Illustration 96C. Mark of Figure D. *Maurine S. Popp Collection.*

Illustration 97. 12 inch (31cm) incised: "STEINER//PARIS//Fre D 5," this charming Figure D is an especially appealing child. Despite her small size, she stands out in a crowd.

Featured here simply to provide a stunning comparison with the Figure D is an extremely fine quality *Bébé Phénix*. Incised " ☆ 96," she is 24 inches (61 cm) of unsurpassed quality. The similarities between the two are striking. The very uniform eye cuts, the shapely nose and the mouth and philtrum modeling are all very much alike. The eyebrow painting is not as well balanced and it looks as though the paint flowed more in the *Phénix* painting; however, the similarities cannot be ignored. Her body, while not marked, is definitely of Steiner composition, with straight limbs and a well-separated large toe. A beautiful doll, she is also an interesting one for comparative study.

While the word "Phénix" was originally used in advertising by Henri Alexandre, the trademark "Bébé Phénix" was taken out in 1895 by Madame Lafosse and carried into the 20th century by Jules Mettais, both while heading the Steiner firm.

These two handsome bébés, The Figure D in *Color Plate 44* and the *Phenix* in *Color Plate 45* are quality products of the gay nineties.

FIGURE E

———————— COLOR PLATES 46 - 47 - 48 ————————

The Figure E Steiner is an exciting find. Probably not one of the original group of Figure marked heads introduced in the late 1880s, she seems instead to be a product of the mid 1890s. However, in her case the adage "it's later than you think" could well be wrong...it can be very hard to pinpoint a doll's date!

While the Figure A had been a competitive response, and a very successful one to Emile Jumeau's ever popular bébé, it is worth considering that the period of the 1890s saw new competition — German competition.

With the pendulum swinging back toward a German domination of the doll making industry, the French doll makers were forced into a new competitive situation, which eventually led many to band together under the canopy of S.F.B.J. (the Société Francaise de Fabrication des Bébés et Jouets). While the Steiner firm was not a member, it was not unaffected by the times. Many French manufacturers were importing their doll heads from Germany; and many of these heads were lovely, especially those marked "DEP," products of the Simon & Halbig firm. The "new kid on the block" was not only pretty, but in growing demand and could possibly have influenced the Steiner firm into creating a competitive face — Figure E.

And what a face it is! Unlike any other in the Steiner repertoire, she has a definite pouty mouth with the corners both molded and painted downward. It is a mouth so reminiscent of a 900 series Simon & Halbig that finding her incised "J. STEINER//Bte S.G.D.G.//PARIS//Fre E 3" as seen in *Illustration 98* is astounding! The bottom bar of the "E" is very faint. She has the small hole in the bisque for wire-lever eyes but has her originally set jewel-like paperweight eyes that are identical to those of the Figure C in the middle in *Color Plate 43*. Her feathered eyebrows say "Steiner," her fine bisque quality and evenly pale pink coloring with a hint of shading above the eyes say "Figure," while the deeply modeled ears say both "Steiner" and "Figure." Her very fine translucent pressed bisque clearly says "Jules Steiner," and yet the face, wonderful, rare, and so very appealing in its very sadness says "Allemand." French-German, she gives renewed impetus to all sorts of suppositions as to what was going on within the Steiner firm and renewed hope that more answers will be found.

Her body is stamped in blue "Le Petit Parisien//BÉBÉ STEINER" and it is with its original but dried up stringing, this limpness adding to her charm. The body, of gray papier-mâché, has the usual fine Steiner form, but is unusual in that it has metal hands, *Illustration 99*, just as the Arab and soldiers which will be seen in Section IV. She has a molded gray papier-mâché pate and the inside of her long blonde mohair wig is marked "3" in ink.

Illustration 100 shows well a three-quarter view of her full-cheeked solemn face with its expressive mouth intensified by a definite overbite. An endearing face, the Figure E is extremely rare.

A study of dolls marked "Figure" could fill an entire volume, for even small variations make each unique. *Illustration 101* shows a summary group of bébés with "Thaddeus," a 1904 Steiff Teddy Bear, who has an eye for a cute little Figure and a lap with room to spare.

As mentioned before, the next section will look at some additional unusual Figure A Steiners in addition to a number of other rarities — all simply special Steiners!

TOP LEFT: Illustration 98. Mark of Figure E seen in *Color Plates* 46 through 48. Note that bottom bar of "E" is very faint, but that it is an E.

TOP RIGHT: Illustration 99. Metal hand of Figure E. The doll is 10¼ inches (26cm) tall.

BOTTOM LEFT: Illustration 100. 10¼ inch (26cm) Figure E 3 seen in three-quarter profile shows the very full modeling of her cheeks and her downturned mouth with its definite overbite.

BOTTOM RIGHT: Illustration 101. Four Figure bébé Steiners are, clockwise from top, 10¼ inch (26cm) mulatto Figure A, 8¼ inch (21cm) incised only: "A-1," 8¼ inch (21cm) Figure C 4/0 and 10¼ inch (26cm) Figure E 3. The Teddy Bear is a 1904 Steiff, 18 inch (46cm) long, with room to spare on his accommodating lap.

142

Section Four

RARITIES,
NOVELTIES and MYSTERIES
SOME SIMPLY SPECIAL STEINERS

COLOR PLATES — Section Four

Plate 49. Series C Steiner with Kubelka patent for inserted hair, circa 1887. *Fidelia Lence Collection.*

Plate 50. Arab and French soldiers of tiny size and immense detail, circa 1890. *Dorothy Dixon Collection.*

Plate 51. 10½ inch (27cm) young soldier. *Dorothy Dixon Collection.*

Plate 52. 11½ inch (29cm) older soldier. *Dorothy Dixon Collection.*

Plate 53. 10 inch (26cm) Arab cavalryman. *Dorothy Dixon Collection.*

Plate 54. 13 inch (33cm) Whistler marked: "Le Parisien," a Lafosse trademark, circa 1895. *The Strong Museum, Rochester, New York.*

Plate 55. Oriental costumed, kid-bodied bébé, 11½ inch (29cm), circa 1880. *Mary Lou Rubright Collection.*

Plate 56. 14 inch (36cm) papier-mâché in traditional costume of Pont-Aven region of Brittany, with lined head as in Lafosse patent of 1898.

Plate 57. 12½ inch (31cm) Figure A clown with multicolored decoration on white bisque, a handsome and charming doll, circa 1890s. *Sidda Sandel Collection.*

Plate 58. Figure A Turkish-garbed boy incised: "A 2," 9½ inch (24cm) with replicas of the 1889 Médaille d'Or and the 1890 Diplôme d'Honneur.

Plate 59. Figure A Turkish dancer in full regalia. *Ann Lloyd Collection.*

Plate 60. Figure A mulatto in original box, 10½ inch (27cm), circa 1890s. *Tom Bugenhagen Collection.*

Plate 61. Three recent discoveries include a rare portrait man, 11 1/2 inches (29cm) tall, a musical and walking black bisque doll, 14 inches (36cm), and the marvelous rifleman of Steiner's last patent.

Plate 62 & 63. Candy box Steiner of great charm, 20 inch (51cm) tall. Doll opens at middle to reveal box for candy, circa 1900.

Plate 64. 10¼ inch (26cm) Series C 3/0 with wonderful original skin wig! Circa 1885.

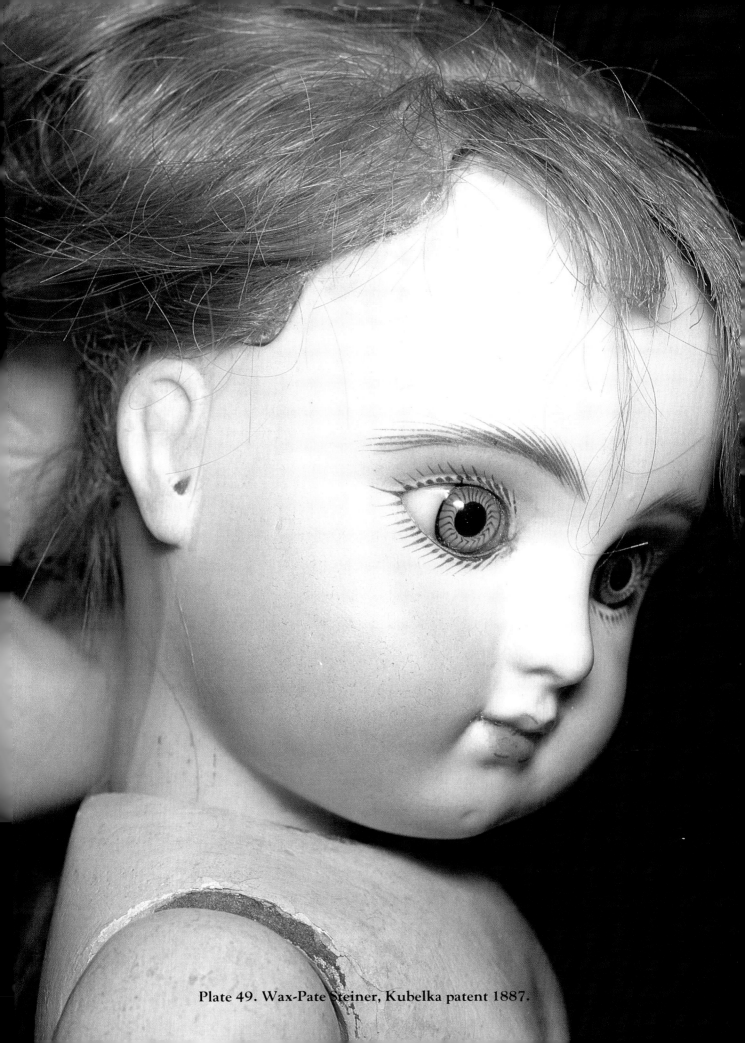

Plate 49. Wax-Pate Steiner, Kubelka patent 1887.

Plate 50. Arab and two French soldiers, circa 1890.

Plate 51. French soldier, circa 1890.

Plate 52. French soldier, circa 1890.

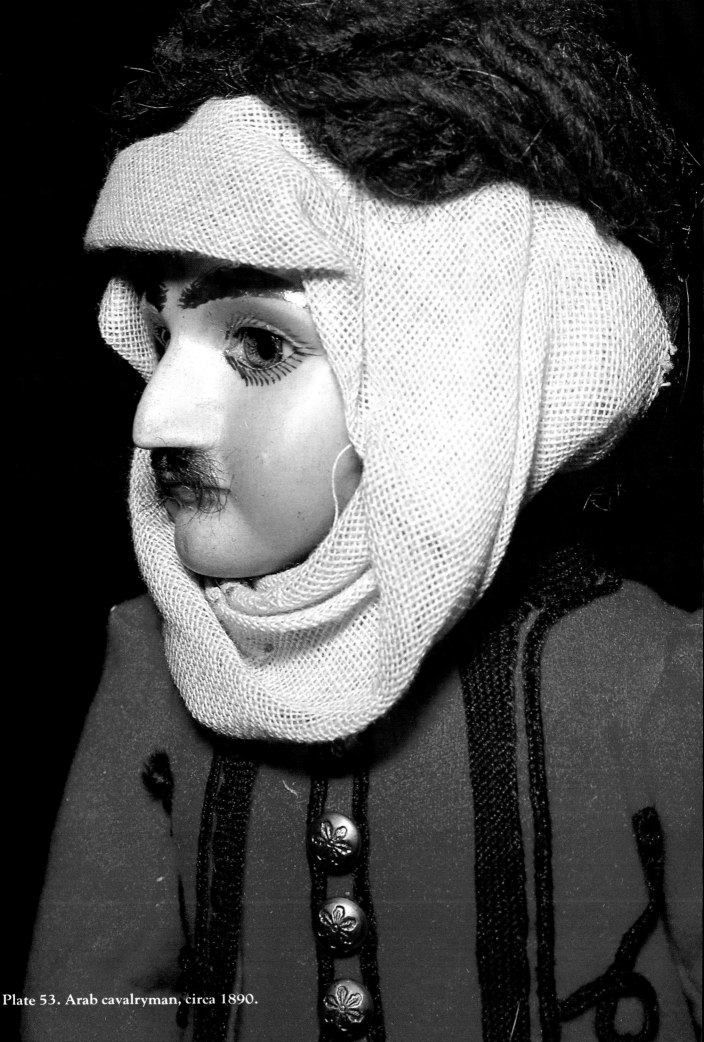

Plate 53. Arab cavalryman, circa 1890.

Plate 54. "Le Parisien"
whistler, circa 1895.

**Plate 55. Oriental costumed,
kid-bodied, circa 1880.**

Plate 56. Papier-mâché in provincial costume, circa 1898.

Plate 57. Figure A clown.

Plate 58. Figure A Turkish boy with replica medals, circa 1890.

Plate 59. Figure A Near East dancer, circa 1895.

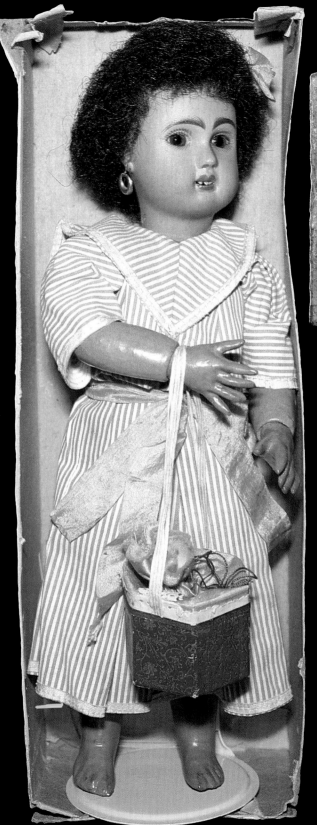

Plate 61. Three recent discoveries.

Plate 62 . Candy box, circa 1900.

Plate 63. Open candy box showing gouache label.

Plate 64. Sie C, 3/0, circa 1885.

RARITIES,
NOVELTIES and MYSTERIES

A number of Jules Nicolas Steiner's dolls have been studied thus far including those with patented mechanisms, bébés with unmarked heads, the group with heads marked "Series" and the group marked "Figure." In addition to these, Steiner produced numerous other dolls including some novelty items throughout the many years that he was active in the doll industry. Some unusual dolls of special interest will be looked at in this section. A number of Figure A dolls, his most extensively manufactured head, are featured here, including a wonderfully expressive clown, a Turkish-garbed boy and several black or mulatto dolls in original costume, one of which has a very unusual open-closed mouth.

An Arab and two soldiers of unparalleled quality and personality, a Series C Steiner utilizing Josef Kubelka's patent for hair imbedded into a wax pate, a whistling boy, a kid-bodied bébé in wonderful Oriental costume and a marvelous candy container are all seen in the color plates of Section Four. They and others illustrated are all part of the phantasmagoria of dolls of Jules Nicolas Steiner.

involved. From that research it is apparent that the Steiner head seen in *Color Plate 49* reflects Kubelka's 1887 patent addition. This detailed a recess made in a solid head along the hairline which is filled with a waxy resinous material and into which the hair was implanted, in a manner similar to that used on wax dolls with inset hair. When found, these rare heads are usually of elegant ladies with strikingly regal features and of superb quality of modeling and painting. One such example is seen in *Illustration 102*.

Many questions surround these elusive heads. As Spadaccini Day points out, at least one has an incised mark "FG" on the shoulder plate. Francois Gaultier was not a doll maker but a manufacturer of bisque heads and limbs, some of which are of extremely high quality. Other heads with the Kubelka method of inserted hair have been found marked "E.D." The use of Kubelka's patent by other doll makers, under license, is a possibility, given additional credence by the finding of Steiner bébés having the Kubelka hair procedure.

--------- COLOR PLATE 49 ---------

Seldom does the opportunity to enjoy rarity and beauty occur as it does in the Steiner bébé seen in *Color Plate 49*. Previous dolls have shown well the workings of the ingenious mind of Jules Steiner. This bébé shows another aspect of his versatility, his adaptation of one of his bébés to accommodate another inventor's patented idea.

In 1884 Josef Kubelka, an Austrian doll maker, obtained patents in Germany, Austria and France for a process of imbedding hair into doll's heads. This was followed by additional and modifying patents in 1887, 1889 and in the 1900s, as well. Barbara Spadaccini Day, in her article, "Exploring The Kubelka Mystery" (*Dolls*, Fall 1983), details the patents and the various processes

Illustration 102. 22 inch (56cm) lady doll with Josef Kubelka patented method for insertion of hair into a recess in head filled with a waxy substance. *The Strong Museum, Rochester, New York.*

The Steiner head in *Color Plate 49* is stamped in red "STEINER B S.G.D.G.//BOURGOIN" as seen in *Illustration 104*. This is the usual stamped mark seen on bébés during the latter part of Bourgoin's management of the Steiner firm. The area of the head by the crown where the incised mark is made is here incorporated into the hair area. However, a study of the facial modeling confirms it is a Series C mold. See *Illustration 103*. She has the typical mouth with the molded flattened M upper lip shape and the ears which are found on Series heads. The block letter Bourgoin stamp coincides with the Kubelka patent addition of 1887; this Steiner bébé thus dates from 1887 or early 1888. While some of the Series heads of this period have a more feathered eyebrow (typical of the fashion of the day), the lushly feathered brow seen here is more like the painting of heads marked "Figure," which gives rise to additional questions. As F.G. has been found marked on the shoulder plate of one or more of the lady dolls, and he possibly made those heads, could he also have been the supplier of Steiner's Figure marked heads? Is this rare and wonderful bébé a link? Surely the period is right. Although no known records exist to confirm this, it must be considered. Another interesting point is that many A.T. heads bear a striking resemblance to some of Steiner's heads, notably early Figure A and some of the Figure C heads. A number of A.T. heads have been found on Steiner bodies, although as Barbara Spadaccini Day notes, Steiner may have supplied these bodies to A. Thuillier, an assembler of dolls. The open mouth A.T. heads are very like Steiner's bébés, especially in the mouth cut and teeth placement. Painting characteristics of the A.T. and Steiner Figure marked heads are very similar as well. (See *Illustration 105*) suggesting the same artists may have painted the heads, indicating that they may well have come from the same manufacturer. According to research done by Madame Florence Poisson, Curator of the Roybet-Fould Museum in Poissy, France, A. Thuillier is known to have purchased heads from Gaultier. This is surely a fertile area for future research.

──────── COLOR PLATES 50 - 51 - 52 - 53 ────────

While the previous bébé is truly a tough act to follow, the ensuing entourage is up to the task! They are an Arab (probably Algerian) and two French soldiers of

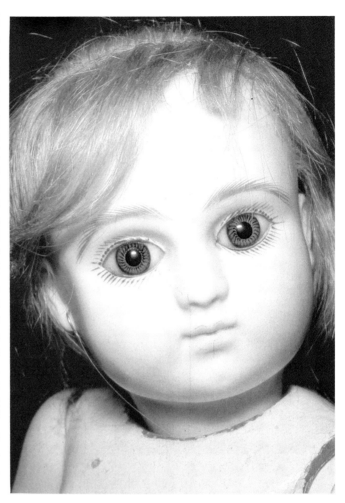

Illustration 103. Classic Series C face of 16 inch (41cm) bébé with lovely blue paperweight eyes, closed mouth and an "I've got a secret" smile. *Fidelia Lence Collection.*

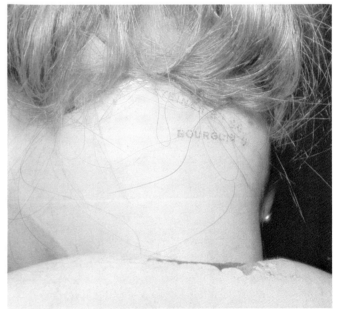

Illustration 104. The Steiner and Bourgoin stamp on the back of the head of the doll in *Illustration 103* and *Color Plate 49* shows the scalloped line with the hair inserted into the waxy resinous material, the Kubelka patented idea. This is sure reason for the doll to smile. *Fidelia Lence Collection.*

162

incomparable individuality. The period of the 1880s within France had seen continued growth and improvement in relations between France and Algeria, one of France's most important colonies. At that time, too, ethnic and regional costumed dolls were quite popular.

These three, however, are in a class by themselves. Very different and very special, they are real people. It is possible this trio was part of a larger group, perhaps depicting an important event between the two countries. While these dolls may have been a special personal order, as an assemblage, they would surely have presented a significant and impressive exhibit and one worthy of display at a major exposition such as the Universal Exposition in Paris in 1889. It is well known that Jules Nicolas Steiner won the Gold Medal at that Exposition. He likely had a new line of dolls to offer and he probably also presented a simply fabulous, eye-catching, spectacular display of which these dolls could easily have been a part. They are extraordinary, and make such speculation seem logical.

———————— COLOR PLATE 50 ————————

Color Plate 50 shows these three unique dolls in a front view, in which it can readily be seen that a trend toward naturalism has been completed. Jules Steiner has reached the pinnacle of success! These three dolls came together from Paris years ago in the same shipment. The head of each is incised "J. STEINER//PARIS." Each has, glued in the middle of his back, the paper label proudly proclaiming the Gold Medal won in 1889.

Illustration 106 shows the three full view, the Arab astride his horse, the soldiers at his side. Each soldier wears a navy blue wool uniform but they seem to represent different regiments or rank. Their trousers are the same, with striped red cording down the sides of each leg. The brass buttons of all three uniforms are identical.

The fully-articulated composition bodies of the soldiers are of fine quality and are unusual in that they have metal hands, just as was seen on the rare Figure E.

Illustration 105. 24 inch (61 cm) A. 10 T. with open mouth, two rows of teeth and bearing strong similarity to Jules Steiner's bébés. Articulated composition body is also typically Steiner; Steiner may have sold bodies to Thuillier. Heads may have been made by the same manufacturer for both Jules Steiner and Thuillier. *Dorothy Dixon Collection.*

———————— COLOR PLATE 51 ————————

The soldier on the right in *Color Plates 50* and *51* is 10½ inches (27cm) tall. His features are delicate and more subtle than those of the other soldier, who is also larger. This soldier does not have spats, and his helmet, called a *shako*, has a replaced emblem of crossed

163

Illustration 106. Arab cavalryman, called a Spahi, and two French soldiers, 10½ to 11½ inches (27 to 29cm) tall, in full and accurate uniform, seen also in *Color Plates 50* through *53*. Specialty dolls of the highest caliber, they are unique and wonderful. *Dorothy Dixon Collection.*

cannons copied from the second soldier's hat, so it is not known if his original assignment was to the artillery. This uniform was worn during the Third Republic (1850 to 1900) which included the time of Napoléon III. The mandarin collar of his jacket is trimmed in red wool and marked "3;" his buddy's is marked "B." He has no cuffs and only one row of figural brass buttons with bound buttonholes down the center of his jacket. His epaulets are of the same dark blue wool.

As can be seen in *Illustrations 107* and *108*, his face is that of a young man, barely more than a boy. His nose is slightly aqualine, without a hint of exaggeration. His large brown stationary eyes are shaded above the long eyelashes which gives them an interesting depth. Also, his eyebrow treatment is heavy but realistically masculine. His dark brown mohair wig perfectly suits him and matches his coloring. His mouth is subtly natural, with only the corners accented. No sharp modeling or furrowed brows have disturbed this young soldier's serenity.

Illustration 107. 10½ inch (27cm) young soldier of gentle features which have a strong impact. Seen also in *Color Plates 50* and *51* and detailed in text. *Dorothy Dixon Collection.*

Illustration 108. Close-up detail of soldier in *Illustration 107* and *Color Plates 50* and *51. Dorothy Dixon Collection.*

The larger soldier seen in *Color Plate 52* is an extraordinary piece of sculpture. At 11½ inches (29cm), he has everything but his given name and rank. His uniform is complete. From spats to the panache of his shako — helmet — he is completely wonderful. His collar is marked "B," but it is not known what that represents. Could it be the rank of Brigadier? His jacket has red wool cuffs and red epaulets. It also has three rows of brass buttons with black soutache braid trim in frog closings. His more elaborate uniform and his maturity imply a higher rank.

His face is an impressionistic human portrait of great impact, particularly in this small size. A larger, broader nose is accentuated by a deeply furrowed forehead which angles sharply back, as seen in *Illustrations 109* and *110*. The *Color Plate 52* and illustrations were taken from the same side to show how much a slight change in the viewing angle affects the look of this man — just as with a human being. His wide set brown eyes are also deep and compelling with their beautiful shading. An accented philtrum and lines around his mouth add to his character. His expressive mouth surely has spoken French all his life. His cleft chin adds an air of authority and a firmness to the set of his jaw. He is a <u>soldier</u>...

...and he is an Arab. Words fail to adequately describe this doll. He should be seen from every angle. It is difficult to believe that this much personality can be translated into a doll standing — or more accurately, straddling — 10 inches tall (26cm). The chiseled rendering of his features and his overall demeanor exude Sheik-like authority. He is apparently a Spahi, a native cavalryman from Algeria serving under the French government. His body is molded in one piece with his

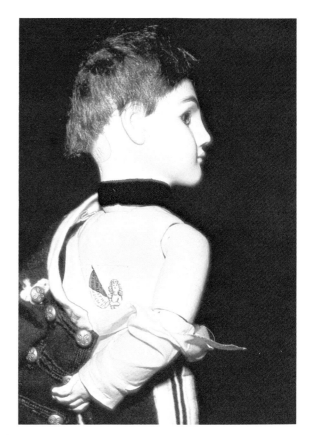

Illustration 109. 11½ inch (29cm) French cannoneer with dramatic facial modeling. Note strong profile and label in the middle of his back. Seen in *Color Plates 50 & 52. Dorothy Dixon Collection.*

Illustration 110. 11½ inch (29cm) seen in *Illustration 109*. Note detailed cleft of his chin. Seen in *Color Plates 50* and *52. Dorothy Dixon Collection.*

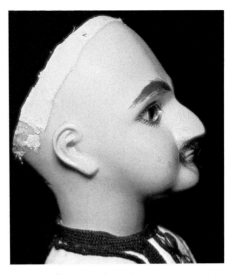

Illustration 113. What does this Algerian wear under his kaffiyeh? Only his forehead, an especially dramatic one. The nose is not to be overlooked either. *Dorothy Dixon Collection.*

Illustration 111. 10 inch (26cm) (in seated position), the Arab (Algerian) looks bewildered at being a horseless cavalryman. His torso and legs are molded in one piece. Note the inside of leg is flat to closely fit on horse. *Dorothy Dixon Collection.*

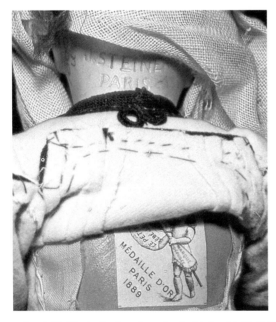

Illustration 112. The incised mark on the Arab's head is "J. STEINER PARIS." The soldiers are identically marked and all three have the paper label on their bodies. *Dorothy Dixon Collection.*

Illustrations 114 & 115. Properly attired and close-up. *Dorothy Dixon Collection.*

166

legs which are flattened on the insides to better hug the horse's flanks. See *Illustration 111*. His feet have painted toenails and a molded bootlike heel, a curious combination. His arms are jointed and, like the soldiers, his hands are metal. He bears the paper label on his back, as seen in *Illustration 112*. It looks as though the label may have been added after he was dressed, giving rise to speculation that he might have been part of Steiner's 1889 Paris exposition exhibit.

His uniform consists of a red wool jacket with black soutache braid trim and brass buttons down the front. His white wool baggy pantaloons, generally called chalwar, go to the tops of his nearly knee-length black riding boots. His head gear is wonderfully complete in its detail. The coarse white cotton kaffiyeh is properly folded and held in place by a black goat hair agal (rope).

But it is his face, his strong Semitic features (*Illustrations 113, 114* and *115*) which capture one's attention and refuse to leave one's memory. His warm brown eyes have immense depth and the shadowing is a rich burnished puce color against the olive brown of his bisque. His fine tight mouth seems at times stern, at others gentle. His applied moustache is perfectly trimmed and a little discoloration on his cheek seems to be completely intentional. He is a powerful and dramatic figure.

One can hope that some questions will not remain unanswered: of who they are, if there are others and of what the inspiration was for the creation of this epitome of art. Small realistic sculptures recreating human form are not necessarily extraordinary in themselves. What is remarkable in these three is that in their creation, the artist has never lost the language of the DOLL.

———————— COLOR PLATE 54 ————————

Perhaps the unusual character doll seen in *Color Plate 54* cannot believe what he has just seen in the previous four plates! Actually, he is a whistler, bearing a red stamp "LE PARISIEN" on the back of his head. As we have seen, the Steiner firm was making character dolls, which were in increasing demand in the 1890s. The head of this doll is of very fine quality bisque.

The doll measures 13 inches (33cm) tall and is on a fully-articulated composition body. The mechanism consists of a reeded whistle attached inside the head at the crown, and operated by a rubber tube and bulb. It is

Illustration 116. Mechanism of *Le Parisien* whistling doll as seen in *Color Plate 54.*

Illustration 117. 16 inch (41cm) poured bisque head incised: "PARIS//6" has a very carefully modeled closed mouth and blue deeply paperweight eyes. Her face is very expressive, alert-looking and carefully painted. While the details of the head are not typically Steiner, there are aspects which indicates Steiner involvement. She is on an articulated Steiner body with slender fingers which are shaped slightly differently and are more on one plane than is usually found. There is a similarity in the expression of this doll to the one in *Illustration 118*. Another example marked identically is seen on pages 92 and 93 of Lydia Richter's *Puppenstars PuppenAlbum 6*. She is a part of the mystery of the Steiner firm releases of the 1890s. *Anarene Barr Collection.*

improbable that any working mechanisms exist for the rubber has, after nearly a century, disintegrated. Generally, all that remains is the hole in the back of the head through which the tube emerged. Another example is seen in Mary Hillier's *Automata*, as well as a drawing of the head showing the bulb and whistle arrangement from which *Illustration 116* has been adapted. Dating from the mid 1890s, this rare novelty character shows the Steiner firm, under Madame Lafosse, adapting to the times.

Several other interesting dolls from this period are seen in *Illustrations 117* through *121*.

———————————— COLOR PLATE 55 ————————————

Illustration 118. 16 inch (41cm) incised: "11//PARIS" has superb modeling of facial features. Her head is of pressed bisque, in typical Steiner fashion, and is thin and clear. She has deep blue paperweight eyes and an aura of Jumeau seen in many of the Figure A bébés. She is basically a Figure A mold, perhaps the next in the pattern of decreasing abbreviation of head marks. Her articulated body is marked: "Le Petit Parisien//BÉBÉ STEINER."

Featured in *Color Plate 55* is an 11½ inch (29cm) Steiner bébé in splendid Oriental costume. A lovely doll with pale bisque and the typical early round face, she is inconsistent in her marking, an incised "5/0," but is unmistakably a Steiner bébé. She is uncommon, also, in that she is kid-bodied with a bisque shoulder plate and bisque arms, as seen in *Illustration 122*. Her bisque hands are lovely with excellent finger and nail detail, as one might expect to find given the beauty of Jules Steiner's bisque hands on articulated bodies.

This unusual Steiner has two exquisitely embroidered silk costumes of late 19th century Chinese design. The details of *Illustrations 123* and *124* show the figural buttons and the embossed markings on the back, which are old Chinese characters for "trust" and "clock." This is the type of clothing worn by the ruling Manchus of the Ching Dynasty, the last Imperial family of China. This was the period of the Dowager Empress, Tsyshi, who ruled her Emperor son with an iron hand for 50 years until their deaths in 1908. She was a contemporary of Queen Victoria but her antithesis. It may be that this doll was dressed to represent her courtly elegance and

LEFT: Illustration 119. 18 inch (46cm) *Bébé Phénix* in original marked chemise. Another *Phénix* was seen in *Color Plate 45*. The mark was registered May 3, 1895, by Madame Lafosse, #47043. The *Phénix* is consistently painted with its eyebrows close to the eyes and nearly meeting in the center. Her paperweight blue eyes have a nice clarity; her nose is long and sharp with larger than usual red dots at the nostrils. The grooved modeling of the philtrum is, as usual, sharply defined. The range of quality of bisque and painting of the *Phénix* is considerable, reflecting the pressures of increased production costs and competition. This bébé has her original lace-trimmed chemise with the paper label "BEBE PHENIX" at the waist. She also has jointed wrists, making her a more expensive variant. *Chantal Dagommer Collection.*

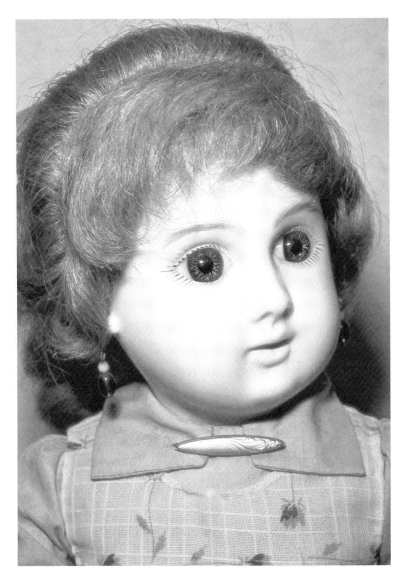

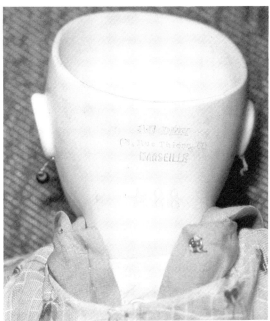

LEFT: **Illustration 120A.** 16 inch (41cm) *Bébé Phénix* is incised: " ☆ **88** " and stamped in red: "AU DÉFI// 68, Rue Thiers, 68//MARSEILLE." Her body also bears the shop name, stamped in blue. Her head is of fine pressed bisque with very crisp modeling. Her expressive closed mouth is unoutlined but nicely shaded between the lips and there is a groove on the lower lip. She has rich blue paperweight eyes, lightly feathered eyebrows and delicately painted lashes; her coloring was done with a light hand. She also has her original brown human hair wig which is pulled back with a ring of bangs framing her face.

BELOW: **Illustration 120B.** The mark as it appears on her head.

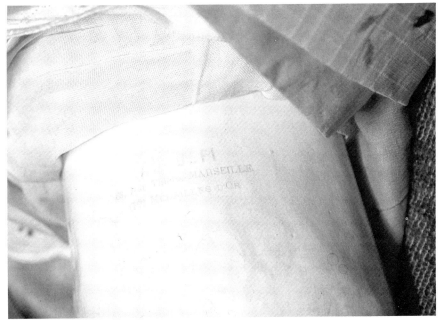

Illustration 120C. Her classic Steiner body is fully articulated and has long slender fingers, but they are more on one plane than the traditional hand. The stamp on her left hip reads: "AU DÉFI//68, Rue Thiers, MARSEILLE//Gdes MEDAILLES D'Or." "Gdes" (grandes) - Medailles (plural) indicates the shop *AU DÉFI* received many gold medals. The name also implies the store defies one to find a better price. If this doll is an example, quality was also of importance to *AU DÉFI*, and makes it easy to understand their being awarded medals.

Illustration 121. This 24 inch (61cm) bébé may well have had nothing to do with the Steiner firm, but she has more Steiner characteristics than of any other maker. Her head is of apparently pressed bisque. Her only incised mark, at the top of the crown, is indecipherable, but is possibly an "M," possibly a mark of Mascotte, the relationship of which to Steiner is not firmly established as fact. However, the modeling of her mouth is very similar to that of a Series C Steiner with the "flattened M" line shape of the upper lip. Her mouth is placed quite close under her nose giving her face a rounder look, and the basic head sculpture is quite similar to that of Series C. Her eyes are lovely, big blue paperweight, but it is her eyelashes that are most unusual, particularly her upper left eye which was never painted! Perhaps the lunch whistle blew early or the wine was flowing..."Lucille" has gone through life this way, a unique testimony to the delight of handwork!

intrigue at a time when France was involved expanding its empire in the Far East and China.

Another interesting kid-bodied Steiner is seen in *Illustrations 125A* and *125B.* She is 17½ inches (45cm) tall. She is a shoulder head with wonderfully detailed muscular modeling of her chest and shoulder blades, similar to that of the bisque hip seen in Section One. She does not have the molded upper arm and full rounded shoulders of the bisque hip, but actually has a greater amount of sculpted musculature. Her head is solid

dome, her mouth open with two rows of teeth and she has narrow blue oval eyes with fine eyebrow painting. An unusual doll, she exhibits very caring treatment.

―――――― COLOR PLATE 56 ――――――

The especially charming bébé in *Color Plate 56* and *Illustration 126* is a papier-mâché Steiner. Measuring 14 inches (36cm), she has a five-piece composition body with long slender fingers. It is stamped in blue on her left hip "BÉBÉ 'LE PARISIEN'//Médaille d'Or//PARIS." She dates from the end of the 1890s or the early 1900s.

She was seen in Section One, (*Illustration 23.*) under a discussion of patents. She reflects patent #276,458, registered March 29, 1898, to the Widow Lafosse, then head of the Steiner firm. That patent was for a method of making lightweight papier-mâché heads and limbs lined with fabric. As seen again in *Illustration 127*, this head is lined with a glue-saturated gauze-like fabric in the manner detailed.

In addition to being an unusual papier-mâché doll, she is in her totally original Provincial costume. These embroidered costumes evolved from the peasants desire for festive Sunday garments. The embroidery was done by both men and women. Whole families spent long winter evenings when they could not be working in the fields in designing and stitching the colorful patterns on their clothes. While these costumes were not uniform in style and color, there was enough similarity in the dress of a given village to tell an outsider where the wearer lived and even his social status. The early 1900s was a fast-paced time of modern ideas and change. It also saw a nostalgic reaction to the loss of tradition and a renewed interest in dolls in regional costume as a means of preserving that heritage.

This doll's costume represents the Pont-Aven region of Brittany. It consists of a black wool dress with an attached white wool vest. They are trimmed with gold silk thread featherstitching on velvet ribbon trim at the wrists, neck and vest sleeves and front. It has gold and silver metallic braid at the hem. The bodice is elaborately decorated with featherstitching and applied multicolor metallic sequin-like flowers and leaves. She also wears a robin's egg blue cotton satin apron with silver metallic

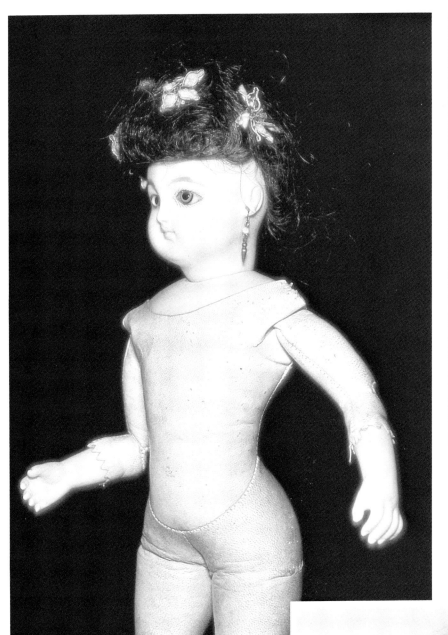

Illustration 124. Back of buttons showing embossed markings including letters "G.K.L." and old Chinese symbols for "trust" and "clock." This authentic and exquisite costuming quite possibly done in China. *Mary Lou Rubright Collection.*

ABOVE: Illustration 122. 11½ inch (29cm) kid-bodied Steiner with lovely bisque arms, detailed in *Color Plate 55. Mary Lou Rubright Collection.*

RIGHT: Illustration 123. Close-up of face also showing figural button on Oriental costume. *Mary Lou Rubright Collection.*

braid at the hem and around her waist. The dress has a white organdy lace-trimmed two-tier pleated collar. A matching white cap is bordered in red satin ribbon with white lace trim all around and with a looped lace band in the front. It is tied under her chin with aqua silk ribbon.

Her face has the rectangular shape of Figure A without the depth of modeling seen in bisque examples. Its painting is reminiscent of a *Phénix*. She has an open mouth, one row of teeth and a nose rub revealing a little brown papier-mâché. Original and unusual, she has a sweet charm.

——————— COLOR PLATE 57 ———————

The next five color plates are of very special dolls from Jules Steiner's Figure A mold; all are original and unique. *Color Plate 57* shows one of the most wistfully appealing renditions of any Steiner white-faced clown noted. As are most, he is 12½ inches (31cm) and incised "STEINER//PARIS//F^E A 6." His body is a five-piece composition with long slender fingers. His costume is of red and green velvet in a harlequin pattern. His wig is curly blonde mohair and his brown eyes are softly expressive.

As noted in Section Three, a study of Figure marked dolls, the Steiner firm almost exclusively used the Figure A mold for their clowns. While many variations exist in the painting, there were likely models for the workmen to paint from, as was usual with the bébé heads. A Series F clown was shown in *Color Plate 29*; that doll has identical facial painting to this mellow fellow. However, while that clown is funny or cute, because of his basic modeling this clown is downright handsome! He is most worthy of being enjoyed in color.

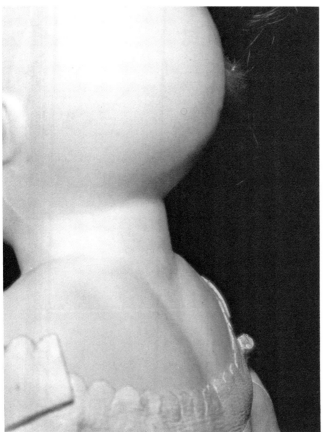

Illustrations 125A & 125B. 17½ inch (45cm) shoulder head Steiner with very pale coloring, narrow blue eyes, open mouth with two rows of teeth, solid dome head, and incredibly detailed chest and back musculature, a sculpture of note. *Courtesy of Richard W. Withington.*

Illustration 126. 14 inch (36cm) papier-mâché in full costume representing the Pont-Aven region of Brittany.

Illustration 127. 14 inch (36cm) papier-mâché with head lined with glue-saturated fabric as detailed in Lafosse patent #276458 of 1898.

173

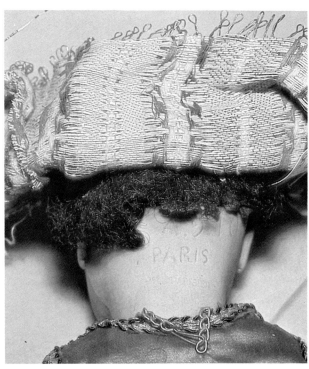

Illustration 129. Incised mark: "A.9-10//PARIS" on head of doll in *Illustration 128* is an unusual in-between size found on some Figure A Steiners. *Ann Lloyd Collection.*

Illustration 128. 16 inch (41cm) Turkish dancer in full costume. Gold coins in jewelry represent her dowry earned in Mediterranean ports. Warm brown coloring, open mouth with one row of teeth, detailed in *Color Plate 59. Ann Lloyd Collection.*

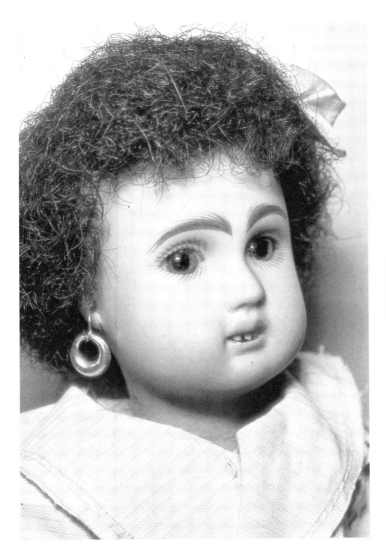

Illustration 130. 10½ inch (27cm) mulatto bébé with open mouth and one row of teeth. She also has original box, seen in *Color Plate 60. Tom Bugenhagen Collection.*

———————COLOR PLATES 58 & 59———————

The small doll in Turkish regalia is incised "J. STEINER//Bte S.G.D.G.//PARIS//A-2." Only 9½ inches (24cm) tall, he is one of the in-between sizes seen after the new size numbering system was adopted about 1890. His body is five-piece composition with long slender fingers and is stamped "Le Petit Parisien//BÉBÉ STEINER," a mark found for over a decade on dolls.

His coloring is more Caucasian; he has lovely deep blue paperweight eyes and even painting, but it is his Turkish influenced costume which is of primary interest. Bright fuschia cotton satin *chalwar* (pantaloons) are worn over a standard Steiner chemise. A red and bronze brocaded dickey ties around his neck, and a gold metallic cummerbund is around his waist. His gold cotton satin coat is deeply cut and has dalmation sleeves. It is entirely trimmed in gold metallic braid, and is another fine example of Steiner attention to detail.

While he likely originally had a fez, an improper but period hat was added for the photograph, for it seems unlikely he would have stepped out in this attire bareheaded.

Most notable is the golden crown and shield pin he wears to which are attached tiny paper replicas of the Médaille d'Or (Gold Medal) won at the 1889 Paris Universal Exposition and the 1890 Diplôme d'Honneur (diploma of honor). They are seen in the corners of *Color Plate 58.*

An exciting Turkish woman, a dancer, is seen in *Color Plate 59*, and *Illustration 128.* At 16 inches (41cm), she is incised "A.9-10//PARIS" with "LE PARISIEN" stamped in red. She has warm brown coloring, dark eyes and black eyebrows painted very close to her eyes. Her open mouth has one row of teeth.

175

Gill Stribling-Wright, producer for London Weekend Television writes:

"Belly dancing is known as the oldest dance. It belonged to a race of people who wandered the world and came originally from India, migrating west towards Europe. These were the original "gypsies" who earned their livelihood from singing and dancing. They made their way across the land routes of Afghanistan to the ancient Middle East and divided on the shore of the Mediterranean, some going west via present day Iran, Turkey and Greece, others via Egypt and the northern shores of Africa. The gypsies retained a remnant of the old birth mime and transformed it into an entertainment and as they progressed west it was influenced by the cultures it encountered and became what we call today the belly dance. The cabaret costume of tinsel, tassels and bared flesh has little to do with the real folk art of belly dancing. The most famous belly dancers have always been gypsies, especially the ghawazee of Egypt and the Turkish çengi — the old Turkish word for female dancers, believed to derive from their word for gypsy which is çingeni. The dancers were lavishly dressed..."

This doll wears the traditional *shintiyan*, the brightly colored harem trousers tied at the waist. She also wears Turkish style peak-toed gold slippers. Her satin bolero with full white net embroidered attached sleeves is called an *anteree*. Folk dancers generally cover their heads; attached to her multi-colored brocaded headdress is a gold silk "fall" or veil. The headdress is adorned with gold bangle jewelry, stars and cups, and she wears a matching necklace. Generally, the jewelry included gold coins which even the poorest wore. In some Algerian tribes, is represented the dancer's dowry, amassed by performing in Mediterranean ports; after having acquired it, she would return home to marriage and a quiet life among her own people.

This wonderful doll was responsible for hours of digression into her fascinating background!

──────────── COLOR PLATE 60 ────────────

The 10 1/2 inch (26cm) bébé seen here and in *Illlustration 130* is one of Jules Steiner's mulatto dolls. Totally original, she even has two boxes — the one she came in and the one she carries! Her head is incised "A3-4//PARIS" and her fully-articulated composition body is stamped "BÉBÉ 'LE PARISIEN'//Médaille d'Or//PARIS." Her eyes are stationary brown paperweight and her mouth is open with one row of teeth, as is often found with this doll. Her coloring is very good, even, and of medium hue. A yellow ribbon is pinned in her very curly black mohair wig. She wears a red and white striped cotton dress with a yellow sash and she carries her marvelous original "purse," a six-sided red

and white striped paper-covered box with a gold paper lid. Alas, no West Indies treasure lies hidden within.

Such originality is to be prized, and even more so when it includes the original box marked "LE PARISIEN" and stamped "Mulâtre." SHE is the treasure.

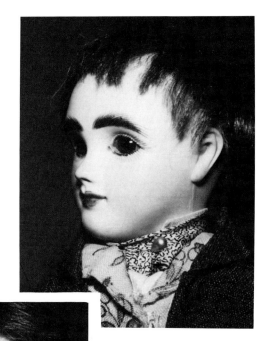

Illustrations 131, 132. Two studies of the rare Steiner man, 11 1/2 inches (29cm) tall. Note in front view, color plate 61, he bears a noticeable resemblance to Julie Andrews!

──────────── COLOR PLATE 61 ────────────

Since the first printing of this book, several interesting and unusual dolls have surfaced. They span the many decades of Steiner's production and include both patented and unpatented novelties. These range from a papier-mâché tightrope walking man of the 1860s to a kicking and crying Steiner baby from pre-1880 modified with an oscillating mechanism to the legs which produces a walking movement similar to the Bébé Premier Pas patented more than a decade later. The Series D Steiner remains unfound, but a character man of singular beauty has emerged, pictured in *Color Plate 61* and *Illustrations 131 and 132.*

This gentle man is very similar to the two soldiers seen in *Color Plates 50-52,* and is likely from the same series of dolls. He is incised in exactly the same manner: J STEINER on one line, PARIS below; he measures 11 1/2 inches (29cm). The bisque of his oval face is clear and beautifully tinted, his eyebrows are lushly masculine, and his large brown paperweight eyes are like those of the soldiers. His profile shows a sharp but slightly upturned nose, while his outlined and shaded mouth captures the suggestion of a smile. The philtrum is deeply grooved but delicate. This sensitive portraiture renders him unique among his colleagues. His composition body has unjointed legs but fully jointed arms and he, too, bears the paper label on the back of his torso. While his blue serge suit is of the nineteenth century, it is possible he became a businessman after a brief period in the service of his country. He is truly extraordinary!

Also pictured in *Color Plate 61* is a black bisque-headed doll, an apparently unpatented musical novelty. Standing 14 inches (36cm) tall, her head is incised A-7 and is stamped in black ink Le Parisien. She has dark brown stationary eyes and an open mouth with four molded upper teeth. Her head is attached to a threaded rod from the mechanism in her torso which contains a small cylindrical music box. As the wooden piece covering the mechanism is pressed the cylinder revolves and plays an as-yet unidentified tune, and causes the unjointed arms and legs to move as if walking, and her head to turn. The limbs have distinctive Steiner modeling and her classic long slender fingers are typical of the mid 1890s. Like the whistler seen in *Color Plate 54,* it shows Madame Lafosse modifying production to appeal to the whims of the time. An intriguing toy, it is the only one of its type noted thus far.

The extraordinary rifleman is Jules Nicolas Steiner's last patent, dated April 24, 1894. Its operation is precisely as described by Steiner, with the soldier dropping to one knee and cocking his head before firing the rifle. The firing sound is produced by a flat spring attached to the underside of the wooden carriage box which is drawn off the wood by a cam, then sharply released to slap against the wood. The soldier, 9 inches (23cm) tall, wears a field uniform appropriate to the North African desert, an area convincingly depicted by the sand and stones glued all over the box. The doll's head is unmarked, but is distinctively that of a man. He has a generous moustache and a serious expression, consistent with the theme of this wonderful toy. A similar head to this has recently been seen on a small fully articulated Steiner body, which furthers the intrigue of the final years of the Steiner production, and the degree to which Jules Nicolas Steiner maintained an interest in his field. These finds, along with his myriad other curiosities, constitute a store of wonders that confirms Steiner's place at the forefront of the nineteenth century toy and doll industry.

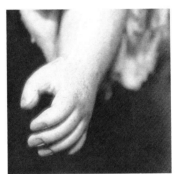

ABOVE: **Illustration 133.** Face of 20 inch (50cm) candy container is delicate and pretty. A socket head, incised: "3," it is fitted into torso of body. Skirt covers the box.

LEFT: **Illustration 134.** Detail of hands of candy container.

Illustration 135. Advertisment from supplement to *Femina,* a French magazine for women, dated Dec. 15, 1901, shows the new featured candy box creation from the Gouache establishment, a confectioner in Paris. The candy box in *Color Plates 62* and *63* is also marked "Gouache." *Bibliothéque, Musée des Arts Décoratifs, Paris.*

One can almost see the happy smile on the face of the recipient of this sweet token of affection. As a doll, she is sheer delight. She stands 20 inches (51cm) tall. Her early round face with overall pink coloring is the setting for her amber eyes of true paperweight depth. She has an open mouth with just one row of teeth; she seems about to speak, and she could tell us stories...

Her Provincial costume, probably representing a region of Brittany, is marvelous in its detail and in the quality of its construction. A fine white wool challis guimpe with full sleeves is worn under a deep forest green wool dress and apron. The green is so dark it invariably photographs black. Trimmed in gold metallic braid and sequins in a reverse loop meander pattern, it required yards of braid and considerable skill and patience to evenly assemble. Her white cotton petticoat is trimmed with a red wool pleated ruffle matching the shawl worn around her shoulders. Her tall bonnet has a ring of blonde mohair curls attached to its edge. Bright green silk ribbons hang from the back.

Her beautifully formed bisque hands (*Illustration 134*) are small, perhaps so she will not eat too much of the treasure hidden within — she is a candy container! Her torso is attached to the top of an oval box and her legs to the bottom. The lace trimmed white cotton underpants cover the box. As seen in *Color Plate 63*, the inside of the box lid is marked "GOUACHE," a Parisien confectioner.

Illustration 135 shows an advertisement from the December 15, 1901, supplement to *Femina*, a woman's magazine for the Gouache establishment featuring that year's special offering, a Japanese candy box doll. It is likely this piece never went through Steiner's hands; the firm may have sold the heads, by then old stock, to the box maker.

Were the affections of the turn-of-the-century suitor accepted? We know only that the candy is gone and the doll well-preserved; surely she was cherished. Who could help but be smitten with a wooer with this sense of *joie de vivre*, of taste, and yes, this sense of humor!

One picture is worth a thousand words! This again is "Felice Delaire," seen in full view in *Color Plate 24* wearing her hat. As she was put away nearly a hundred years ago and shows no evidence of play, one wonders if hers was a little known hairstyle that swept the continent so long ago. Her curved tortoiseshell comb is untouched by time and her very being a timeless delight!

She is one SIMPLY SPECIAL STEINER!

RIGHT: Illustration 136. 10¼ inch (26cm) Series C 3/0, as seen in *Color Plates 24* and *64*.

Section Five

A LITTLE REVIEW:
COMPARISONS FOR STUDY

A Group of Petite Bébés
Series & Figure Faces
Bodies
Marks
Size Chart
Advertising
Trademarks

COLOR PLATES — Section Five

Plate 65. 8¼ inch (21cm) Series C 4/0 with fully-articulated body and BISQUE hands, blue wire-operated sleep eyes, circa 1885.

Plate 66. Series B 3/0 with papier-mâché "Motschmann-type" body. Series C 3/0 with fully-articulated body. *Maurine S. Popp Collection.* Figure A, (A - 2) with five-piece body. Series C 3/0 with fully-articulated body. Figure C 4/0 with fully-articulated body.

Plate 67. Marked only 3/0 on six-ball articulated body. Series C 3/0 on articulated body. Figure E (Fre E 3) on articulated body with metal hands. Figure C No 3/0, on articulated body. Series C 4/0 with fully-articulated body with bisque hands.

Plate 68. Figure A (A 3) *Le Parisien, Au Nain Bleu* costume. *Beulah Franklin Collection.* Series A 3/0 on papier-mâché "Motschmann-type" body. *Beulah Franklin Collection.* Series A 3/0 on articulated body. *Sylvia MacNeil Collection.* Figure C No 4/0 on fully-articulated body.

Plate 69. Figure A (Fre A 3) mulatto, fully-articulated body. Figure C No 3/0, articulated body, Au Nain Bleu costume. Figure A (Fre A 1) on fully-articulated body. Series A 3/0 on papier-mâché "Motschmann-type" body. *Nancy A. Smith Collection.* Series E 3/0 on six-ball articulated body.

Plate 70. Series A 3/0 boy, "Motschmann-type" body, natty clothing. Detailed in *Plate 17. Beulah Franklin Collection.*

Plate 71. Figure A (Fre A 1) on fully-articulated body, blue wire-operated eyes, detailed in *Plate 36.*

Plate 72. Series B 3/0 on "Motschmann-type" body has unusual modeling around mouth. *Courtesy of Richard Wright and Rick Saxman.*

Plate 73. Figure B (B 1) on fully-articulated body, early marking, 16 inch (41cm), detailed in *Plate 39.*

Plate 74. Two Series C 3/0 bébés with blue paperweight eyes and articulated bodies, detailed in *Plate 23.*

Plate 75. Three Figure C bébés, two size 3/0 and one 4/0 with squeak toy lamb.

Plate 76. Series E 3/0 bébé with six-ball articulated body, wistful expression, detailed in *Plate 27.*

Plate 77. Figure E (Fre E 3), very rare mold, unusual look of Simon Halbig, fully-articulated body with metal hands, detailed in *Plates 46-48.*

Plate 78. Series A, B, C, E, F, G seen close up.

Plate 79. Figure A, B, C, D, E faces seen close up.

Plate 80. Series C 4/0 seen in *Plate 65* relaxing with Steiff Lesser Panda who is 3½ inch (9cm) long. Doll is 8¼ inch (21cm).

Plate 65. Sie C 4/0, circa 1885.

Plate 66.

Plate 67.

Plate 68.

Plate 69.

Plate 70. Series A, circa 1880.

Plate 71. Figure A, circa 1890.

Plate 72. Series B, circa 188[...]

Plate 73. Figure B, circa 1888.

Plate 74. Series C, circa 1885.

Plate 75. Figure C, circa 1890.

Plate 76. Series E, circa 1885.

Plate 77. Figure E, circa 1890.

A

G

B

F

C

E

Plate 78. "Series" Faces.

A

E   B

D   C

Plate 79. "Figure" Faces.

Plate 80. Sie C 4/0 with Lesser Panda, circa 1885.

A LITTLE REVIEW:
COMPARISONS FOR STUDY

This final section, a little review, brings Series and Figure marked dolls into side-by-side comparisons for study. It also features my personal favorites, the small dolls of Jules Nicolas Steiner, his multifaceted petite jewels. With the exception of his mechanical dolls and the bisque hip Motschmann-type, Steiner's dolls were all made in the 10¼ inch (26cm) size, marked 3/0 or 3. Many were made in the smallest size, 8¼ inches (21cm), size 4/0 or, in later dolls size 1. All of the dolls in this section are in these two sizes with the exception of repeated dolls in *Color Plates 78* and *79* and the Figure B in *Color Plate 73* which has not yet been found in that size. Where possible they are printed actual size.

A number of factors contributed to the success of these small bébés. A fine clean kaolin paste was used in the production of Jules Steiner's heads, creating the flawless bisque so often found on these precious, high quality, tiny dolls. As we have seen, the facial features were distinctly and sharply sculpted. Clean molds yielded crisp features; standards were high and were met. Jules Nicolas Steiner had no serious French competitors in this size range. It is interesting to note that some of the tiny dolls of the German firm of J. D. Kestner show exquisite detail not unlike Steiner's. Some with open mouths even have the cut dip in the center of the upper lip. Like the dolls of Jules Nicolas Steiner, these dolls also have crisp modeling and finishing of details both of the heads and their tiny bodies. Many of the French manufacturers' small dolls were of inferior quality and few, if any, even made an articulated doll only 8 inches (21cm) tall.

The Steiner composition bodies are also perfect miniatures of the larger bodies, even to an 8¼ inch (21cm) fully-articulated bébé with bisque hands. This little treasure is seen in *Color Plates 65* and *80*. She also has blue wire-operated eyes with enameled lids, each about the size of a medium green pea and each fully incised "STEINER 4/0 B.S.G.D.G." I love it! The later all-glass wire-operated eyes are seen in the equally tiny Figure A in *Color Plate 71*, who is shown actual size. Ears of all types, including those with the deeply incised canal, and wigs in perfect miniature coiffure are other features of these bewitching little bébés to be savored.

Futhermore, these dolls must have been delightful for a child to play with, for they comfortably fit even a small child's hands. One can easily imagine that many petite Steiner bébés were Sunday dolls not just to be looked at, but were taken to church (perhaps in Mama's purse) to quietly occupy its young owner. As the price comparisons on pages 205-207 show, these dolls were, additionally, a good buy.

Many were sold through *Au Nain Bleu* and were dressed in the fancy frilly lacy beribboned style so typical of the period and of that wonderful toy shop. Some dolls described in detail in other sections of the book are seen again in *Plates 66* through *77*. We are fortunate that a number of these gems have survived as historical documents and personal treasures.

Plates 78 and *79* show a "typical" face of each Series and Figure mold, while the concluding pages contain body types, details of features, body and head marks, trademarks, two copies of Steiner's signature, and some advertising with comparative prices. Shown also is the 1901 insurance plan diagram which, in conjunction with the insurance descriptions, provided the basis for the drawing of the factory on the Frontispiece. The Appendix lists and summarizes each of the patents of Jules Nicolas Steiner and his successors, the Lafosses.

The dolls of Jules Nicolas Steiner truly deserve our study and our accolades. Their production spanned several decades during which time many other firms came and went. His dolls are varied, encompassing the spectrum from simple to technically complex and from cute to hauntingly beautiful. The dolls which survive today, the patents and those toys which hopefully will surface as well as the awareness of his many other patented inventions are all part of the legacy of Jules Nicolas Steiner. His prodigious work filled a lifetime which this work attempts to honor.

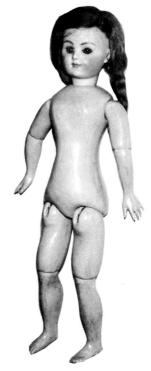

1. *Bébé Parlant Automatique* or kicking-crying Steiner. Produced 1860s through 1890s with variations. See feet on following page.

2. Waltzing lady on molded cardboard base, circa 1880. Produced 1860s through 1890s.

3. Young lady body stamped "La Patricienne." Mark used by Edmond Daspres, last successor of Steiner firm in 1904. Found with a variety of heads including this Series F.

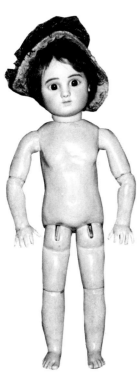

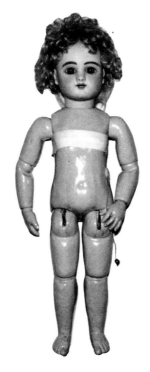

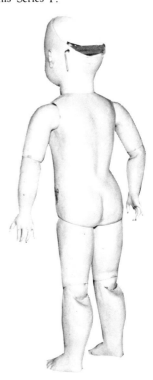

7. 1880s, 1890s. Traditional sleek articulated body with short fat fingers made by use of compressed air. Usually of purple papier-mâché with Series heads in 1880s, gray papier-mâché with Figure heads in 1890s. Occasionally with pull-string voice box.

8. Later 1880s, 1890s. Same body form as No. 7 but with articulated wrists. Various types of hands seen on following page. Stamp on hip is often body mark #3, Steiner & Bourgoin. May have pull-string voice box.

9. 1890s. Traditional body form but with long slender fingers. Gray papier-mâché. Figure marked heads. May have pull-strong voice box.

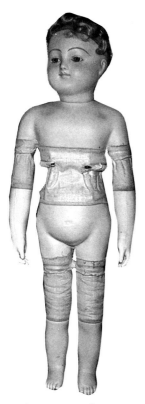

4. Bisque hip or Motschmann-type, circa 1870s.

5. Papier-mâché Motschmann-type, circa 1880s. Note similarities to body No. 6 at right.

6. 1870s introduction. First articulated bébé body, hand-pressed, with separate ball joints. Note icicle-like fingers. Usually found with unmarked heads and occasionally Series heads.

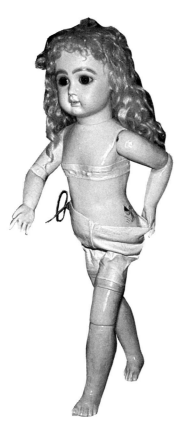

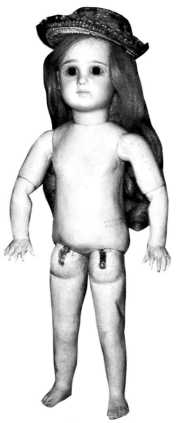

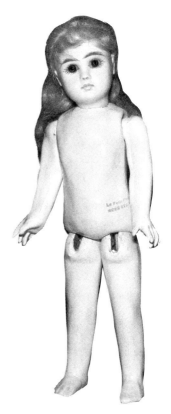

10. *Bébé Premier Pas*, patented 1890. Traditional body with keywind mechanism. Other variants have fewer body articulations.

11. 1890s. Seven-piece body has straight legs and articulated elbows. Found with either long slender or short-fat fingers and usually Figure marked heads.

12. 1890s +. Five-piece body usually has long slender fingers, occasionally a mitt-like hand. Figure marked heads and novelty pieces, some of very fine quality.

HANDS
STRAIGHT WRIST:

   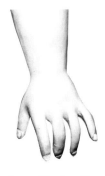

1. Bisque Arm Motschmann-Type   2. First Articulated Body with Separate Ball Joints. "Icicle-like" Fingers.   3. Short Stubby Fingers   4. Long Slender Fingers

ARTICULATED WRIST:

5. Bisque   6. "Banana"   7. Long Slender   8. Metal

FEET

Kicking-crying *Bébé Parlant Automatique*. 1860s through 1890s. Shows variations over the decades.

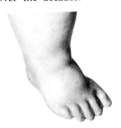 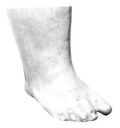 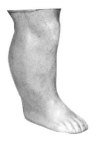

1. 1860s   2. 1880s   3. 1890s

  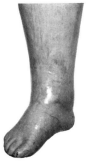 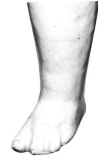

4. Bisque Hip Motschmann-Type (Body #4)   5. Papier-Mâché Motschmann-Type (Body #5)   6. First Articulated Body (Body #6)   7. Foot of Traditional Body - circa 1890. (Degrees of modeling exist) (Bodies #7-12)

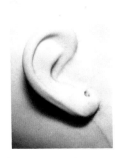

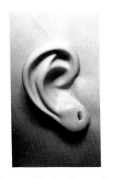

1. Early Unmarked Heads. 1860s 1870s

2. Series Heads. 1880s

3. Figure Heads. Ear with canal. 1888 through 1890s

4. Figure Ear — Flat. 1890s

SIZE CHART: The Dolls of Jules Nicolas Steiner

Inches	Centimeters	Old Sizes 1880s Series Heads Some Figure Heads	New Sizes from 1890 Figure Heads	Additional and In Between Sizes — Figure Marks	
8¼	21	4/0	1	0	
10¼	26	3/0	3	2	2.3
12¼	31	2/0	5	4	3.4 4.5
14	36	0	7	6	5.6
16	41	1	9	8	9.10
18	46	2	11	10	
20	51	3	13	12	
22	56	4	15	14	
24	61	5	17	*16	
28	71	6	19	18	
32-33	84	7	20		
37-38	96	8	21		

Occasionally a doll will not quite fit this chart.
Largest sizes can vary by several centimeters (an inch or two).

*Size not as yet verified.

S^{le} A · 2 S^{le} B · 1 S^{le} C · 4

S^{le} E · 1 S^{le} F · 2/0 S^{le} G · 6

J. STEINER, B. S.G.D.G
J. BOURGOIN, succr

J. Steiner Bte Sgdg J. Bourgoin

FIGURE A

Marks incised except where noted.
These marks reflect old sizing.

A 3/0 ——— Handwritten in black

J. STEINER, B. S.G.D.G. ——— Red Stamp
J. BOURGOIN, succr

FIGURE A N° 5
J. STEINER B^{te} S.G.D.G.
PARIS

These marks reflect new sizing.
Note pattern of abbreviation. Other marks may be found.
Some marks do not have "J" before STEINER.

J. STEINER
B^{TE} S.G.D.G.
PARIS
F^{IRE} A 15

J. STEINER
B^{TE} S.G.D.G.
PARIS
F^{RE} A 9

J. STEINER
B^{TE} S.G.D.G
PARIS
A·2

STEINER
PARIS
F^{RE} A 7

STEINER
PARIS
F^{E} A 6

STEINER
PARIS
F A·11

Heads incised simply A show a variety of incised sizes with red or black stamps. Incised marks shown by heavy line, stamps by lighter.

A·1

A 2.3
PARIS
"LE PARISIEN"

A 3.4
PARIS

A 5.6
PARIS "LE PARISIEN"

A 7
LE PARISIEN
SGDG
A 7

A.3
LE PARISIEN
BTE SGDG
A 3

A.5
Le Parisien

A.9.10
PARIS
LE PARISIEN

A-15
PARIS
NAIN BLEU

A _ 15
PARIS
Le PARISIEN

FIGURE B

Marks reflect old & new sizing
as indicated

B 1 —— Handwritten in black

(old)

J. STEINER, B.S G.D.G. —— Red Stamp
J. BOURGOIN, SUCCᵣ

FIGURE B Nº 1
J. STEINER BTE SGDG
PARIS

(old)

FIGURE B Nº 10
STEINER BTE SGDG
PARIS

(new)

FIGURE B Nº 7
STEINER BTE SGDG
PARIS

(old)
Red Ink over

B 7

J. STEINER
BTE SGDG
PARIS
FIᴿᴱ B 20

(new)

FIGURE C

FIGURE C 4/0
J. STEINER BTE SGDG
PARIS

(old)

FIGURE C Nº 3/0
J. STEINER BTE SGDG
PARIS

(old)

STEINER
PARIS
FRE C 4/0

(old)

FIGURE C Nº 12
J. STEINER BTE SGDG
PARIS

(new)

STEINER
PARIS
FRE C 11

(new)

STEINER
PARIS
FRE C 15

(new)
number
embossed

STEINER
PARIS
C . 3

(new)

FIGURE D

STEINER
PARIS
FRE D · 15

(new)

FIGURE E

J. STEINER
BTE. S.G.D.G.
PARIS
FRE E 3

(new)

BODY MARKS

	Mark	Description	Dates Used	Dolls Found On
1.	J. STEINER, fabricant, de Saintonge, No 21, à P...	Paper label printed 1867, glued to body	1867	Waltzing ladies Bébé Parlant Automatique (kicking-crying baby)
2.	J ST (Caduceus)	Caduceus, ink stamp. Probably steel die, mark sometimes cut into body surface.	1880s	First articulated body (#6) or Traditional body (#7). Unmarked & Series heads.
3.	LE PETIT PARISIEN J. ST. Bté S.G.D.G. J. B. Succr PARIS	Ink Stamp (probably rubber). Note Steiner & Bourgoin. Earliest usage of "Le Petit Parisien."	1887-88	Often on body #8. Later Series or earlier Figure heads. Also with Bourgoin stamp.
4.		Paper label, glued to body	1889+	Traditional articulated bodies, usually Figure marked heads.
5.	Le Petit Parisien BÉBÉ STEINER Médaille d'Or PARIS 1889	Ink Stamp	1890s	Various articulated bodies, Figure marked heads.
6.	Le Petit Parisien BÉBÉ STEINER	Ink Stamp	1890s	Various articulated bodies, Figure marked heads.
7.	BÉBÉ "LE PARISIEN" MÉDAILLE D'OR PARIS	Ink Stamp	1895+	Various articulated bodies, Figure marked heads.
8.	LE PARISIEN BÉBÉ STEINER	Ink Stamp	1895+	Various articulated bodies, Figure marked heads.
9.	MARQUE DÉPOSÉE ARTICLE FRANÇAIS Nº 84	Ink Stamp of Chambre Syndicale des Fabricants de Jouets et Jeaux Francais.	ca 1900	Figure A, 5-piece body, and probably others.
10.	LA PATRICIENNE (DÉPOSE)	Ink Stamp	1905	E. Daspres, Sie F 2/0 and non-Steiner heads.

ADVERTISING and COMPARATIVE PRICES

Prices are converted at five francs to the dollar.

An 1891 catalog from the department store Maison du Petit Saint Thomas featured Jules Steiner's Le Petit Parisien bébé on its cover (above.) The price list on the following page shows the wonderful 21cm (8¼ inch) size bébé was offered at 2 francs 25 (45 cents) while in the larger sized dolls an additional two francs purchased the mama — papa speaking version.

The 1892 Marshall Field & Co. catalog presented an 18 inch (46cm) Premier Dressed bébé Steiner at $90 a dozen ($7.50 each), the most expensive of their offerings. A similar sized Jumeau, but wearing only a chemise was priced at $48 a dozen ($4.00 each). Typically, however, a dressed Jumeau bébé sold for three times the cost of one in a chemise. (An interesting chart of comparative Jumeau prices can be found in Constance King's *Jumeau: Prince of Dollmakers*.) Using the United States Government Consumer Index figures, $7.50 in 1892 is almost $93 in 1988. With these facts in mind, the dressed Bébé Steiner as offered by Marshall Field & Co., while definitely a luxury item, was surely less costly than a comparable Bébé Jumeau.

The 1898 Au Bon Marche advertisement provides a greater comparative pricing study. The Steiner bébé in the bottom row, second from right, is shown with a *Bébé Le Parisien* label on her chemise. The 53cm (21 inch) "*parlant et pleurant*" (speaking and crying) doll with an open mouth and teeth sold for 10 francs 50, ($2.10) compared with a similarly articulate Jumeau at 19,50 ($3.90). The store's own labeled *Bébé du Bon Marche* (made for them by Jumeau) was offered at 16,25 ($3.15). Franc for franc, the Steiner bébé was a very good buy.

Apropos, a report on dolls in *La Grande Encyclopedie*, published in Paris in the late 1880s notes that accessories for dolls are considerable and states that male workers in this general industry earn in the vicinity of 6 francs per day ($1.20) and women, 2F to 3F50 (40 to 70 cents). These wages confirm that wonderful dolls such as these were out of the reach of the ordinary working person and as much to be treasured then as now.

205

Detail from 1891 Maison du Petit Saint Thomas catalog which featured Steiner's *Le Petit Parisien*, an articulated bébé with a bisque head and wearing a necklace and earrings and a muslin dress with lacework.

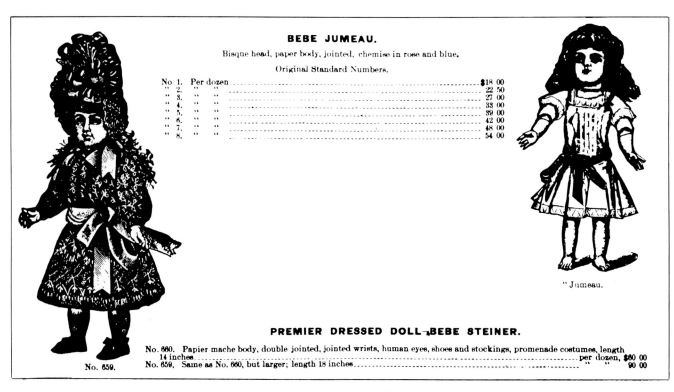

Offerings from the 1892 Marshall Field & Company wholesale catalog included the Jumeau and Steiner bébés above. A study of their respective prices indicate the well-dressed Steiner bébé was a comparatively good buy.

The 1898 *Au Bon Marche* catalog featured this page of lovely dolls. In the bottom row, second from right, is a Bébé Le Parisien, a Steiner whose price is very attractive compared to her counterparts. Note that most dolls are open mouth (bouche à dents) and many walk, talk, cry or kiss, typical of the period.

1901 INSURANCE PLAN

Plan of the Establishment of Mr. Steiner, manufacturer of mechanical dolls, 60 rue d'Avron

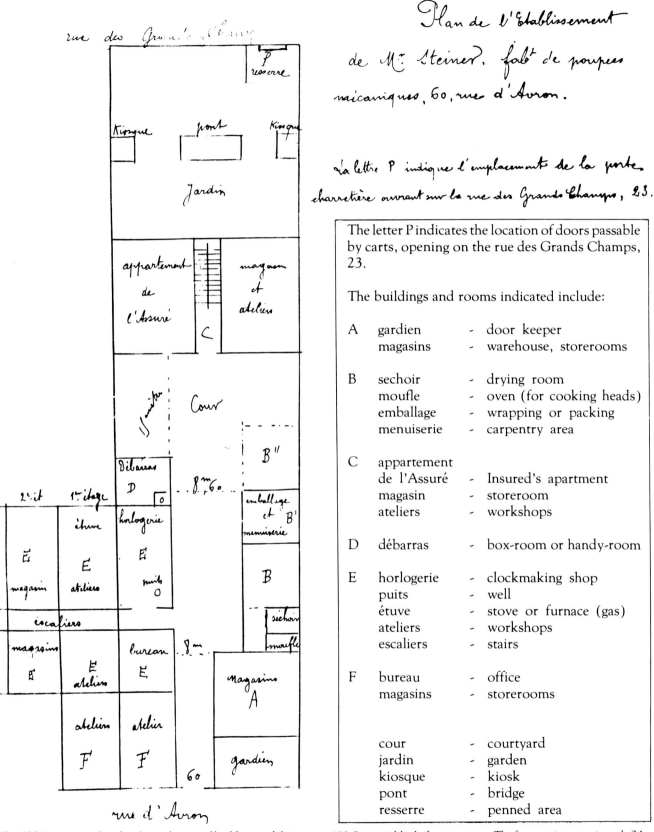

Plan de l'Etablissement de M: Steiner. fab⁺ de poupees mécaniques, 60, rue d'Avron.

La lettre P indique l'emplacement de la porte charretière ouvrant sur la rue des Grands Champs, 23.

The letter P indicates the location of doors passable by carts, opening on the rue des Grands Champs, 23.

The buildings and rooms indicated include:

A	gardien	-	door keeper
	magasins	-	warehouse, storerooms
B	sechoir	-	drying room
	moufle	-	oven (for cooking heads)
	emballage	-	wrapping or packing
	menuiserie	-	carpentry area
C	appartement de l'Assuré	-	Insured's apartment
	magasin	-	storeroom
	ateliers	-	workshops
D	débarras	-	box-room or handy-room
E	horlogerie	-	clockmaking shop
	puits	-	well
	étuve	-	stove or furnace (gas)
	ateliers	-	workshops
	escaliers	-	stairs
F	bureau	-	office
	magasins	-	storerooms
	cour	-	courtyard
	jardin	-	garden
	kiosque	-	kiosk
	pont	-	bridge
	resserre	-	penned area

This 1901 insurance plot plan shows the several buildings and their uses at J.N. Steiner's block-deep property. The frontage is approximately 24 meters (78 feet) and its depth over 92 meters (300 feet). The inset box contains both the French designations and English translations. At this date, Jules Mettais was leasing the property from Jules Steiner. This plan was instrumental in the creation of the drawing on the Frontispiece.

REGISTERED TRADEMARKS

3823   November 9, 1869
Mark stamped in relief on metal plaques to be put on toys, velocipedes, mechanical toys, registered Nov. 9, 1869 at 1 p.m. at the office of the Commercial Court of the County of Seine by Jules Nicolas Steiner. Constructor in Paris, 25 rue de Saintonge.

Registered by
Jules Nicolas Steiner

31596   October 29, 1889
Mark to be affixed to bébés, and their wrappings, registered Oct. 29, 1889 at 3:20 p.m. at the office of the Commercial Court of the County of Seine by Monsieur Steiner (Jules Nicolas) maker in Paris.

Jules Nicolas Steiner

39514   August 12, 1892 at 1:30 p.m. Mark to designate dolls and bebes.

LE PARISIEN

Amédée Onésime Lafosse

47043   May 3, 1895 at 11:00 a.m. Mark to designate dolls.

BÉBÉ PHÉNIX

Madame Marie Lafosse

63872
63873
63874   October 21, 1899

BABY
PHÉNIX-BABY
BÉBÉ-LIÈGE

Jules Mettais

64701   January 12, 1900

POUPEE MERVEILLEUSE

Jules Mettais

70426   June 10, 1901

"BÉBÉ MODÈLE"

Jules Mettais

Comparison of Jules Nicolas Steiner's signatures.

The less mature signature is from his first patent, September 17, 1855, at age 23. The more flourished is from March 11, 1891, age 58.

Appendix
THE PATENTS OF JULES NICOLAS STEINER
Trademarks and Patents from INPI in Paris

PATENTS OF JULES NICOLAS STEINER

1.	24,828	September 17, 1855	Mechanical Doll
2.	35,726	March 8, 1858	Mechanical Stopping System
3.	52,929	February 7, 1862	"Bébé Parlant Automatique"
4.	57,803	March 13, 1863	Mechanical Doll with Single Pullstring
5.	74,679	January 25, 1867	Mechanical Horse
6.	81,091	May 26, 1868	Magical Optical Box
7.	85,858	May 29, 1869	Improvements for Velocipedes
	1 Add.	November 6, 1869	
	2 Add.	April 19, 1870	
	England #2729	September 20, 1869	
8.	88,803	February 2, 1870	Odorless Toilet with Automatic Valve
9.	137,333	June 18, 1880	New System for Moving Eyes
	1 Add.	December 13, 1880	
	2 Add.	May 19, 1881	
	3 Add.	June 20, 1881	
	Germany #14292	July 29, 1881	
10.	140,916	February 2, 1881	New Method for Manufacturing Eyes
	1 Add.	May 19, 1881	
11.	160,564	February 26, 1884	Landing System for Balloons
12.	162,061	May 15, 1884	Molding Method Via Compressed Air for Toys Made of Cardboard
13.	199,084	June 20, 1889	Unbreakable Heads of Porcelain, a lining process
14.	206,131	June 4, 1890	"Bébé Premier Pas"
	1 Add.	October 7, 1890	
15.	238,101	April 24, 1894	Firing Toy Soldier
	1 Add.	October 23, 1894	

PATENTS OF SUCCESSORS
Amédée Onésime Lafosse

16.	221,582	May 12, 1892	Improved Bellows for Dolls

The Widow Lafosse

17.	229,995	May 10, 1893	Improvements in Moving Eyes
18.	234,713	December 11, 1893	Bébé Walker and Talker with Simplified Mechanism
	1 Add.	March 24, 1894	
19.	238,710	May 22, 1894	Walking Mechanism with Optional Movements of the Head
20.	264,464	February 26, 1897	Bébé with Single Pullstring For Speaking, Crying and Blowing Kisses
21.	276,458	March 29, 1898	Manufacturing Method for Heads and Limbs, a lining process

Edmond Daspres

22.	323,175	July 21, 1902	New Walking and Talking Doll

Patents of Jules Nicolas Steiner

24,828   *Jules Nicolas Steiner*   *September 17, 1855*

POUPÉE MÉCANIQUE

DESCRIPTION DE DEUX MÉCANISMES DESTINÉE A FAIRE MOUVOIR LES BRAS, LES JAMBES, LA TÊTE ET LA BOUCHE D'UNE POUPÉE, ET LA FAISANT CRIER QUAND ELLE EST COUCHÉE.

(DESCRIPTION OF TWO MECHANISMS USED TO CAUSE THE MOVEMENT OF ARMS, LEGS, HEAD AND MOUTH OF A DOLL, AND OF CAUSING IT TO CRY OUT WHEN LAID DOWN.)

DESCRIPTION:

The first of these mechanisms is made of a small cage formed by two copper plates mounted together by three pillars. A spring casing holding a spring serves as the part's motor. The teethwork of the spring case is fashioned so as to mesh with the pinion of an open-ended screw serving as the piston rod to a governing wheel which controls the deployment of the spring. An ordinary ratchet, taken up by the spring's axle controls the rewinding. A tiny cone-shaped roller, mounted on the bridge coming from the left with the upper plate is attached to the bottom of the spring casing to assure the proper meshing action with the open-ended screw in the operating position. This is done in a way heretofore impossible to achieve.

At the bottom of the spring casing comes a cylindrical ferrule whose generating mechanism of uneven lengths makes of the upper stop a propellor-like plane. On this plane roll three small conical rollers, two of which are mounted on the edge of the levers which activate the arm motion. The third is affixed to another lever mounted on the lower bearing of the cage, and this has as its function to open the bellows which an elastic spring tends toward keeping closed. From this alternating movement comes the sound produced by the bellows.

Two cords or jointed steel wires join the movement of the legs to that of the arms when the doll is in a standing position or placed horizontally. When seated, these cords stretch out (or the steel wires bend one on the other), stopping all movement in the legs.

In one of the sides of the bellows' moveable part is implanted a pin which, upon entering the slot of a diverter mounted on the fixed part of the bellows, prevents the bellows from closing when the mechanism is in a vertical position. The eccentric position the diverter has with its stop, and the shallowness of the slot, allow the diverter to fall as soon as the position is no longer vertical. To one of the spooled levers, used for the movement of the arms, is placed a small addition made of a copper bevel and of two steel wire stoppers

which forces the turning of a steel shaft on which is attached the doll's head. This movement simulates pretty well the life-like motion of a child who looks to its right and left.

All the pieces of copper are soldered. The plates, pillars, bridges come from a single cast. This arrangement, by avoiding considerable manual labor, greatly reduces the cost involved.

This then is the arrangement of the workings for which we reserve all rights and hereby establish proprietary rights so that neither all nor part may be used by others without our authorization.

The second device for the movement of the lower lip of the mouth would be completely different from the first were it not for the necessary accompanying circular movement of the head. This entire little mechanism, which is quite simple, is set in the interior of the head by means of a steel wire shaft imbedded in a piece of wood glued in the forehead. This way the whole device moves with the head.

The lip is made of wood, hollowed out inside and mounted on a little copper shell by means of two steel wire pins counterbent at a right angle. A counterweight placed at the edge of a shaft found in the lower part of the lip keeps the mouth in a closed position. On a spindle attached to the shell is placed another counterweight at whose edge are affixed two lever arms of steel wire of unequal lengths.

In no matter what position the head is found, this counterweight always seeks its center of gravity. Thus, the result is an oscillating movement produced by the play of the head, and each of the lever arms comes, one after the other, to rest against one or the other of the elbowed pins which control the lip. In this movement, the weight of the lever's weight being greater than that of the counterweight on the lip, this latter weight when it moves in one direction or the other, the pressure of either one of the levers opens and closes alternately.

This is the general description of these two devices for which we renew our request to establish our proprietary rights, and reserving the additional right to make modifications and improvements that time and experience may suggest to us, or prohibiting by any means the use or positions pertaining to each of these devices by anyone not having authority to do so granted by us.

NOTE: *It goes without saying that the dolls can be either dressed or undressed at will and that the mechanism can also be made to stop and start voluntarily.*

Paris, September 17, 1855

Recorded, November 9, 1855

Patent translations, in their entirety or excerpted, are printed in Italic face. Author's Summarizations of Patents and Commentary are printed in Roman face.

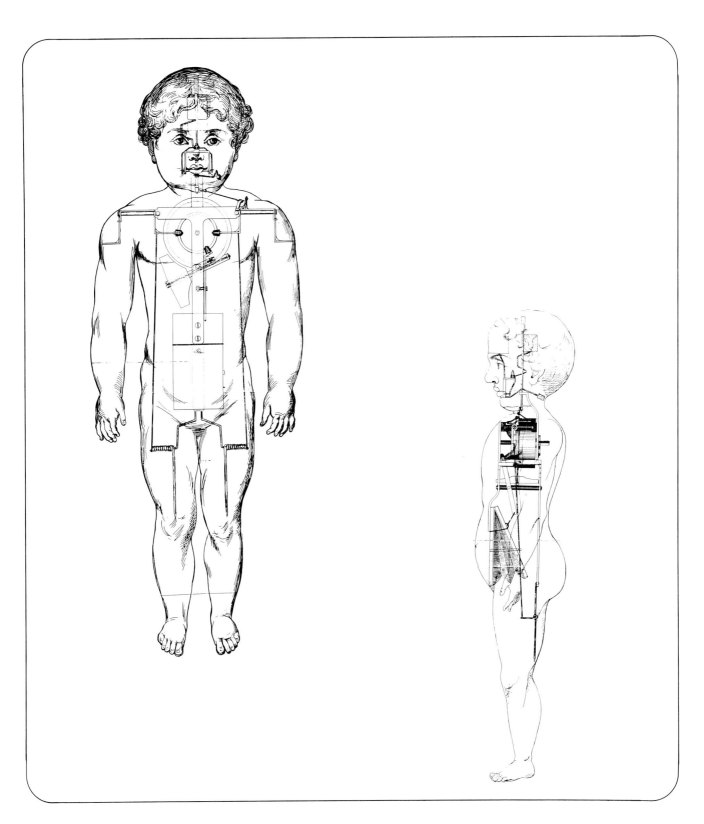

This patent is given the best translation possible considering its technical nature and that the original is in handwritten script with several words unclear. It does, however, clearly show Jules Nicolas Steiner's detailed knowledge of clockworks and his ingenius modifications of same for this mechanism. The patent also contains Steiner's signature on the last page, as seen on page 209.

Paris le Septembre —

35,726   *Jules Nicolas Steiner*   March 8, 1858

DEMANDE D'UN BREVET D'INVENTION DE 15 ANS POUR UN ARRET MÉCANIQUE APPLIQUE AUX JOUETS MÉCANIQUES ROULANTS EN GENERAL Par M. Steiner (Jules Nicolas) fabricant de jouets mecaniques 108 Rue Vielle du Temple, Paris

(APPLICATION FOR A 15 YEAR PATENT INVENTION FOR A MECHANICAL STOPPING SYSTEM FOR ROLLING MECHANICAL TOYS IN GENERAL)

DESCRIPTION:

For quite some time there have been toy vehicles, boats, guns, and even animals made using automatic movement, that is, tractionless toys using mechanical rollers. The mechanism in these toys consists of a clockwork-type barrel set up by means of a key, and which unwound acts upon a series of grooved wheels arranged so as to give the car or other object the capacity to move quite rapidly. Now one changes this ordinary system by winding a spring-type barrel, but one must take care to hold one wheel in the hand, or else the spring unravels even as one winds it up. Additionally, one must hold the wheel in place before setting the toy down so as not to loose any tension from the unwinding spring.

This double inconvenience is the result of the absence of a regulator, or of any stopping mechanism, brake or gripping mechanism. This coordination of movement carries with it another complication concerning the grooved wheel which I have sought to solve to the highest degree possible. The various refinements that I have brought to automatic childrens' toys, and which I highlight in this patent application, are:

1-the arrangement of different stopping systems rendering motionless the toy's works while not in contact with the ground and allowing the same to move freely once in contact with the ground or any surface.

2-the adaptation of the clockwork mechanism of a flying regulator which allows a regulation of the spring barrel.

3-the simplification and new arrangement of the meshing portion due to the improvements included herein.

4-the mechanical stopping feature in boats and other toys, and

5-the economy resulting from making the barrel of zinc or iron instead of copper.

With the help of the enclosed diagram, I shall describe the varied improvements mentioned above. Figure 1 shows my stopping mechanism as used in a toy car. Figure 2 is a side view from the rear. Figure 3 shows two additional stopping mechanisms for toys. Figure 4 shows yet another very simple stopping mechanism. Figure 5 is of a toy boat's stopping mechanism engaged only when the boat is placed in water...

This is a significant patent for it documents Jules Nicolas Steiner as a toy maker in Paris. Further, the mechanism patented herein is one to which Steiner makes reference in his commercial advertising. While the first page of the patent has been given here in direct translation of the original, the remaining pages, which detail the several variations designed to keep the mechanisms from unraveling as they are wound, are best summarized:

Figures 1 and 2 show a split or hinged axle for vehicles. One wheel is driven by the mechanism geared to the spring. When the toy is not on the ground, the hinged wheel falls and its attached stop-start rod impedes the flying regulator. When the toy is set down on the ground or on any surface, the weight of the object and gravity combine to effectively disengage the stop-rod from the flying regulator allowing the spring to drive the mechanism. A second arrangement based on this principle is also detailed and illustrated in Figure 3.

A simple arrangement, seen in Figure 4, consists of cutting a vertical slot in one side of the mounting plates holding the axle of the toy's wheels. When the toy is lifted to be wound, the weight of the axle causes it to drop to the bottom of the slot where a pin attached to the axle engages a bar which stops all movement. When the toy is set onto a surface, the axle lifts in the grooved slot, the pin separates from the bar and the mechanism and wheels are once again freed to move.

A flotation device for use in toy boats (Figures 5 and 6) works in much the same way. The mechanism can also be adapted for use with toy animals' limbs.

A flying regulator is a normal part of many clockwork mechanisms and automatons of the period. Noteworthy with this patent is the assertion by JNS that this is "the first of its kind used in children's toys." In the patent resume he further states, "I hereby claim this automatic or mechanical stopping mechanism as my exclusive property. Along with it, I claim all rights to change or modify the design as to having or not having a regulator or bladed flywheel...I claim as well the right to apply the mechanical stop to any and all toys no matter their size, dimension, or material."

Jules Nicolas Steiner's own *Bébé Parlant Automatique*, his next patent (1862) will employ one in its mechanism, but its stop-start will, logically, be manually controlled by a lever.

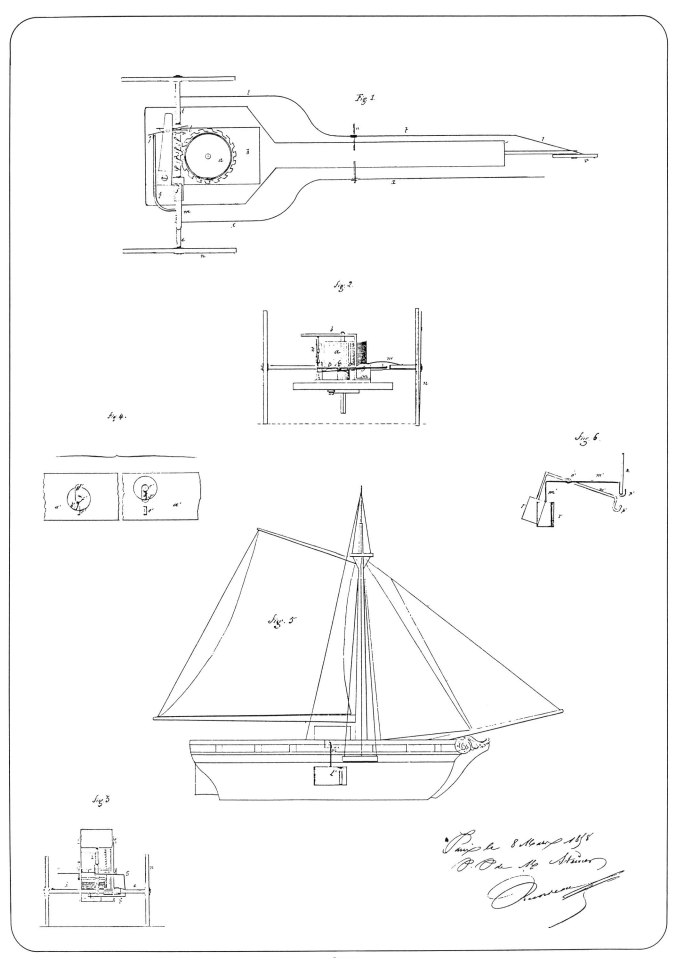

Fig. 1.

fig. 2.

fig. 4.

fig. 6.

fig. 5.

fig. 3.

Paris le 8 Mars 1858
P. O. de M. Steiner

DEMANDE D'UN BREVET D'INVENTION DE 15 ANS POUR UN BÉBÉ PARLANT AUTOMATIQUE Par M. J.N. Steiner, fabricant de jouets à Paris

(APPLICATION FOR A 15-YEAR INVENTION PATENT FOR AN AUTOMATIC TALKING BABY Submitted by Mr. J.N. Steiner, Toymaker of Paris)

DESCRIPTION:

There already exist dolls which can say "papa and mama" as well as dolls whose prolonged cry simulates the weeping of a real child, by means of an interior bellows controlled by a pull cord and a counterweight.

Likewise, the jointed movements in dolls and bébés have been accomplished in a way that allows the movement or arms or legs as the baby cries out. However these different combinations don't present anything mechanical and have so far been realized by the pull of a rod or of a cord.

The automatic talking baby, the patent for which I hereby make application by this document, has the following unique characteristics:

First, the adaptation of a mechanical system which can produce at the same time a movement of the head, the eyelids, the arms and the legs, and in addition provides the bébé with the ability to speak the words "papa and mama" to a degree never before attained.

Secondly, the change in omitted sounds by the mechanism to differentiate the baby's cries, which standing, says "papa and mama" and, lying down, imitates the weeping of a real child.

Thirdly, the replacement of the acoustical piece, ordinarily made of wood or of hard metal, with an acoustical piece made of rubber, capable of various positions and making the sound emitted change according to the bébé's position.

This results in a mechanical system which can produce, at the same time, a jointed movement of the leg and a speaking doll applicable to all kinds of dolls, bébés and toy animals. In addition, the omitted sound can be modified for any kind of mechanical toy. ...All operations are controlled by the watch-like movement of Part A, which carries a flywheel (a)...

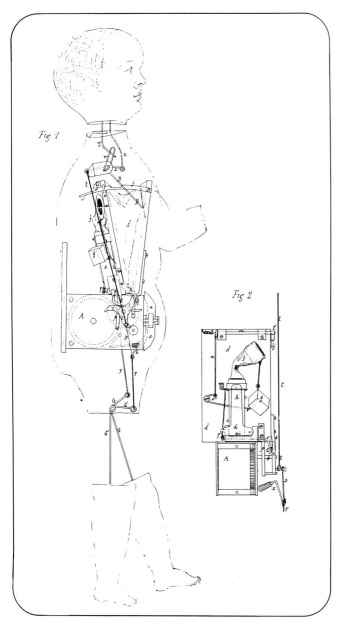

Fig 1

Fig 2

A very detailed description of the mechanical system is contained in the patent including that producing the alternating sounds, "...a soft sound corresponding to the plaintive cry of 'mama' in which the two syllables are emitted with great sweetness contrary to the cry 'papa,' whose every syllable is accented and hammered out." Additionally, a modification is outlined which enables the doll to say "papa" and "mama" when horizontal. The concluding sentence is, typically, very broad: "I reserve the right to construct bébés and poupées of the type described in all forms, sizes and materials."

57,803   *Jules Nicolas Steiner*   *March 13, 1863*

DEMANDE D'UN BREVET D'INVENTION DE 15 ANS
Pour une poupee a disposition mecanique et a simple tirage. Par Mr.
Jules Nicolas STEINER Fabricant de jouets à Paris.

(APPLICATION FOR AN INVENTION PATENT OF
FIFTEEN YEARS FOR A MECHANICAL DOLL WITH A
SINGLE PULLSTRING. Made by Jules Nicolas STEINER,
Toymaker of Paris)

DESCRIPTION:

Up until now the application of a talking mechanism has been
accomplished in dolls identified as bébés, either of wood or of
cardboard, but no one had yet thought of this adaptation for
kid-bodied dolls, filled with bran or sawdust.

The first part of my invention consists of a stuffed leather-
bodied doll containing a talking mechanism...which gives the
advantage of an automatic or mechanical doll into which a child
can put pins just as in an ordinary leather-bodied doll.

The other part of my invention is a perfected talking mechanism
which produces the two words: "papa" and "mama" with one
operation, an accomplishment which heretofore has required two
distinct operations. ... I may at my option vary the forms, materials
and dimensions of any and all parts used depending on the various
applications sought.

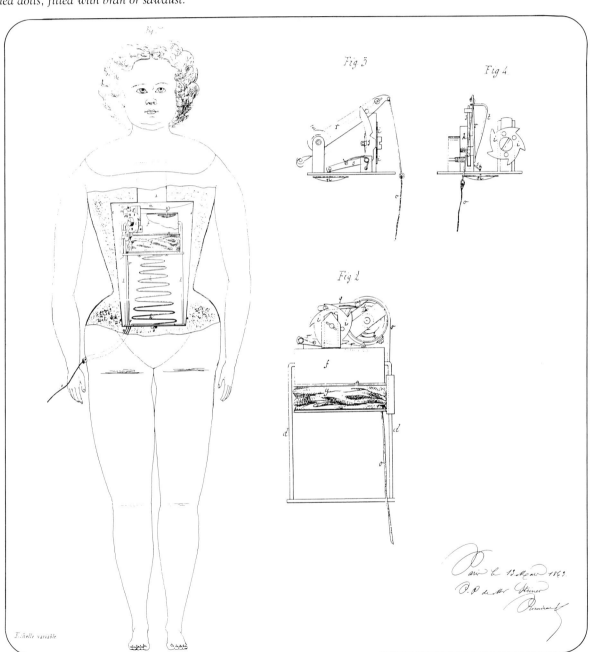

The patent details the assembly and operation of the
mechanism which expands the bellows and at the same time
advances a gear tooth of the ratchet wheel so that on alternate
pulls of the single string the "mama" or "papa" sound is
emitted.

217

74,679   *Jules Nicolas Steiner*   January 25, 1867

UN CHEVAL MÉCANIQUE ANIMÉ
(MOVING MECHANICAL HORSE)

DESCRIPTION:

The most admirable toys without any doubt are those automatons or mechanical ones which by mimicking the life and motion of real things they purport to be offer instruction as well as enjoyment for the child.

Unfortunatly, mechanical difficulties presented in their manufacture prevent them from realizing perfection as to solidity, stability and automatic movement.

Thus up to now mechanical toy horses unable to move by themselves have been made so as to be attached to rolling vehicles or supported by other means, all lacking genuine jointed motion.

Recognizing these considerations, I envisioned a moving mechanical horse which walks by means of its own legs without the help of any support, and which can move its head and bend the knee like a real horse, which has never been achieved before.

My mechanical horse invention is based on the idea of having at all times three points of contact with the ground (two back feet and one front), and all the weight of the motor in the back to assure the greatest stability.

Another important point of this invention is my adoption of a combined mechanism which transfers the force and motion to separate legs, thereby producing the best illusion of the actual motion of a real horse.

To understand the significance of this, consult the attached diagram. Figure 1 shows the full animal in profile. The outside covering has been removed to allow an examination of the workings inside...

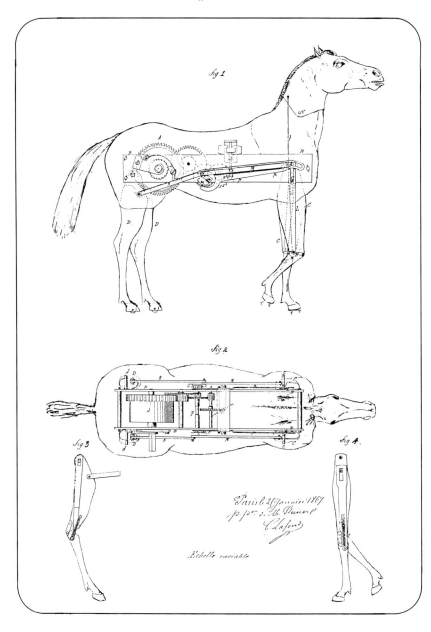

The patent further details the clockwork mechanism for the front leg driven horse whose rear legs are unjointed but glide forward in tandem with the opposing front leg, a natural walking action found in real quadrupeds. Figure 3 diagrams a jointed back leg which permits a bending action; Jules Steiner reserved the right to apply one or the other of these methods at his own choosing.

81,091   *Jules Nicolas Steiner*   May 26, 1868

UNE BOITE MAGIQUE JOUET
(MAGICAL OPTICAL BOX)

DESCRIPTION:

This invention is based on the well-known scientific principle called phenakisticopy, which can be defined as follows: When an object or several images (at different angles) are represented successively on the curve of a cardboard disk, and when these are seen through equally spaced, equally sized openings cut near the curve of a second, larger disk which is set on the same visual axis and turned at the same speed, the resulting impression the eye sees as the object moves in sequence is of a seemingly moving object capable of all the motion represented.

There are already several toys made with this principle, however the toy seeking patent herein is made along special and more simplified lines aimed at expanding the capabilities of the toy.

My description relies on the attached diagrams which show my invention in Figure 1 (longitudinally) and in Figure 2 (front view). This toy invention consists of a cardboard cylindrical box A, covered with like material B, and attached thereto by rubber D. The lateral walls of box A are cut with equidistant grooves aa across which the viewer sees the object(s) inside box A. Cover B has at its center a small vertical shaft b, which is gently brought into play within a small metal barrel d (which can be made of other appropriate material as well).

When one lifts cover B from the upper position on top of the box (having it take its opposite position below the base), shaft b acts as a pivot from box A's rotating motion. Within box A is placed a piece of paper or cardboard C cut in segments, wrapped into a cone shape, and set with glue along a starter formed like a backwards sunshade. On cone C's interior surface are painted the object's different positions, displayed so as to simulate movement.

This arrangement affords the instrument a great simplicity and will lead to a more wide spread use as a popular toy.

RÉSUMÉ In accordance with the law, I claim the exclusive right to production of my new magical optical box based on the natural phenomenon of persistence of vision whereby an object seen in rapid succession tends to impress its image upon the eye after it has in fact disappeared from view. This box as herein described has these notable features: an upper cover fashioned in such a way as to

first - allow placement below the box, and thereby serving as a support to the box's point of rotation

second - the free movement of the paper upon which the object(s) appear by use of the cone shape.

I reserve the right to modify the form, materials and dimensions of this optical toy, as for example to join the cover with the box by means of an elastic strap D.

May 26, 1868

Signed at Paris

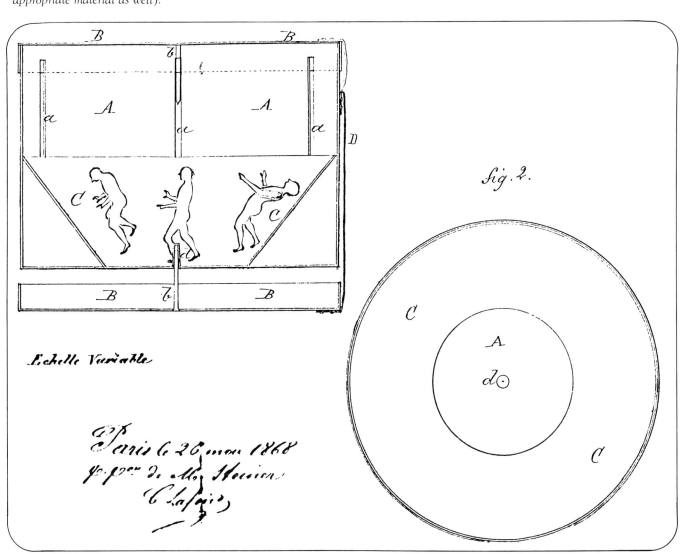

Echelle Variable

fig. 2.

85,858   *Jules Nicolas Steiner*   May 29, 1869
Add. 1. November 6, 1869
Add. 2. April 19, 1870
Also: England #2729 September 20, 1869

PERFECTIONNEMENTS APPORTES DANS LA CON-
STRUCTION DES VÉLOCIPÈDES ET DANS LES
MOYENS PROPRES À LEUR PROPULSION

(IMPROVEMENTS IN THE CONSTRUCTION AND
DRIVE MECHANISMS OF VELOCIPEDES)

INTRODUCTION - *The improvements which concern the filing
of this patent application include the following features:*

1. *a special means of propulsion or operating a velocipede
surpassing outmoded ones, while increasing speed and also
reducing the attendant fatigue associated with riding, all the*
*while eliminating problems in this regard with remarkable
ease*

2. *a new braking system.*

*These modifications which I am introducing to the construction
of velocipedes of two, three or four wheels will be readily
comprehensible by use of diagrams attached to this description.*

*...my system is useful for the making of toy velocipedes. (Figure
7)...*

1st Addendum - November 6, 1869 - makes modifications
and introduces a velocipede in the shape of a locomotive
for children.

2nd Addendum - April 19, 1870 - makes further modifications concerning efficient pedaling of the velocipede.

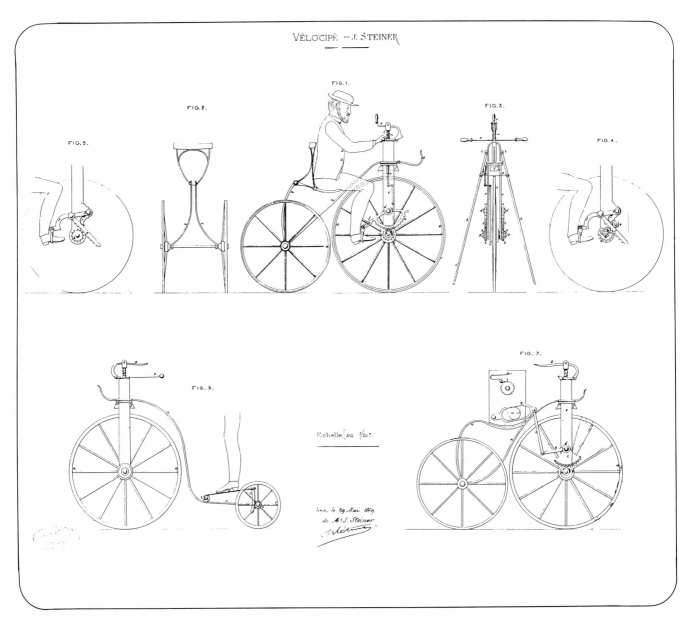

Details of the rake gears, springs and rack-and-pinions
have been omitted here, but as can be seen in the drawings,
some of the machinery is common clockwork. One can
assume that with 19th century steel alloys being inferior to
those of today, these toothed gears must have worn out very
quickly.

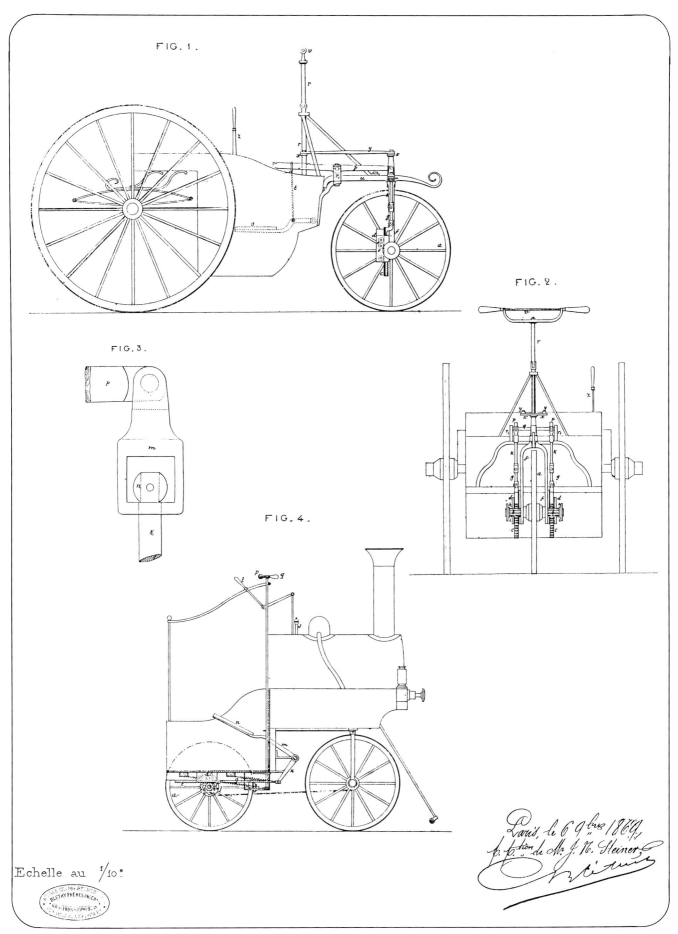

FIG. 1.

FIG. 2.

FIG. 3.

FIG. 4.

Echelle au 1/10°

1st Addendum — November 6, 1869

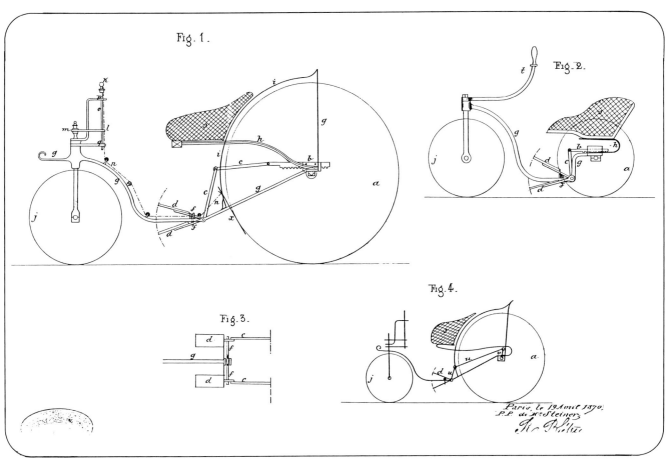

2nd Addendum — April 19, 1870

88,803   *Jules Nicolas Steiner*   *February 2, 1870*
UN SYSTEME DE GARDE-ROBE À CUVETTE INODORE,
ET VALVE AUTOMATIQUE

(ODORLESS TOILET WITH AUTOMATIC VALVE)

INTRODUCTION - My invention is for a toilet for apartments and public latrines, etc. As can be seen in the attached diagram, this apparatus has various advantages: its simplicity of operation, its odorlessness, its ease of cleaning, and its reliability of operation, accomplished automatically. When a person sits down, the valve remains closed, and as soon as he/she rises, the same valve opens by the very act of leaving, then closes shut.

There is no point in mentioning here the numerous advantages of my toilet system, rather the diagram itself should suffice to point out its merit...

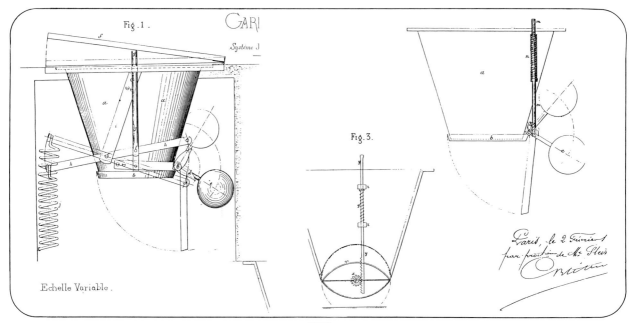

NOUVEAU SYSTEME DE MOBILISATION DES YEUX DANS LES TÊTES DE POUPÉES ET BÉBÉS

(NEW METHOD OF EYE MOVEMENT IN THE HEADS OF DOLLS AND BÉBÉS)

Patent 137,333 consists of the main patent dated June 18, 1880, and three additions, filed: 1. December 13, 1880

                                  2. May 19, 1881

                                  3. June 20, 1881

     Also: Germany #14292 July 29, 1881

Lengthy and technically detailed, these patents contain some general comments reflecting Jules Nicolas Steiner's pride as a French doll maker and some bordering on braggadocio while he establishes his proprietary rights to the various ideas he patented. They are summarized here with excerpts from each.

The main patent, June 1880, describes "how eyes are made to move at the present time." One method, Steiner stated, was by the use of a wire rod from the eyes going through the neck and emerging from the body, an impossibility with socket head dolls. (In 1880, this method was no longer widely used.) The second method "has been and still is much used in dolls and bébés coming from German manufacturers, those whose heads are made of waxed plaster. This method consists simply in fashioning a lead weight in the shape of a horse shoe, which depending on whether the doll is standing or lying down, holds the eyes open or closed, but does not allow the waking or sleeping action at will. In addition, this method is used only in the more common toys of Germany."

The patent then details the eye mechanism contained in the head, consisting of a series of wire linkages terminating at and operated by a button or a bent part of the wire on the side of the head, "so that heads equipped with my little device can be placed on all manner of dolls and bébés without the slightest difficulty nor any special arrangement and the child can open and close its toy's eyes in whatever position, laying down, standing, even stood on its head..." The diagrams show that in this system the support and operating button is toward the back of the head. The eyes described are of Parisian enamel, wired together to keep them securely and properly positioned in the head. The main patent concludes: "Of course, it goes without saying that in place of the button one can substitue wheel-drive or a tripping device and that the placement of either can vary. As long as the mechanism is contained in either side of the head, it remains within the scope of my invention, without which heads with movable eyes would not be able to be used in the manufacturing of Parisian dolls and bébés; an invention which from here on in makes possible the voluntary movement of the eyes in jointed heads of biscuit, and also of oval eyes of hard Parisian enamel, with prominent iris, which makes for quite an important advancement in this industry since up until now all eyes were rounded and made of blown glass which does not offer either the grace or the natural look given by the oval eye and above all the prominent iris.

"On the pivoting points I shall of necessity place a covering of zinc or something similar so as to provide for the softening effect in the wax in warmer climates and to facilitate the movement of the eyes.

"I hereby make claim to the exclusive property of the system described herein for the movement of eyes in the heads of dolls and bébés, a system whose operating mechanism is placed anywhere within the head of the toy, and reserving the right to modify the process by way of materials, shapes and sizes."

1st Addendum, December 13, 1880, makes modifications in the framework connecting the eyes and in the connecting linkage of the mechanism. The patent drawings illustrate a grooved horizontal cross piece with the wire embedded in it and leaving the head "near the ear so as to be accessible and controllable by the child." This is the basic Steiner production configuration for the connecting rods. The drawings appear to show "paperweight" or French enamel eyes. In less than two months from this date, Jules Nicolas Steiner's next patent (#140,916) will be filed which describes the unique porcelain globe eye associated with this system. The German patent uses the same illustrations found with this addendum.

2nd Addendum, May 19, 1881, makes modifications to more rigidly join the eyes together as well as to secure the linkage rod to the framework between the eyes to eliminate slippage. This is done by tightly crimping the end loop of the brass linkage around the dowel into a triangular groove before the eyes are attached to the dowel. On this same date, an addition is also filed to his next patent, concerning the manufacture of eye globes.

3rd Addendum, June 20, 1881, reaffirms Jules Nicolas Steiner's proprietary rights to his eye movement system whether for eyes or eyelids, though he does not detail a system for eyelid movement. He takes "formal exception to the use of my frameworks to unitize the eyes and also to the activating lever, the whole thing grouped in and around the head..." This addendum also makes provision for a counterweight assist which he claims the two previous additions to the main patent had also allowed for, even though not detailed therein. Primarily he seems to object to other people using his design to improve ordinary sleep eyes, as he concludes: "I seek to prohibit the use of my framework by anyone who chooses to take it to make closing eyes when the baby is laid down and opening when raised up as is seen in dolls from Germany, those called rocking eyes that everyone knows. Therefore, I am the only one in France or elsewhere who has succeeded in making the eyes move at will in a sure and simple way in the heads of poupées and bébés, either of pasteboard or of porcelain, and this thanks to my framework invention which unites the eyes between them, and thanks to my lever arrangement using a pulling action, or of counterweights combined and arranged entirely within the head and in a completely independent fashion from the rest of the toy."

At the risk of being redundant, there is considerable repetition in these patents.

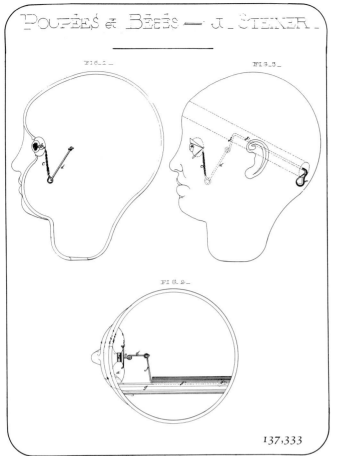

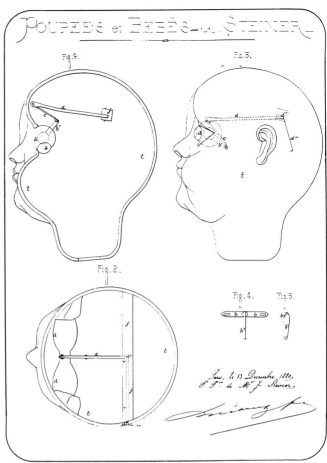

137,333

1st Addendum — December 13, 1880

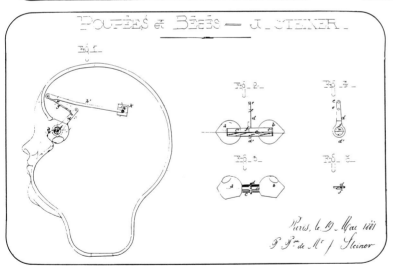

2nd Addendum — May 19, 1881

3rd Addendum — June 20, 1881

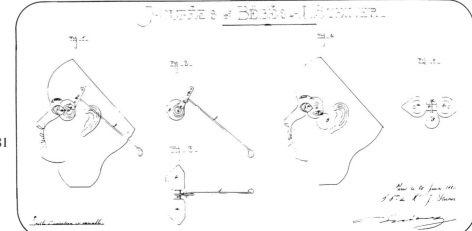

NOUVEAU MODE DE FABRICATION DES YEUX ARTIFICIELS POUR JOUETS D'ENFANTS, POUPÉES ET ANIMAUX.

(NEW METHOD OF MANUFACTURING ARTIFICIAL EYES FOR CHILDREN'S TOYS, DOLLS AND ANIMALS.)

DESCRIPTION:

It has been an aim for all time to give toys a life-like appearance, especially with an expressive look.

Different methods have been used to make artificial eyes either fixed or movable (refer to Enclopedia Roret, 1859 Edition, page 349). German manufacturers prefer the use of blown eyes, oval-shaped for fixed, round for the mobile type. The French makers favor the oval eye but solid, not hollow, and made of hard Parisian enamel. I myself used this method to create the movable eyes described in my patent dated June 18, 1880, but here I finished the globe of the eye with wax, plaster, sulphur, alabaster or powdered stucco and many other mixable and fusible substances. However all showed serious drawbacks either for lack of durability or lack of beauty. To site but one example, wax, which is the easiest and most elegant material, has the problem of hardening to the point of breaking in cold climates and of softening in hot climates. In the latter case, the wax surrounding the eye globe to finish it sticks to the wax inside the head which forms the eye socket.

Faced with these obstacles, I was led to explore a manufacturing method far off the beaten path. I imagined a way of making the globes in porcelain having exactly the shape of the natural eye. This way, for any competent man, is of immeasurable progress from the point of view of beauty and of durability of the finished product. Thus, instead of setting the eyes with wax, which is both meltable and breakable, I simply set them with plaster, for I no longer fear ruining the gloss of the globe and my movable eyes are resistant under any climate.

But the globe of the eye is not sufficient to give expression and life to the look and here arises a real difficulty which I have overcome in several ways, notably by the four following means:

1. The first thought has been to paint the iris with colored enamels to obtain the radiating rays, the circle (iris) and the pupil. For the ordinary eye, this is sufficient; chromo-ceramic does me a great service for by this procedure I obtain an absolutely regular and natural iris. Figures 1 and 2 of the attached drawing show the frontal view and cross-section of this first solution.

  a) refers to the iris in a general way
  b) the rays
  c) the circle
  d) the pupil

2. For a finer and more expressive eye (Figures 3 and 4) I have covered the paint or the chromo with a portion of a ball of crystal e which gives luster and life to the look of the eye. This drop of crystal is deposited hot or cold; the same effect is obtained and to a further degree more sparkling is obtained by painting directly behind the drop of crystal either by hand or with the aid of a decal or chromo.

3. The same effect is obtained (Figures 5 and 6) by hollowing out the iris in the eye f and adapting into this empty cavity a complete iris a made with special enamels. This system gives admirable results.

4. Finally, the method indicated in Figures 7 and 8 consists of making the globes of the eyes in porcelain f as hollow as an empty eggshell, of cutting out the place of the eye and adapting in it an ordinary eye g full or blown. By this last procedure one obtains the results and appearance of a fixed eye, however it is mobile, seeing the round shape of the porcelain globe into which this eye has been placed.

RÉSUMÉ

It is easy to understand from the preceding text that my invention consists of a new application of porcelain in the making of eye globes, to which I apply enamels or paints in an entirely new way. This facilitates the movement of the eyes in dolls and bébés to such a point as to render these objects at the same price as dolls having fixed eyes. In fact, nothing can change or deteriorate these porcelain globes and the enamels or paints applied to them. As I have said, I can make these eye globes with many other fusible or mixable materials, even with enamelled metal. This is what leads me to claim exclusively the absolute rights and ownership of this invention of a porcelain eye, painted, covered or not with crystal or with a glass iris or with enamel applied, or, indeed, any other element having the appearance of a natural eye.

Paris, February 2, 1881

Patent applied for February 2, 1881
Paris, March 21, 1881

NOUVEAU MODE DE FABRICATION DES YEUX ARTIFICIELS POUR JOUETS d'ENFANTS POUPÉES, BÉBÉS et ANIMAUX.

(NEW METHOD OF MANUFACTURING ARTIFICIAL EYES IN CHILDREN'S TOYS, DOLLS, BÉBÉS AND ANIMALS.)

DESCRIPTION:

To the new idea of manufacturing in porcelain the globes of artificial eyes for children's toys as I outlined in descriptive material accompanying my patent application, I have added different methods aimed at achieving a natural appearance for the iris, crystalline lens, and the overall look. In particular I described the new application of chromolithography (printed decal) in this type of industry.

The tests that I continued to undertake in that direction have brought me towards a well defined procedure which produces with considerable economy products in perfect imitation and of great beauty.

Here is the process.

Looking at the attached diagram, one can see that I take a spherical dome a (Figures 1 and 2) of glass or preferably crystal of the appropriate dimension to that of the eye that I want to reproduce; that is to say equal in size to that of the eye's iris. Then I attach the paper image b (Figure 3) by glue or otherwise, which faithfully represents the iris and the crystalline lens which I have already made by chromolithography. The new chromolithography printed color is determined by the shade that the iris is to be given, so as to represent blue eyes, black eyes, grey or any other color.

When the adhesion between the crystal a and the paper b (Figures 4 and 5) is complete, then the assembled iris is placed into the cavity reserved for this purpose in the porcelain globe. To do this a drop of liquid wax or gutta-percha is poured into this place c (Figure 8) and then the iris is fitted into it. The results of the wax or gutta-percha overflowing partially around the eye can be to form a border d (Figures 6 and 7) that gives to the look a life-like appearance.

The chromolithography which in the end gives life to the small crystal sphere which forms the iris is of an extremely low cost. Its adhesion to the crystal can be done in all the known ways and is not costly. This new procedure consequently produces very economical products and at the same time brings a finish that has been difficult to attain until now.

EN RÉSUMÉ   Summary

Without limiting in any way the generalities which I previously formulated in my patent claims, I hereby add to that claim by this document the exclusive property of applying chromolithography in the manufacture of artificial eyes for bébés, dolls or toy animals. This application of new artificial eyes which I have already mentioned, will be used in accordance with the conditions stated above, to produce an image of the iris for the eye with the crystalline lens, then fix this image, by glue or otherwise, behind the spherical dome of glass or crystal which will determine the outer dimensions of this part of the eye. Thus adorned with the chromo image, all that remains is to fix with wax or gutta-percha this iris in the empty cavity of the globe of the eye.

PARIS, May 19, 1881

Patent applied for May 19, 1881
Paris, August 4, 1881

This addition, applied for the same day an addition to the previous patent was filed, details the method of making irises for the porcelain eye globes. The process involves a spherical ball of crystal with a chromolithographed paper iris glued behind and set into the hollowed out globe with wax or gutta percha. This method was mentioned in the main patent as the second possible means of producing the eye. This addition fully describes that method, likely the one most often employed in the production of these eyes.

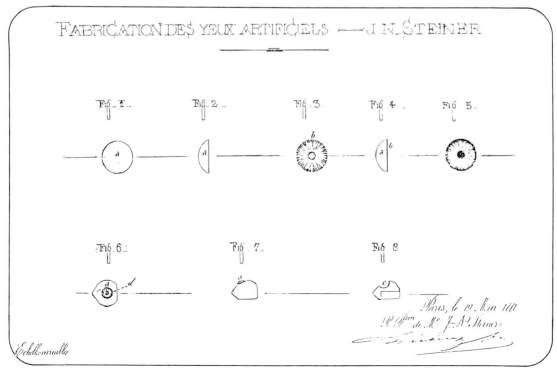

Addendum — May 19, 1881

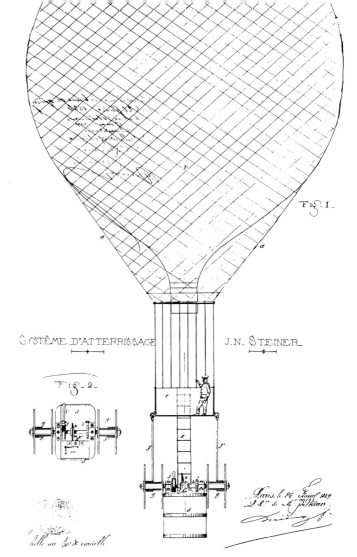

SYSTÈME d'ATTERRISSAGE DES BALLONS
(LANDING SYSTEM FOR HOT AIR BALLOONS)

DESCRIPTION:

Several studies I've come across in past years have convinced me of the necessity for having a practical means of landing flying craft, since every ascension up to now has shown that the descent is the perilous part, indeed the cause of certain catastrophes. To rectify this state of affairs I've envisaged a system or two, and settled upon the one which is the subject of this patent application, and which surmounts all difficulties by affording landing when and where desired, and this without either deflation or gas escape, and what's more, landing by design while keeping the balloon safe from damage due to wind or storms.

Refer to the attached diagram to see: Figure One, showing an overview, and Figure 2 showing the landing gear. Balloon b is covered by ordinary netting a, to which passenger basket c is suspended. Beneath basket c I place another basket d, connected to the former by cord ladder x, which is itself attached via two cables f f' separated one from the other so as to prevent twisting upon descent...

OPERATION - *On approach to landing area, one of the flyers takes his place in winch basket d, then lifts cog rachet i's lever. This frees the cable's unwinding mechanism. As he directs the descent, the flyer keeps careful control of brake j. A certain distance from the ground, and while still controlling descent by unwinding the braking mechanism, the flyer moderates the rate of descent as he spies out the desired landing spot. Close to the ground, he tosses the anchor toward a suitable hooking spot. He chooses a solid target wherever he can find one in the given terrain.*

Then setting cog i into the rachet's teeth, the pilot may (in calm winds) use crank m to effect the simultaneous unwinding of cables f f', resulting in the balloon's landing. In bad weather at ground level, he and his balloon are safely attached to places in higher elevations (and can wait out a storm). When the flyer wishes to ascend all he has to do is cut the moorings holding the basket to the ground, then the balloon ascends with both baskets as usual, so long as the balloon isn't deflated or hasn't lost gas. The flyer gets back in the air by turning the winch crank, unwinding cables f f' as he ascends.

To emphasize my new system's practicality, I figure the winding drums g g' should allow for 2000 meters of cord, one centimeter thick. At an altitude of 1000 meters mobile basket c has only 1000 meters of ground clearance. This way, there remains 1000 meters of cord on each drum, which allows the flyer to land the craft on the ground, attach it to a tree, etc. Once safe haven is achieved, the flyer puts the cog within the rachet's teeth arrangement; then turning crank m, he draws the balloon to him as previously explained.

Should the crew be equipped with electrical means of communication, the flyer who has already landed can keep in touch with a partner still in the basket and receive appropriate instructions.

RÉSUMÉ

I claim the invention herein described for a new means of balloon landing, which consists of:

1-Suspending from the usual balloon basket another basket drawn toward and away from the first by the arrangement of a winch installed within and operating mechanically or by hand by one of a balloon's crew descending inside this mobile basket.

2-Supplying the winch's movement with a cog rachet, which prevents cable untracking as the basket rises or as the balloon descends.

3-Supplying this same winch with a locking brake, thereby permitting variation in the speed of descent and a flexibility in landing choices.

This new way of landing, which affords a greater choice in both time and place, effected without deflation or loss of gas, also offers a means of guiding the balloon. This invention features not only a new arrangement for raising and lowering the craft, but also a parking system permitting stopping, ascending and descending at will. It overcomes many of the dangers of balloon landing, fulfills all the conditions I have sought to impose, and forms the basis of the industrial application of balloons.

As previously mentioned, with the addition of electricity, my landing system is capable of being of great use since it establishes practical communication between those on the ground and the flight crew without the necessity of bringing the latter down to earth.

signed, Feb. 26, 1884
at Paris

An intelligent young pilot who has studied this patent suggests that while this is an intriguing idea, well thought out and with good mechanical detail, it is probable that Jules Nicolas Steiner never flew and that this basic principle would not work because it does not take into account the layers of irregularly moving air at the earth's surface which would wreak havoc with a floating balloon. "You can't just park a balloon."

This is perhaps an example of why JNS is remembered for his dolls.

162,061   *Jules Nicolas Steiner*   May 15, 1884
PROCÉDÉ DE MOULAGE PAR L'AIR COMPRIMÉ DES JOUETS EN CARTON OU AUTRE MATIÈRE SIMILAIRE TELS QUE BÉBÉS, POUPÉES, STATUETTES, ETC.
(MOLDING METHOD VIA COMPRESSED AIR FOR THE CONSTRUCTION OF TOYS MADE OF CARDBOARD OR SIMILAR MATERIAL FOR BÉBÉS, DOLLS, STATUETTES, ETC.)

The use of compressed air in the casting of children's toys is effected by the arrangement presented in the attached diagram, which shows an ordinary balance wheel whose screw controls a piston which, operating within a cylinder, compresses air to the required level in the mold placed under the air cylinder.

I realize full well that other means, with or without a balance wheel, can be designed and used to take advantage of compressed air to mold objects made of paper, pasteboard or other material, generally used in the manufacture of bébés, dolls and other children's toys, statuettes, etc.

My patent application is specifically based upon the adaptation of compressed air in this industry, and upon both the industrial and economic results that this adaptation can bring to the perfection, the elegance and quality of the products produced.

Figure #1 is a sectional diagram showing the connections involved in the balanced air compressor with the bébé mold at the center.

Figure #2 shows the same thing in a side view...

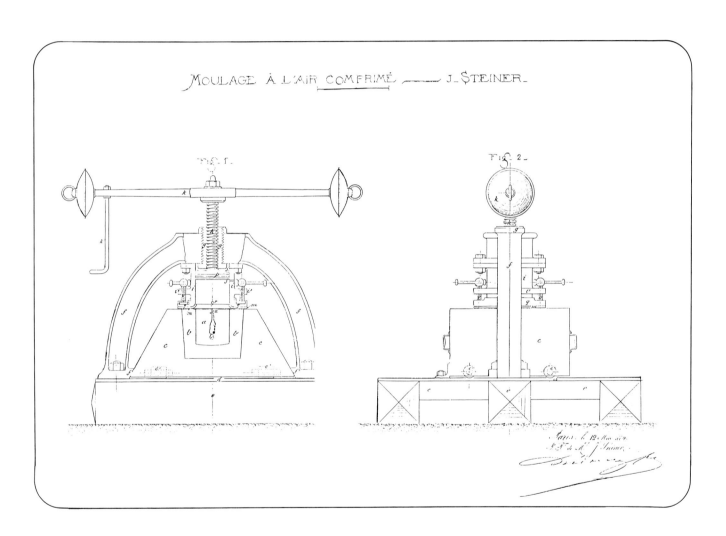

This patent describes in detail the workings of the machinery. The mold is prepared "in the ordinary way," with cardboard pieces layered in the mold to achieve a desired uniformity. These stick together and adhere to the inner wall of the mold so that it can be closed. The closed mold is joined to the cylinder. Air is compressed by the descent of a piston and then forced through one or more jets into the mold, compressing the molding materials everywhere they have been placed, and assuring a tight joining of the pieces of the mold for each body part.

Compressed air machinery was a child of the Industrial Revolution, a relatively new idea with widespread application; Jules Nicolas Steiner's adaptation of it to this use was ingenious and produced superb results.

228

TÊTES INCASSABLES EN PORCELAINE, BISCUIT, ETC. POUR POUPÉES ET BÉBÉS

(UNBREAKABLE HEADS MADE OF PORCELAIN, BISQUE, ETC. FOR DOLLS AND BÉBÉS)

DESCRIPTION:

Heads made of bisque, porcelain or any other similar material have the serious disadvantage of breaking into pieces when a child accidentally drops the doll. The unfortunate consequence, then, is that to effect the repair the doll must be sent to the manufacturer, who substitutes a new head for the broken one; and the more dangerous consequence that the child runs the risk of being cut by the broken pieces among which he unexpectedly finds himself.

My invention is intended to, as much as possible, make these porcelain or bisque heads unbreakable, or at the least to make them in such a way that, in the case of a fall followed by a crack where the pieces don't become detached, they will not separate; thus the accidental fall results in cracks which do not require an immediate repair, causing separation of the baby from its clumsy owner. Additionally, no accident will be a dread one for the child no matter how severe the break.

To accomplish this goal, the porcelain, bisque, etc. heads are made in the ordinary manner, then I coat the inside with glue and apply onto this coating a resistant and suitable fabric such as buckram, linen, marli or other more or less tight material. I let it dry and these products have the qualities mentioned above. One can drop the head from a great height or knock it vigorously; either way, if a crack results, all the material remains intact, still attached to the lining and the accident produces but traces of cracks or star-shaped dents. One may repeat this experiment, and no fragment falls loose; a child cannot be injured from a break of this kind.

In the course of my experiments, I have obtained good results from using both strong glue or paste glue, using any and all of the fabrics mentioned, and what's more, using hide pieces or felt, even nap or oakum. Fabric made of rubber may be used as well.

To the advantages already mentioned, my invention adds yet another:

Today, the eyes are fixed in plaster in porcelain, bisque, etc. heads. Now, at the first fall of even a slight impact, the plaster comes apart and the eyes fall from their settings. With my lining process, the eyes are sandwiched between porcelain, bisque or whatever and the lining fabric. Consequently, the lining, no matter what happens, withstands the shock and prevents the falling out of the eyes, which are doubly fixed in place.

The skullcap, either of cork or of pasteboard, is set up in the ordinary way.

RÉSUMÉ

My invention essentially consists of making these porcelain, bisque, etc. heads unbreakable in dolls and bébés, in an interior lining made of the appropriate fabric, of hide, nap or oakum applied to a bed of suitable glue — strong glue, paste glue or otherwise, spread throughout the interior surface of the head, which itself is constructed by means already widely known.

I claim title to the new products with which I endow the industry with new porcelain, bisque, etc. heads thus lined and reinforced, these products characterized by their new properties and the means used for their manufacture.

Paris, June 20, 1889

Patent applied for June 20, 1889
Paris, September 11, 1889

This is an interesting process for lining heads and one to which Jules Nicolas Steiner made reference in his commercial advertising. However, bisque heads have not as yet been found lined as described herein. A similar process is described in the Widow Lafosse's patent #276,458 of March 29, 1898.

Jules Nicolas Steiner June 4, 1890

Addendum Oct. 7, 1890

BÉBÉ MARCHEUR DIT "BÉBÉ PREMIER PAS"
(BABY WALKER CALLED "BÉBÉ PREMIER PAS" [BABY FIRST STEP])

My invention is for a solid, simple mechanism in a new arrangement whose function gives to dolls and bébés so equipped a completely natural walk, one that imitates perfectly childhood's first steps whether the bébé is controlled by hand or led by holding it under the arms, or taking its little up-held hands much like handling a toddler, able to take a step yet still cautious in its movements.

There are already automatic bébés and I myself have already made walking dolls able to move head, arms, etc. However these accomplishments differ totally from my new bébé walkers, first by a

mechanical motor and transmitter, and also by the nature of the motion sent to the legs and by the total freedom given the legs to seat the bébé, have it walk (hop) on one foot, etc. without any precautionary instructions to the child-owner nor constraints on his/her enjoyment.

The design enclosed with this description explains the system I wish to patent since, as will be shown, the motor mechanism changes with the shape and size of the doll or with the desired stride of the walk.

Figure #1 is a side view, sectionalized, to show the internal mechanism.

Figure #2 is a back view, also secitonalized for the same purpose.

Figure #3 shows the detail of the leg motion...

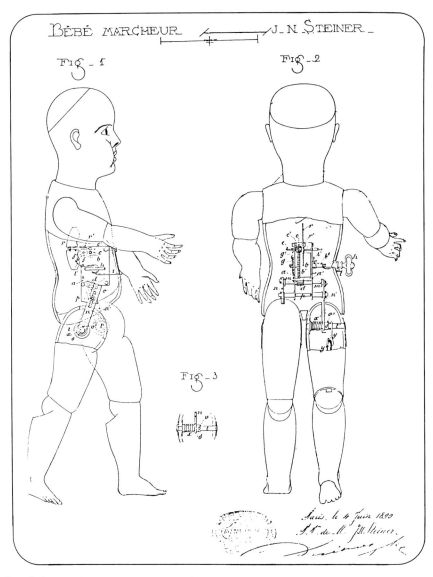

The ratchet details of the mechanism's operation have been omitted here, but the natural walking effect is achieved by an oscillating or circular movement, up and down, forward and back. When the doll is seated, the mechanism is automatically disengaged and the motor stops. The mechanism is, not surprisingly, comprised of clockwork parts, including a fly manually controlled by a stop-start lever.

Addendum, October 7, 1890, adds a talking mechanism, the traditional Jules Nicolas Steiner bellows which says "Mama" and "Papa" when standing and cries when horizontal. A special cart is also added which holds up *Bébé Premier Pas* and allows it to move even without the support and direction of a child.

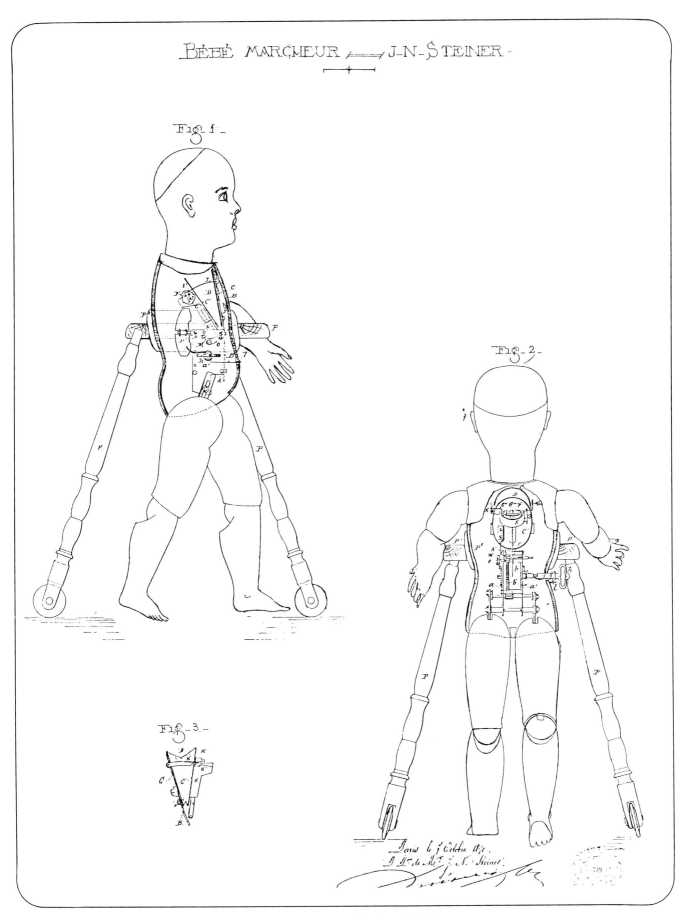

Addendum — October 7, 1890

TIREUR AUTOMATE
(FIRING TOY SOLDIER)

DESCRIPTION:

I have created a new toy called "The Firing Soldier," made of a small mannequin figure who, after taking one step forward, from either a standing or kneeling position, is made to set, fire, shoulder the firearm, and do so repeatedly.

At the toy's base is placed a bar spring movement strong enough to assure a repeated series of actions. The soldiers are dressed in the uniform of any nation. They can be made of any height, and can be set on different bases — wood, metal, cardboard. One can also place several objects on the same platform, having the soldier perform general motions either standing or kneeling...

This is a lengthy patent which details the operation of this complex and wonderful toy. Its spring activated motor moves both the base and toy's mechanism. The firing automaton is made to move via a system of levers, cranks, tie rods and other rods which allows various movements of legs, arms, head and firearm. The repertoire allows the marksman complete movement from "present arms" to "at rest." The firing sound is produced by a hammer striking a plaque under the base by means of a cam and a tension spring which is set to make the sound coincide with the precise moment the marksman lowers the rifle to the horizontal firing position.

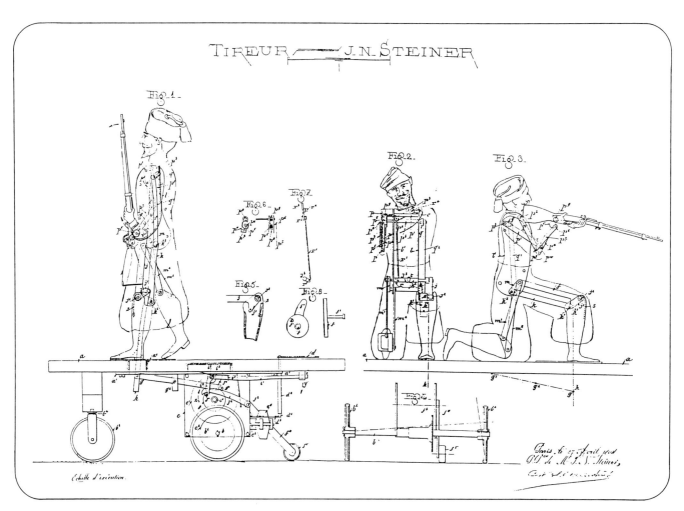

238,101   Addendum, filed October 23, 1894

"This application for a patent addition is submitted to guarantee my proprietary rights to improvements made in my invention called 'The Firing Soldier.' These improvements consist of:

1. As a substitute for producing the sound of a rifle firing, a special mechanism for sounding at will with exploding capsules.

2. As an optional equipment to the Firing Soldier, an automatic music box...."

The complex new method detailed in this addition which creates a more realistic firing sound consists of "A magazine cartridge for the firing caps (bullets), a distributor which isolates a bullet, then leads it and keeps it in place in the firing position; a firing pin, and finally a barrel sweeper to replace spent shells much like the extractor used in a real firearm." The music box which plays military marches, war songs, national anthems and the like as the soldier goes through his firing sequence can be disengaged and made to play only when desired or eliminated altogether.

This patent (and its addition) was the last known to be filed by Jules Nicolas Steiner, at the age of 62, after he had ceded his business to Amédée Lafosse. Steiner's creative genius glistens through the patent's descriptive workings of this fantastic toy, a toy which it is fervently hoped will some day surface.

Second Printing: see Color Plate 61.

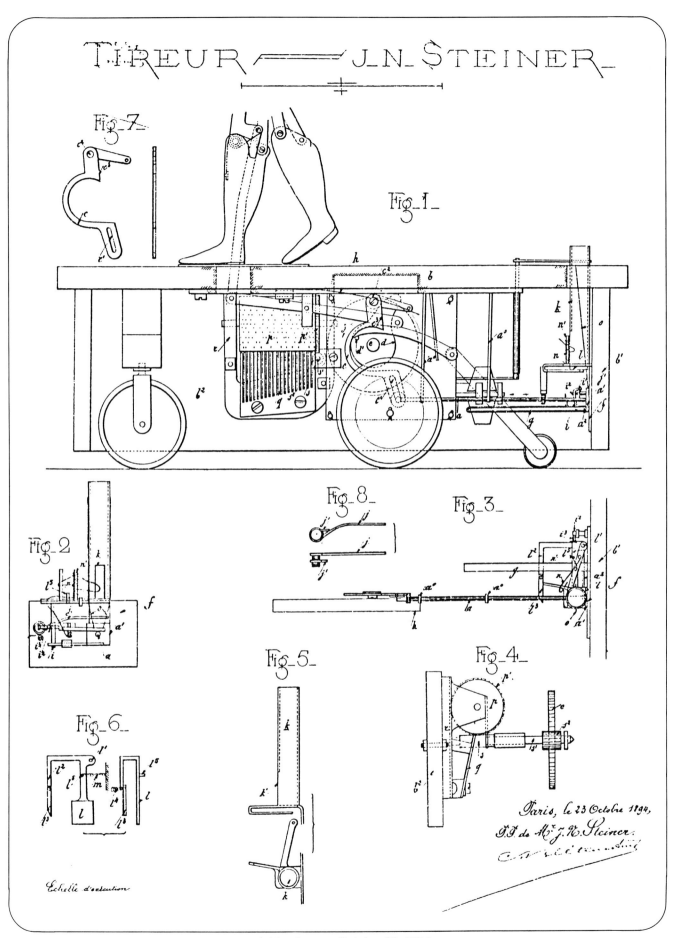

Patents Of Successors

221,582   *Amédée Onésime Lafosse*   May 12, 1892

SOUFFLET PARLANT PERFECTIONNE POUR BÉBÉS ET POUPÉES MÉCANIQUES OU NON

(TALKING BELLOWS IMPROVED FOR USE IN MECHANICAL OR NON—MECHANICAL DOLLS AND BÉBÉS)

My invention is intended to realize certain improvements I have made in talking bellows in a way that makes the mechanism simpler, less costly and lighter...

This Mama-Papa bellows has two cords. When one is pulled, a valve opens and the sound heard is "Mama." When the other cord is pulled, it closes the valve and one hears the sound of "Papa." It is a variation of the Steiner mechanism. The trumpet is described as being made of "carton moulé" (molded cardboard), definitely cheaper to manufacture. However, dolls examined that were made during the Lafosse years of operating the Steiner firm have the more traditional metal trumpet sometimes signed "J. STEINER" and sometimes not signed at all. The concluding sentence of the patent is: "I reserve the right to vary the shapes, materials and sizes of all pieces according to the applications and various models of dolls and bébés."

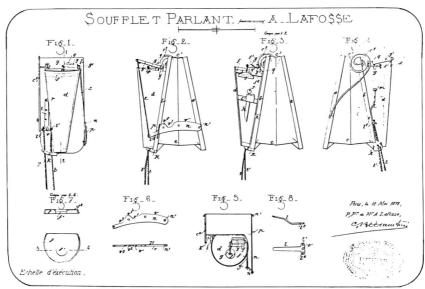

229,995   *Madame Vve Lafosse*   May 10, 1893
(nee Marie Lambert)   The Widow Mrs. Lafosse

PERFECTIONNEMENTS AUX MOYENS DE MOBILISATION DES YEUX DES BÉBÉS ET POUPÉES

(IMPROVEMENTS IN THE EYE MOVEMENTS IN BÉBÉS AND DOLLS)

This patent makes modifications in the lever-operated eye mechanism system seen in Jules Nicolas Steiner's patent #137,333. The operation is still by a lever found on the outside of the doll's head and still allows the bébé's eyes to be opened or closed at will, regardless of the position of the doll. The changes include the configuration of the linkage methods and the use of a counterweight to perform the basic opening and closing operation with the lever used to deter or release the weight. Figure 9 of this patent shows a geared mechanism at the eye which replaces the linkage and eliminates the need for a weight. These systems may never have been put into production.

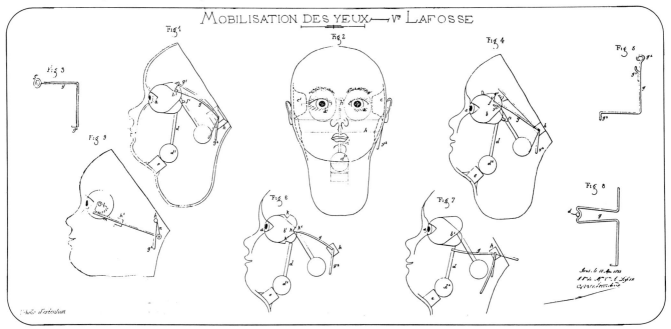

BÉBÉ MARCHEUR ET PARLEUR A MÉCANISME SIMPLIFIE

(BÉBÉ WALKER AND TALKER WITH SIMPLIFIED MECHANISM)

This Lafosse patent does NOT contain a spring driven keywind mechanism. The original patent basically calls for assembling a three-gear axle inside the torso of the doll with the outside gears attached to each leg. The middle gear trapped between them causes the legs to go in opposite directions as the doll is walked (by being pushed) either forward or backward. Attached to this mechanism is a toggle that engages and expands the bellows, then releases it, alternating the ratchet valve for the "Mama" and "Papa" sounds. The patent also allows the option to omit the speaking mechanism.

The addendum to #234,713 dated March 24, 1894, is primarily for production improvements to facilitate assembly. The mechanism is to be preassembled on a board and this assembly then mounted onto a plate attached to the inside of the back of the torso, rather than directly to the torso. This method was designed to solve difficulties which arose from differences in the shape of individual torsos. The addition also describes a simplified toggle or lever connection to the voice box.

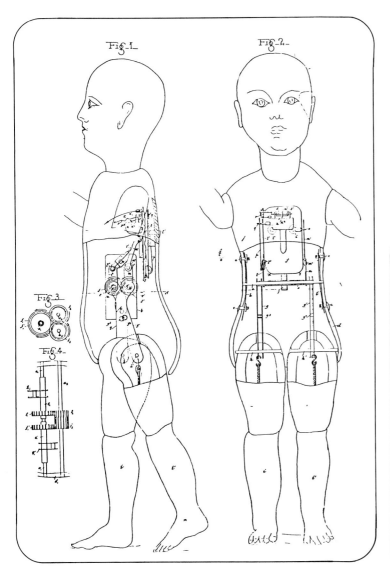

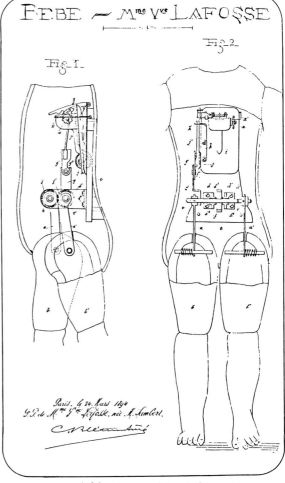

Addendum — March 24, 1894

238,710   The Widow Mrs. Lafosse   May 22, 1894

MÉCANISME MARCHEUR AVEC MOUVEMENTS FACULTATIFS DE LA TÊTE, APPLICABLE AUX BÉBÉS, POUPÉES, ETC

(WALKING MECHANISM WITH OPTIONAL MOVEMENTS OF THE HEAD IN BÉBÉS, DOLLS, ETC.)

The walking mechanism for this doll is similar to the previous patent except that the third gear drives a shaft which extends into and is fastened in the doll's head by a coiled spring screwed onto the axis. Walking the doll's legs forward or backward causes the head to turn right and left.

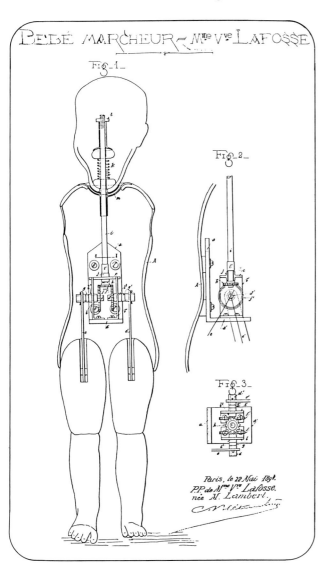

264,464   Madame Vve Lafosse   February 26, 1897
(nee Marie Lambert)   The Widow Mrs. Lafosse

BÉBÉ A TIRAGE UNIQUE PARLANT, PLEURANT & ENVOYANT DES BAISERS

(BÉBÉ WITH A SINGLE PULL MECHANISM FOR SPEAKING, CRYING AND BLOWING KISSES)

This patent describes the mechanism which enables a bébé to speak, cry and blow kisses, with all action coming from a single pull string at the doll's hip. The string operates the bellows and connects to the moving arm. However, the path of the string in the arm would not normally be long enough to allow the bellows to open wide enough to "speak," hence the patented idea for a block and tackle arrangement which doubles the path the string travels in the arm and allows the bellows to open fully. The bébé speaks and simultaneously blows a kiss. This patent of the Widow Lafosse further describes the speaking mechanism which says "Mama" and "Papa" when the doll is standing and cries when laid down, a concept and working arrangement seen in many earlier dolls of Jules Nicolas Steiner.

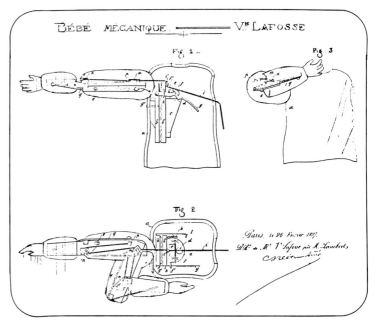

276,458   Madame Vve Lafosse   March 29, 1898
(nee Marie Lambert)   The Widow Mrs. Lafosse

BREVET d'INVENTION de QUINZE ANS POUR PROCEDE DE FABRICATION DES TÊTES & MEMBRES POUR POUPÉES & BÉBÉS

(15-YEAR INVENTION PATENT FOR A MANUFACTURING METHOD FOR HEADS AND LIMBS FOR DOLLS AND BÉBÉS)

DESCRIPTION:

My invention's purpose is for a manufacturing method for the heads and limbs of "bébés" so as to make them lighter, more pliant, more break-resistant and more finely detailed than that given by methods used up until now.

Today, to make the heads and limbs of bébés and dolls, after having made a hollow mold representing the desired piece, one goes about superimposing again and again, while making them layer deeper and deeper into the mold's recesses, three or four sheets of non-glued paper which one then wets with paste glue; then one removes it from the mold and sets it to dry. The necessity of using paper sheets of a certain thickness to obtain a sufficient strength also makes the piece thus formed heavy, breakable, inelastic, and the surfaces rough (due to the grain of thick paper stock).

My method allows one to by-pass these disadvantages because it uses a very thin paper stock to form the mask, and the application on the paper's backing of fabric strips, tarlatan or otherwise, which gives the piece great strength combined with great elasticity and a

*fineness unobtainable up until now. My method is distinguished by
an arrangement of superimposing a paper coated in strong glue,
without which, following the separate shrinkages of these two
materials, there would be wrinkles, tearing or weaknesses evident on
the outside surface of the piece.*

*On the attached diagram by way of demonstration, is displayed
a bébé's head in vertical view made according to my invention...*

The use of thin paper stock reinforced as described in this
patent produced light and strong dolls with excellent detail.
This patent is very similar to Jules Nicolas Steiner's patent
#199,034 of June 20, 1889, which may have been the
inspiration for Madame Lafosse or have created the necessity
for her to register this patent.

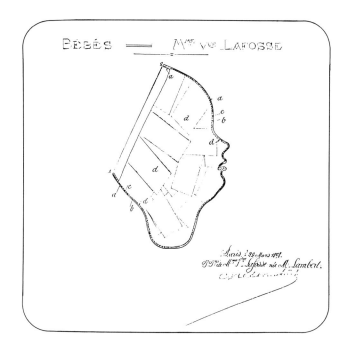

323,175   *Edmond Daspres*   July 21, 1902

*BREVET DE QUINZE ANS POUR NOUVELLE POUPÉE
MARCHANT ET PARLANT*

(15-YEAR INVENTION PATENT FOR NEW WALKING
AND TALKING DOLL)

Although this patent was registered before Edmond
Daspres became the final successor in the Steiner firm, it is
nonetheless included here. It is an interesting coincidence that
his patent is also for a walking and talking doll, although this
was an item of great interest to toy makers of the period. As
can be seen in the diagrams, the Daspres walking doll differs
from those of Steiner and Lafosse. It is described in the patent
as having a keywound mechanism "with a built-in spring
much like that seen in clockworks" and which, he later adds,
"contains a regulator (fly) and, in a general way, all those gears

demanded by a machine of that nature," a description far less
technical than that given by the clock maker Steiner! The
mechanism in this doll extends down through the legs and is
hinged to allow the legs to bend and slide forward and
backward on rollers or wheels attached to the base or feet.
During the oscillating movement from the legs the shaft
moves and expands the bellows which produces the alternating
sounds of "Mama" and "Papa." Additionally, the arms move
up and down, activating a bar which moves the head from side
to side. Although of a substantially different design, this
walking and talking doll has a similar range of movement by
the use of clockwork parts to the 40 years prior to *Bébé Parlant
Automatique* of Jules Nicolas Steiner. While symbolic of the
cyclical nature of the industry, it seems to define the Steiner
firm as having come full circle.

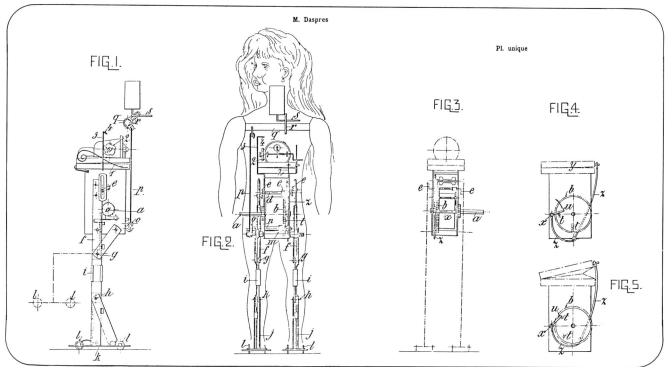

SELECTED BIBLIOGRAPHY

Beers, Burton F. *China in Old Photographs, 1860-1910*. New York: Chas. Scribner's Sons, 1979.

Capia, Robert. *Les Poupées Françaises*. Paris: Hachette 1979.

_____ . *Poupées, Les Edition Arthaud*. Paris: Hachette, 1984.

Chapuis, A. and Droz, E. *Automata*. Neuchâtel: Editions du Griffon, 1958.

Cieslik, Jürgen and Marianne. *German Doll Encyclopedia, 1800-1939*. Cumberland, Md.: Hobby House Press, Inc., 1985.

Clayre, Alasdair. *The Heart of the Dragon*. Boston: Houghton Mifflin Co., 1985.

Coleman, Dorothy S., Elizabeth Ann and Evelyn Jane. *The Collector's Book of Dolls Clothes, Costumes in Miniature: 1700-1929*. New York: Crown Publishers, Inc., 1975.

_____ . *The Collector's Encyclopedia of Dolls*. New York: Crown Publishers, Inc., 1968.

_____ . *The Collector's Encyclopedia of Dolls, Vol. 2*. New York: Crown Publishers, Inc., 1986.

Cooper, Marlowe and Selfridge, Madalaine. *Dimples and Sawdust*. Privately published, n.d.

Cooper, Marlowe. *Dimples and Sawdust, Vol. 2*. Privately published, n.d.

Daryl, P. *La Vélocipédie Pour Tous par un Veteran*. Reunies: Librairies Imprimeries, 1892.

Foulke, Jan. *Doll Classics*. Cumberland, Md.: Hobby House Press, Inc., 1987.

Green, Felix. *Peking*. New York: Mayflower Books, Inc., 1978.

Hart, Luella. *Complete French Doll Directory, 1801-1964, Part III*. Privately published, 1965.

Hillier, Mary. *Automata and Mechanical Toys*. London: Jupiter Books, 1976.

King, Constance Eileen. *The Collector's History of Dolls*. New York: St. Martin's Press, 1978.

_____ . *Jumeau Prince of Dollmakers*. Cumberland, Md.: Hobby House Press, Inc., 1983.

La Grande Encyclopedie. H. Lamirault et Cie, Editeurs. Paris: 1886-1906.

Merrill, Madeline O. *The Art of Dolls, 1700-1940*. Cumberland, Md.: Hobby House Press, Inc., 1985.

Noble, John. *A Treasury of Beautiful Dolls*. New York: Hawthorn Books, Inc., 1971.

_____ . *Dolls*. New York: Walker and Co., 1967.

Richter, Lydia. *Puppenstars*. Munich: Verlag Laterna magica Joachim F. Richter, 1984.

Selfridge, Madalaine. *Wendy and Friends*. Escondido, Ca.: Swadell Lithographers, 1969.

_____ . *Dolls, Images of Love*. Jim and Madalaine Selfridge, 1973.

United Federation of Doll Clubs, Inc. *Glossary*. 1978.

The Velocipede; Its History, Varieties and Practice. New York: Hurd & Houghton Cambridge Riverside Press, 1869.

Victorian Fashions & Costumes from Harper's Bazar, 1867-1898. Edited and introduction by Stella Blum. New York: Dover Publications, Inc., 1974.

Von Boehn, Max. *Dolls and Puppets*. London: George G. Harrap & Company Ltd., 1932.

Wellard, James. *The French Foreign Legion*. Boston: Little, Brown and Co., 1974.

Wilcox, R. Turner. *Folk and Festival Costume of the World*. New York: Chas. Scribner's Sons, 1965.

Yamada, Tokubei. *Japanese Dolls*. Tokyo: Japan Travel Bureau, 1955.

PERIODICALS and CATALOGS

(Various issues for each entry)

Annuaire-Almanach du Commerce, 1858 ff.

Doll News, 1965 ff.

Doll Reader, Cumberland, Maryland, Hobby House Press, 1979 ff.

Dolls, The Collector's Magazine, New York. Collector Communications Corp. 1983 ff.

Galerie des Chartres (Lelievre), Chartres, France, 1981 ff.

Neret, Minet, Paris, 1982 ff.

Polichinelle, Paris. 1983 ff.

INDEX

Numbers in bold face type refer to illustrations. "CP" refers to color plates.

239